Modern Terrestrials

7 38759 80382 4

Suzy's Yellow Mini Skirt

Modern Terrestrials

TYING AND FISHING THE WORLD'S MOST EFFECTIVE PATTERNS

Rick Takahashi and Jerry Hubka

HEADWATER BOOKS

STACKPOLE BOOKS

I would like to dedicate this book to my parents, Henry C. Takahashi and Clara T. Takahashi, who always encouraged my sisters and me to show kindness and respect to others.

RT

To my Mom, Helen Dorothy Kurth (Thompson Hubka), who passed away in 2011 at the age of 92. She was a working mom and a woman of grace and principles. She is missed every day.

JH

Published by
HEADWATER BOOKS
PO Box 202
Boiling Springs, PA 17007
www.headwaterbooks.com

STACKPOLE BOOKS
5067 Ritter Road
Mechanicsburg, PA 17055
www.stackpolebooks.com

Printed in China

10 9 8 7 6 5 4 3 2 1

FIRST EDITION

Photography by Jim Browning, Mark Boname, Dennis Collier, Pat Dorsey, Jerry Hubka, Eric Ishiwata, David Iwane, Landon Mayer, Takashi Nakajima, Jay Nichols, Henry Ramsay, Rick Takahashi, Mark Tracy, Brian Yamauchi, Jay Zimmerman, Greg Hoover, Connor Murphy, Joyce Hubka, Jens Buurka, Chris Kennedy, and Doreen Kemp.

Illustrations by Rick Takahashi and Jerry Hubka

Library of Congress Control Number: 2014937365

ISBN 978-1-934753-22-4

CONTENTS

ACKNOWLEDGMENTS

THANK YOU FAMILY! Especially my wife of forty-six years, Joyce, who continually gives her love and support to me and my endeavors. And, especially for her understanding when I told her that I was going to write another book.

My mother and stepfather Helen and Leonard Hubka have passed on, but their influence and guidance remain a part of me.

Much appreciation goes to my other parents, Joyce's father and mother, Stanley and Maude Usel and Joyce's sister, Carolyn Usel Stegner, for her willingness to help me with editing, scanning, and software.

Over the last few years I have had the opportunity to work and fly fish with numerous people in the fly fishing community. My gratitude goes to the following individuals for their professional help and personal influence, advice, and loyal friendship; Herman deGala, Scott Kemp, Al Ritt, Juan Ramirez, Brian Yamauchi, Dennis Collier, John Harder, Eric Ishiwata, Monte Miller, and Gary Okizaki. I would like to thank my co-author, Rick Takahashi, for his help with this book. —JH

I couldn't have attempted to do all of what I've done in the fly-fishing industry without the encouragement, support, love, and advice of my wife of twenty years—Susan Takahashi. Thanks to my son, Josh, and daughter, Haley, for allowing me to spend time with my passion.

Jerry Hubka, my co-author, has been a constant support, a great fishing companion, a wonderful advisor, and great friend who has always had my back. It has been our goal to share all that we have learned from this wonderful sport with others who love all that fly fishing and fly tying has to offer.

I have had the opportunity to tie with some great fly tiers and have learned so much about fly-fishing techniques both on the water and at the bench. Great tiers like Scott Stisser, Tim England, Dr. Donn Johnson, Tim Mack, Deward Yocum, Jude Duran, Dave Mosnik, Brian Yamauchi, Juan Ramirez, Bubba Smith, Jeff Goff, Herman deGala, Charlie Craven, Mark Tracy, Jason Haddix, and Dennis Martin have all had an imprint on my tying. Shop owners like Steve Solano of Rocky Mountain Fly Shop, Gordon Waldmier of Angler's Roost, and Brian Chavet of Elkhorn Fly Rod and Reel have given me the opportunity of spreading the good word in their shops with their customers.

And finally thank you to my parents, Henry and Clara Takahashi, who taught me the value of working hard, character, and sharing. To my sisters Dee Dee Hotta-Lee, Becky Larsen, and Caprice Benz, this book is for our family and the Takahashi Clan. —RT

Our special thanks must go to Robert Younghanz, "The Bug Guy." Robert willingly gave of his time and talents to become involved with our terrestrial book as our entomologist. Our sincere gratitude goes to Eric Ishiwata for his friendship and for his time, research, and writing skill to produce, for this book, an in-depth and thought-provoking chapter that will allow the reader to easily appreciate and understand the relationship between the terrestrial, the water, and the fish.

To Jay Nichols, fly-fishing editor for Stackpole Books and publisher of Headwater Books, for allowing and encouraging us to write our first book, *Modern Midges: Tying and Fishing the World's Most Effective Patterns* that is currently in its third printing. And, for his "wisdom" to ask us if we would like to do it all over again and write a second book.

Thanks to the staff at Stackpole Books for your professionalism, attention to detail, and creativity. You take what we send you and make something truly special that we are sure generations of fly fishers will enjoy.

We are grateful to our friends for their dependable and willing contributions to this book, and contributions in other ways: Landon Mayer, Brian Schmidt, Van Rollo, Ed Engle, Duncan Oswald, Ross Purnell, Eric Ishiwata, John Harder, Dave Young, Tom Whiting, Tom Mullins, Rich Munoz, Pat Dorsey, Jim Cannon, Takashi Nakajima, Tim Mack, Deward Yocum, Juan Ramirez, Ron Yoshimura, Monte Miller, Scott Stisser, Brian Chavet, Yuya Kurihara, Mr. Yonenoi, Mike Kruise, Jim Auman, Steve Schweitzer, Mark Boname, Dennis Collier, Al Ritt, Greg Garcia, Ben Furimsky, Charlie Furimsky,

Scott Kemp, Jesse Riding, Bubba Smith, Bruce Staples, Bill Chase, Tony and Kathi Tomsu, and Kent Grovet.

Without the following companies' assistance and generosity this book would have been difficult for us at best, and their support over the last four years has made the development of a creative work much easier for both of us. These companies provided assistance with fly patterns, tying materials, and fly-fishing and fly-tying equipment. Our sincerest gratitude goes to Whiting Farms, Umpqua Feather Merchants, RIO Products, Montana Fly Company, C&F Designs, Rainy's Flies, Elk Horn Fly Rod and Reel, Spirit River, Clear Cure Goo, River Road Creations, Peak Fishing, Far Bank, Angler's Sport Group, Fly Shack, Hedron Inc., Danville, Laughing Grizzly Fly Shop, Canadian Llama, and Blue Quill Angler.

—Jerry Hubka and Rick Takahashi

Brown and hopper watercolor. RICK TAKAHASHI

Why Not Terrestrials?

WHEN WE BEGAN *Modern Terrestrials*, we discussed our fishing preferences and strategies, and we found that our fly-fishing interests were many and varied. We related stories to each other about our times on the water and we began to slowly realize that some of our most enjoyable times fly fishing and at the tying bench were related to terrestrial insects.

Our experiences throughout the country ranged from fishing ant patterns in the upper Connecticut River to throwing large foam cicada patterns to hungry trout in the A section of Utah's Green River. We reminisced about everything from drifting large black and red-orange beetle patterns to lower Columbia River steelhead when eggs and streamers had little success to casting size 20 cinnamon ant patterns into Rocky Mountain National Park lakes above timberline after huddling for an hour behind a large boulder until the 50 mph wind gusts subsided. We laughed at fond memories of night fishing in Wyoming in the moonlight with large foam grasshopper patterns and then hanging on to large trout that hit this waterskiing

Eric Ishiwata fools a nice brown with a large grasshopper imitation. CONNOR MURPHY

Selecting the right fly. Choosing the right pattern often means having to make a decision about what pattern will best fool the fish into eating what you've chosen. JOYCE HUBKA

At left: Release. A large rainbow that fell for a beetle gets ready to go home. JIM BROWNING

insect with vicious strikes. We remembered the shouts of friends releasing a brown over 25 inches long after plopping a mouse pattern into the water near the bank and the time guests from Japan caught dozens of trout on a small yellow hopper pattern on a local river. The stories went on for hours.

Terrestrials, such as grasshoppers, ants, beetles, cicadas, wasps, bees, moths, and other invertebrates become an important part of a trout's diet spring through fall. Terrestrials provide a "big bite" for trout that have subsisted on smaller fare, and give trout a chance to take a larger meal. Opportunistic trout wait for terrestrials that absently land in the water near the banks, whether due to a flight miscalculation or the misfortune of a strong wind. One only has to lay the fly rod aside, capture a few natural terrestrial insects, and toss them into the flow to watch how trout eagerly feed upon them.

Trout will sometimes travel a great distance to grab a big terrestrial meal. We witnessed large hungry trout on the Green River in Utah come streaking from fifteen feet away to capture a struggling cicada. We have watched our hopper patterns get eaten right in the middle of an enormous Blue Winged Olive hatch on the South Platte and the San Juan Rivers. We have noticed that ant and beetle patterns drifted on the Snake River in Idaho catch the attention of trout that have been accustomed to seeing the usual aquatic born *Baetis* and caddis patterns drifting over their heads all summer long. We have become keenly aware that terrestrial "strike indicators" can have a hook hanging from them along with another fly pattern such as a midge or *Baetis* or a *Callibaetis* nymph attached.

We want to share what we have gathered by way of terrestrial fly patterns from around the world and how innovative tiers have chosen to mimic the terrestrials of their fishing grounds. As with our first book, *Modern Midges*, we have solicited the knowledge of many fly fishers from all over the country and around the world who are skilled at fishing terrestrials to provide you with a glimpse of how they approach fishing terrestrials and the various techniques and fly patterns they employ. We regret that we were not able to find, contact, or represent the many tiers who have been left out of this book; it was not for a lack of effort.

Our purpose is also to stimulate your creativity as a fly tier and encourage you to sit at the bench and take ideas that have been presented in this book and experiment with your own terrestrial patterns. Tie up a few and see what happens! We hope that our efforts open a new world of fly fishing to you or simply strengthen and verify what you already know.

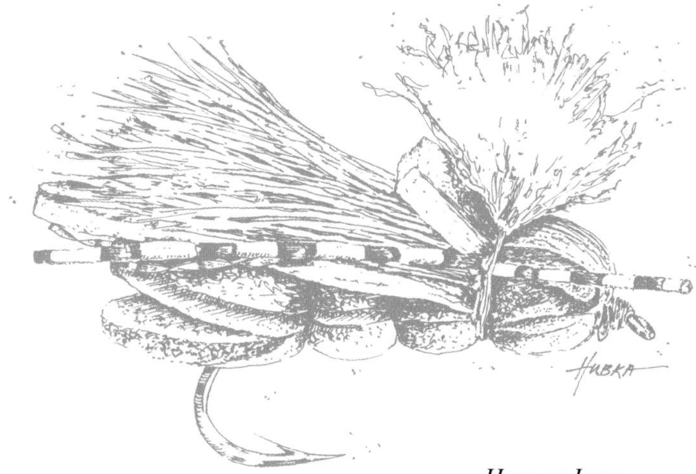

Hopper Juan
by tier Juan Ramirez

10/8/2010
HUBKA

SINKING Ant PATTERN

THREAD. WAIST & HEAD

LEGS: HACKLE or RUBBER ← MOVEMENT!!

ANT COLORS: RED, BLACK
BLUE, ORANGE

LARGE BEADS GLASS OR?

SMALL BEAD to MATCH COLOR OF LG BEADS.

COVER ABDOMEN w/ CCG
&
WAIST THREAD

THREAD TAG OR WIRE?

HOOK?

TRY: TMC 2487
OR
TMC 2302
OR
Daiichi 1250 or 1150?
YES!

PLACE 2 BEADS ON BEND of HOOK!!
UP EYE!

THREAD to MATCH COLOR OF ANT
RED, BLACK
for BLUE ANT USE BLACK THREAD!

1

Designing Fly Patterns

RICK TAKAHASHI AND JERRY HUBKA

FOR THE LAST thirty or more years we have had the opportunity to tie flies and fish those flies on rivers and lakes all over the United States. One of the most satisfying things a fly fisher can do is to design and tie your own flies, catch beautiful trout, and release them back into their natural habitat unharmed.

With both of us, there seems to be a flash of creativity that sparks an idea for a fly pattern. This flash can be out of a need to solve a fishing problem. It can be an answer to a dilemma, issue, or problem created by another fly pattern that just does not seem to work quite right. Maybe the fly does not sink fast enough or float quite right on the water, or maybe when pulled through the water it does not move as well as it should or have the correct profile. Or maybe we are simply browsing the shelves of a fly shop and see a material, a tool, or a hook that sparks an idea. Whatever it is that creates that spark, it can lead to hours of creative fly tying and experimentation that we hope will eventually reap rewards on the water.

The real deal. A grasshopper sits among rows and rows of imposters. HENRY RAMSAY

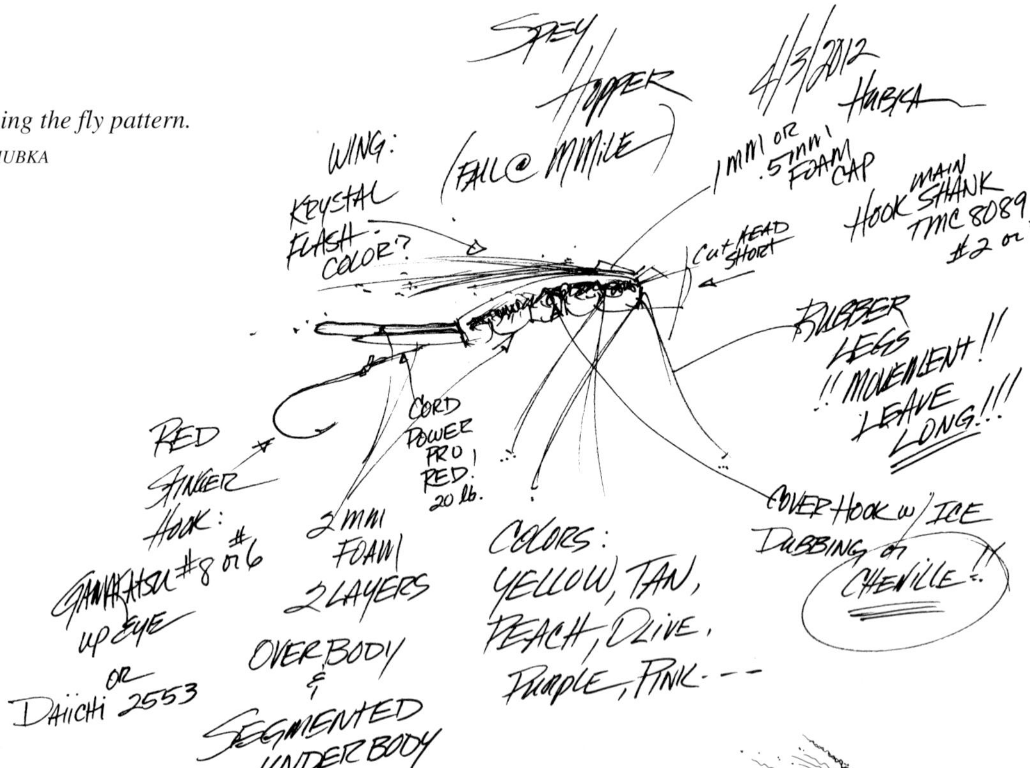

Sketching the fly pattern.
JERRY HUBKA

Rick enthusiastically admits to being a fly-tying-materials junkie. Every time he visits a fly shop (or any store for that matter) he keeps his eyes out for new fly-tying materials. Some of the products he has purchased are not generally associated with fly tying. The Dollar Store has provided several products that have made their way into some of his patterns.

When designing and tying flies, Rick follows a Japanese philosophy called Shibui, which refers to an aesthetic approach to design that incorporates simple, subtle, and unobtrusive beauty. Being an artist, Rick has come to appreciate the minimalist approach of Japanese art; he tries to incorporate the same sense of design in his flies. Some of his patterns may have many tying steps and may be more intricate in design than others, but he always tries to reduce the steps and materials to make a functional pattern. Rick generally starts designing flies after he has studied the insects or food form he is trying to imitate, so that he has an understanding of what he thinks he should incorporate into the design. He often can see in his mind's eye what the pattern will look like and then proceed to the vise to put his vision into reality. He favors the sparse tying style of the Catskills tiers such as Theodore Gordon, Rueben Cross, the Dettes, and Ray Bergman.

We are both of the opinion that craftsmanship is a very important element in the designing flies. Poor craftsmanship can ruin a good design and vice versa. We suggest to students and demonstration participants to always give respect to each fly they tie. If the design is not working out, cut all the materials off the hook and start over.

Rick loves to look at and collect other tiers' fly patterns. He readily acknowledges building on others' flies to create his own version of a pattern. For instance, the Takahopper is Rick's version of Ed Shenk's Letort Hopper. His Split Wing Caddis is his version of Craig Mathews' X-Caddis. Rick has designed flies to meet specific criteria and to solve problems faced while fishing on his home waters.

Whenever we attend fly-fishing shows, we watch as many fly tiers as possible to learn about techniques, materials, and processes that may not be familiar to us. We will sometimes incorporate those methods into our tying if it is appropriate for the design.

Jerry starts the process of designing flies with his pen and sketchbook. Pattern ideas and possible pattern names are written down and likely materials are listed as he sketches out ideas. Drawing the fly is his way of trying out his idea without

At left: Jerry Hubka tying his Señor Ratón Terrestrial mouse pattern at his bench. JOYCE HUBKA

Above: Rick Takahashi takes a break as he ties up patterns for a trip to Idaho's Henry's Fork. JERRY HUBKA

actually sitting at the bench and vise. The fly may not be tied for days or weeks, but he has the idea when he gets in the experimental tying mood. Not all of the ideas work, and he makes changes in materials at the vise. It is possible that several versions come off the vise before he is happy with the look of the pattern. He names his flies based on personal experiences. Three years ago he and his wife, Joyce, were returning from Santa Fe and they traveled over Ratón Pass north into Colorado. Ratón means mouse in Spanish, and his pattern Señor Ratón was born.

Here are some questions to consider when beginning the designing process:

- For what species of fish is the fly intended?
- What part of the water column is the pattern supposed to inhabit?
- What insect, fish, or other species is it designed to represent?
- Will this pattern be an abstract pattern or closely imitate the food the fish likes to eat?
- Is the pattern made to be food for the fish or to anger or excite the fish?
- Is the pattern's profile important from only below the fly or from the side or from all angles?
- What kind of water will the fly be fished on or in? Streams, still water, salt water? Does it matter?
- Will the fly be fished with movement or drifted with the current?
- What kind of movement is the pattern supposed to have in the water, if any?
- What colors are important for this pattern and what colors would be experimental in nature?
- What size should the pattern be?
- Is the fly pattern visible to the fly fisher? Does it need to be visible?
- Does this fly pattern only need to catch fish or does it need to also catch fishermen? In other words, is it marketable or is that not important?
- Is the pattern a stand-alone pattern that is best when fished only by itself, or does the pattern need to be fished in tandem or as an attractor for another fly pattern?
- What materials function best for the purpose of the fly pattern, and will these materials hold up and last during the process of casting, getting wet, and being bitten?
- Does the fly pattern need to "hold up" another fly pattern or help "sink" another fly pattern?
- What style, shape, and size of hook would be best to use for this pattern to allow the materials to be tied on and still allow the fly pattern to function properly?

HUBKA

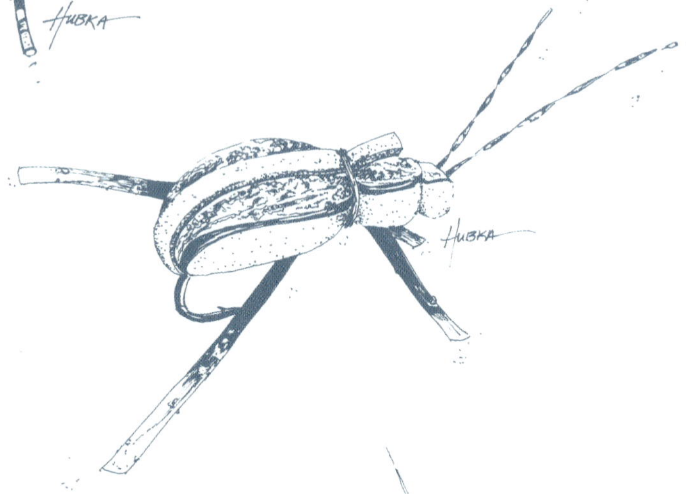
HUBKA

HUBKA

HUBKA

HUBKA

2

Terrestrial Trout Foods

ROBERT YOUNGHANZ (THE BUG GUY)

FLY PATTERNS TEND to imitate aquatic invertebrates. While the benthos is the most accessible source food for trout, terrestrial insects, spiders, mammals, and even small birds—through a variety of ways—often find their way into the water. The first and perhaps the most important step in becoming familiar with the variety of terrestrials available as potential trout food is to become a meticulous observer. More often than not, fly fishers have little consideration for, or awareness of, the abundant biodiversity available to trout that surrounds them as they quickly grab their gear and march toward the water. Truth be told, terrestrial animals far outnumber their aquatic counterparts. Anglers that are willing to spend some quality time investigating the terrestrial environment adjacent to a river or lake that they are about to fish will be rewarded with not only a unique biological perspective but an additional layer of fly-fishing knowledge, and a more successful day on the water.

The diversity of terrestrials most commonly found near water is so rich that a comprehensive assessment of them here is not possible. Furthermore, it is hard to make a distinction

One of the main cast of characters during terrestrial time, the grasshopper is one of the most imitated terrestrials. LANDON MAYER

between exclusively terrestrial insects and semi-aquatic insect that live one part of their life on land and part of their life in the water or vice versa. So from a fly-fishing perspective, a semi-aquatic insect can simultaneously be considered both terrestrial and aquatic. To muddy the waters even further, many families of insects contain species whereby one group within the order is exclusively aquatic and another is exclusively terrestrial. This phenomenon is most often seen with beetles as well as within various families of flies. My goal here is to cover the primary terrestrials that an angler is most likely to encounter while fly fishing in both streams and stillwaters.

GRASSHOPPERS, CRICKETS, KATYDIDS

Orthoptera

The ferocity with which a trout will take a grasshopper imitation is second to none. While grasshoppers do not intentionally land in the water, they often end up in the water due to strong winds while fleeing from predators or simply jumping or flying from one location to another. Grasshoppers of all sizes and stages of development fall victim to nearby water sources, but it is the larger adults that signal a substantial meal for feeding fish. Trout seem to be instinctively aware of the caloric benefits of consuming a large adult hopper, and their aggressive behavior when feeding upon them bears this out. Grasshoppers are most active during the warmest part of the day, and therefore odds dictate that this is when they are most likely to end up in the water.

Grasshoppers come in a wide range of sizes and colors.
MARK BONAME

This cousin of the grasshopper, the common black field cricket, is very important on streams with adjacent woods.
MARK BONAME

Grasshoppers are classified in the order of Orthoptera, which also includes crickets (Gryllidae) and the lesser known katydid (Tettigoniidae). With over 1,200 species occurring in North America and more than 20,000 species worldwide, this group represents an abundant food source for trout. Grasshoppers, crickets, and katydids emerge from early spring to late fall depending on temperatures and can even be present in warmer climates year around.

True to its name, the grasshopper is most often found in open grasslands, as are crickets and katydids, but some species within this group thrive in forested areas and even above tree line. It is for this reason that fishing a generalized "hopper" imitation can be extremely effective even in high mountain ponds and lakes. As the insects in this group metamorphosize, not only do they become larger, but they also can go through dramatic changes in color with each new instar. It is imperative that the angler consider these factors when selecting patterns for this group.

The pygmy grasshopper (Tetrigidae) deserves special mention. Few fly fishers are familiar with this small shore-dwelling grasshopper, yet twenty-nine known species live in North America. Although diminutive, their proximity to the shorelines of rivers and ponds make them a readily available food source for trout. While crickets and katydids are not imitated or fished with the same frequency as grasshoppers, any lake or a river that is near large open meadows or grasslands will likely be rife with these insects.

BEETLES

Coleoptera

With over 350,000 species worldwide and more than 28,000 in North America, beetles are the largest single group of animals on earth. They can be both terrestrial and semi-aquatic and are available as a food source for trout both in the larva and the adult stage. Beetles have demonstrated an unprecedented adaptation to all climates and are found every place on the globe except the North and South poles. Yet, despite this group's unmatched biodiversity and biomass, beetles remain one of the most underfished patterns for anglers across the board. As with all terrestrials, beetles unwittingly find their way into the water due to wind and perhaps their less than adroit flying skills. As an added benefit to the fly fisher, thousands of semi-aquatic species live a considerable portion of their lives in the water. Not only do beetles dramatically vary in size and shape but in coloration as well. They can be black, red, gray, green, orange, yellow, blue, and brown and there is no limit to their color patterns and combinations. It's important to be aware of these numerous size and color distinctions

Beetles provide a tasty meal, and trout love to feed on them in all types of water. LANDON MAYER

The colorful and abundant beetle. MARK BONAME

when choosing a pattern to imitate the local beetle fauna. Patterns tied with foam tend to be the most common method for mimicking beetles and therefore can be a quick and easy tie. Most fly shops offer a limited selection of adult beetle patterns but beetle larva imitations are virtually unheard of.

CICADAS, LEAF HOPPERS

Hemiptera

The order of Hemiptera, commonly known as true bugs, is characterized by their mouthparts, which are modified for piercing or sucking. They can be terrestrial, aquatic, or semi-aquatic. North America is home to 11,000 recognized species, and there are upward of 80,000 species worldwide. They are often mistaken for beetles due to their similarity in size, shape, and color but are in fact a group of insects unique unto themselves. Thousands of different species can be found near water.

For the fly fisher, cicadas (Cicadidae) are the most well known insect in this group of which there are over 160 species in North America. Depending on temperature, cicadas emerge from the soil from late spring through the summer after a period of 2, 13, or 17 years depending on species. These non-annual emergences make cicada hatches all that more extraordinary and a special delicacy for both trout and angler alike. If the emergence happens to be near a river or lake, due to their relatively large size and defenselessness once in the water, they can become a substantial protein source for trout. It is for this reason that the often aggressive manner in which a trout will take a cicada imitation can rival that of a grasshopper.

It is important for anglers to remain educated on which species of cicada occur where they are fishing and to know when the next emergence will take place, given that it is not an annual event as it is with most insects. An angler waiting for a cicada hatch could be standing by the side of a river for an awfully long time if he or she has not done their proper research. Although each species of cicada produces its own unique sound, cicada calls in general are very recognizable and are an obvious sign that they are in your area even if you can't actually see them. Entomologists that specialize in cicada research are able to distinguish one species of cicada from another just by its call. As with beetles and grasshoppers, cicadas have many color variations and combinations. When matching fly patterns to adult cicadas keeping into consideration these color differences dramatically improve fishing productivity.

Not as well known are leaf hoppers (Cicadellidae), which to the untrained eye look like small grasshoppers. Although they are often lumped in with grasshoppers, leaf hoppers, with 3,000 species described in North America and 22,000 worldwide are deserving of their own distinction. They use their modified piercing and sucking mouthparts to collect sap from surrounding vegetation and can be found near water just a abundantly as any other terrestrial insect. As long as the standard rule of size, color, and profile are kept into consideration, a small grasshopper pattern can be a suitable imitation for this prolific family of insects.

ANTS, BEES, WASPS

Hymenoptera

Within the order of Hymenoptera, ants (Formicidae), bees—classified in the sub-order of Apoidea—and wasps, which are so diverse that they cannot broken down into one singular family or even super family, are some of the most well known and important insects on the planet. Collectively, this order encompasses over 18,000 known species in North America and close to 130,000 species worldwide.

While bees and wasps are not an exceedingly abundant food source for trout, they do nonetheless find their way in the water on occasion, especially in areas where there is a plethora of flowering plants, trees, and bushes. A small number of wasp species will intentionally enter the water and are therefore

Taken on occasion, bees and wasps sometimes end up in the water where hungry trout will take advantage of this large bite of protein. MARK BONAME

partially vulnerable to trout. When fishing in these types of habitats it is prudent to keep a few bee and wasp patterns on hand.

Ants are arguably the best known and most often imitated hymenopterans. There are a variety of methods that they can become a food source for trout. They often fly directly into the water, can be blown in by wind, washed in during a rainstorm, or even swept in from the bank due to rising water. Additionally, some species dwell in trees near rivers or lakes, which increases their chances of becoming a meal for a trout. Many species engage in nuptial flights as a means of reproduction and will consequentially fly considerable distances, which can put them near to trout habitat. An ant's coloration can be black, red, brown, or a combination thereof. The use of ant imitations, especially on high mountain lakes, can prove to be an absolutely deadly pattern.

Termites (Termitidae), which look at first like flying ants but do not have a thin "waist" like a flying ant, are often overlooked by fly fishers, yet the sheer size of their swarms can be impressive. Alates, also known as swarmers, are poor flyers and can easily find their way into the water by the thousands while on their nuptial flights. Although no more than 50 recognized species of termites live in North America as compared to over 2,700 worldwide, they are nonetheless found in every

Red cinnamon ant. HENRY RAMSAY

Flying ant. HENRY RAMSAY

state in the Continental U.S. As with ants, some species of termites construct their colonies in trees close to water, making them available to trout on windy days or simply when they accidentally falling into the water. Their swarming behavior is dictated by rises in temperature, and while they tend to favor warmer, more humid climates, they can occur in early spring and throughout the summer depending on location. Given the similarity of size, color, and profile of flying ants and termites, the patterns for either of these two groups are easily interchangeable.

BUTTERFLIES AND MOTHS

Lepidoptera

The order of Lepidoptera is comprised solely of butterflies and moths. In North America, north of Mexico more than 11,000 species of butterflies and moths have been described. On a global level, there are upwards of 175,000 known species and this number continues to rise every year. While it is not unheard of for trout to eat the occasional butterfly, anglers tend to be more focused on moths when it comes to a potential food source for trout. Known as "millers" in the vernacular, this ubiquitous moth is probably the best known of all moths due to its propensity to find its way into people's dwellings. The name Miller Moth is a general term for any moth found in areas where people live or work, but from a purely entomological framework, millers are considered adult army cutworms or caterpillars. They can engage in substantial migrations both in number and distance. Depending on temperatures and moisture, moths can be found in large numbers near rivers and lakes from April through July.

Caterpillars are the larval stage of both butterflies and moths. In is not uncommon for caterpillars to live and construct their chrysalis or cocoon on bushes and trees that overhang lakes and rivers, where they can easily fall, be knocked into, or blown into the water. Trout will not hesitate for a moment to engulf a helpless caterpillar that may drift across its path. As with all insect imitations, size and color are always important considerations. A few species of caterpillars are venomous, so it always best to be familiar with the local taxa especially when collecting specimens.

As with many types of insects, the lines between what is terrestrial and what is aquatic are often blurred. Semi-aquatic moths Pyraloidea, Pyralidae, comprising subfamilies Scopariinae and Nymphulinae, live out their larval stage in aquatic habitats and their adult stage on land. There are 44 known species in North America. When seining for aquatic insect specimens, it is not unusual to collect this larva in the net. It's most often mistaken for a hellgrammite given its similar appearance but is in fact a caterpillar which is flattened dorsally with lateral gills.

Flights of fancy. Butterflies are taken with gusto whenever they land in the feeding lane of a trout. MARK BONAME

Large trout have been seen hanging under low hanging branches waiting for a large juicy caterpillar to drop onto their dining plate. JAY NICHOLS

FLIES

Diptera

Common flies are the insects that humans are often the most familiar with. They belong to the order of Diptera, which means "two wings" and include such groups as house flies, mosquitoes, deer and horse flies, midges, and gnats, just to name a few. North America hosts over 16,000 described species, and over 120,000 species of flies have been classified throughout the world. Flies are also one of the few insects that are found on every continent, including Antarctica. They can be aquatic, semi-aquatic, or terrestrial. Except in cold weather, anglers are almost always certain to encounter flies while fly fishing, yet it is rare to see a fly fisher actually fishing a fly imitation. Flies come in an endless array of colors and color combinations. Complicating matters even more, they are

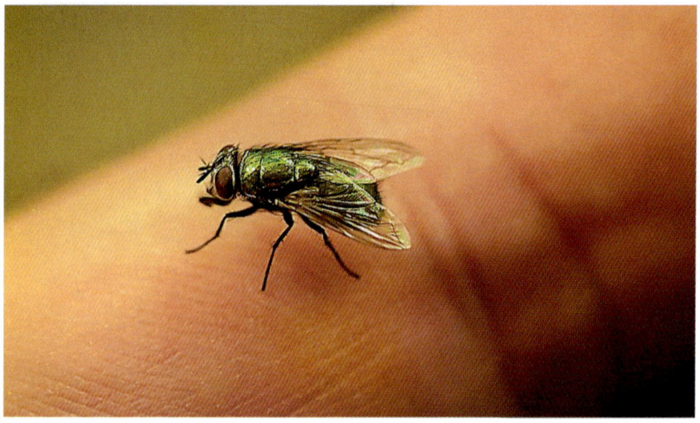

Houseflies and horseflies should not be overlooked as possible candidates for fly patterns. MARK BONAME

mimetic, meaning they have taken on the colors and mannerism of other insects more dangerous insects, particularly ants, wasps, and bees.

SPIDERS

Araneae

There is a common misconception that spiders are insects. In actuality spiders are separated into their own scientific classification. Aside from the obvious difference of all insects having six legs and spiders having eight, insects all share three body segments, known as the tagmata, consisting of the head, thorax, and abdomen, while spiders only have two. Also spiders lack antennae. For the fly fisher and more specifically for those who tie flies, these morphological distinctions are important considerations. Collectively, spiders are known as Arachnids, and of the over 40,000 species in the world, 3,400 live in North America. When collecting terrestrial specimens, there is usually no telling what will show up in your sweep nets, but I always collect a few spiders when sampling areas near river.

A group of spiders of particular interest to both fly fishers as well as fish are fishing spiders (*Dolomedes*). They actually enter the water with their hydrophobic bodies remaining on the surface using the water's surface tension to remain afloat. More amazing, some species are able to swim underwater to catch their prey, which consists of aquatic insects and small fish. It is not beyond a trout to devour a spider that has entered its aquatic habitat.

MICE

Rodentia

Mice are classified in the order of Rodentia, and close to thirty species live in North America. Collectively, rodents are the single largest group of mammals on earth, but realistically, only mice are a potential food source for trout due to their small size. Mice either choose to enter a water source to move from one location to another, or they can be forced in, due to a dramatic rise in water flow or depth, which can flood their dwellings. It is unlikely that there is a single food source that offers as much sustenance for a trout as a mouse swimming its way across a river or lake; consequentially, fishing mouse patterns can be one of the most exciting presentations an angler can experience. Large fish will often explode on to a mouse imitation. It's as if instinctively they know that the amount of energy expended to hunt down such prey will be replenished tenfold with such a substantial, protein-rich meal.

Aquatic insects will always be the primary staple for trout, and it is within this area that the fly fishing community placed its primary focus. On the other hand, terrestrial food sources and their imitations carries with it infinite possibilities. If there is one facet of fly fishing where there is major room for innovation and experimentation, it is within this realm. The sky is truly the limit. For the inquisitive fly fisher willing to expend both the time and energy exploring terrestrial habitats, an entirely endless world of potential trout foods is awaiting to be discovered.

The mouse, an extreme terrestrial, is usually only available to very large trout because they are quite a mouthful. JENS BUURGA

A little lady. Even the ladybug will become prey to an eager trout. MARK BONAME

3

Periodical Cicadas, Methuselahs of the Insect World

Gregory A. Hoover

IN THE EARLY summer of 2008, trout, bass, and even carp that inhabit lakes and rivers within a forested environment were treated to a buffet of adult periodical cicadas that caused them to feed with reckless abandon. Large fish were lured from beneath their overhead cover by these insects to feed during the daytime hours.

It's a time of feasting for a surprising array of creatures when periodical cicadas are on the wing. Birds and fish feed ravenously on the adult stage of these most unusual insects. Grackles and crows voraciously dine on periodical cicadas. Trout will gorge themselves on adult cicadas when they are abundant in trees and shrubs along a stream and fall or fly into the water. Fly fishermen will cast their imitations of the adults so that they enjoy the trout's fondness for this insect. After this unique insect event is over, I've personally heard avid fly fishers admit that they're slightly in a state of depression. The reason for this is they know it will be some time before they can enjoy fly fishing with imitations of the adult stage of this insect

Trout and other fish will key on adult cicadas from early June through late July. During this time birds and other predators will feed ravenously on the adults. GREGORY HOOVER

Three adult western cicadas, Platypedia putnami*, rest on vegetation near the Big Thompson River. These black-eyed cicadas are just over one inch long and become very active as the air temperature warms in June and July. Like periodical cicadas, these cicadas are clumsy fliers and readily fall into the waters of the Colorado's Front Range foothills. They are easy prey as they struggle to escape the water and provide a lot of protein for waiting trout.* JERRY HUBKA

that often yields some huge fish on the surface during daytime hours. Periodical cicadas truly are terrestrial insects worth imitating and fishing

Periodical cicadas are spectacular insects, often making sudden and dramatic appearances. Alexander and Moore wrote in 1962, "The periodical cicadas make up a truly amazing group of animals; since their discovery 300 years ago, the origin and significance of their extended life cycles have been a continual source of puzzlement to biologists. Their incredible ability to merge by the millions as noisy, flying, gregarious, photopositive adults within a matter of hours after having spent 13 or 17 years underground as silent, burrowing, solitary, sedentary juveniles is without parallel in the animal kingdom."

The periodical cicada, *Magicicada septendecim* (Linnaeus), is a native North American species that's found nowhere else in the world. It is the longest-lived insect in North America. No other insects in North America generate as much interest and curiosity as periodical cicada do when they make their sudden, springtime emergence. Periodical cicadas are commonly referred to as "17-year locusts" and are widely distributed over the eastern half of the United States and occur nowhere else in the world.

When early American colonists first arrived to this land they had never seen periodical cicadas. They were familiar with the biblical story of locust plagues in Egypt and Palestine but were not sure what kind of insect was being described. When the cicadas appeared by the millions, some of these early colonists thought a "locust plague" had come upon them. Some American Indians believed their periodic appearance had an evil significance. The confusion between cicadas and locusts exists today in that cicadas are commonly called locusts. The term "locusts" is correctly applied only to certain species of grasshoppers.

There are six different species of periodical cicadas, three with a 17-year cycle and three with a 13-year cycle. The three species in each life-cycle group are distinctive in size, color, and song. The 17-year cicadas are generally northern and the 13-year cicadas southern, with considerable overlap in their distribution. In fact, both life-cycle types may occur in the same forest.

For convenience of reference, each "brood" has been designated by a Roman numeral. The numerals I through XVII were assigned to the 17-year broods and XVIII through XXX to the 13-year broods. The numbering of the 17-year broods

A brown is fooled by one of Rick Takahashi's cicada patterns during a cicada hatch on the Big Thompson River below Estes Park, Colorado. JERRY HUBKA

began with the 1893 brood that was designated as Brood I. In 1909, Brood XVII appeared, and in 1910, Brood I appeared again. There are at least 13 broods of 17-year cicadas and five of 13-year cicadas.

The 2008 brood of periodical cicadas that last emerged in 1991 is referred to as Brood XIV. Based upon historic distribution records, members of this brood emerge in northern Georgia, southern Indiana, most of Kentucky, most of Maryland, eastern Massachusetts (Cape Cod), most of New Jersey, eastern New York (Long Island), western North Carolina, southern Ohio, most of central and eastern Pennsylvania, northern and eastern Tennessee, southwestern West Virginia, and northern, northcentral, and southwestern Virginia.

In Pennsylvania separate populations, referred to as broods, are present during eight different years in different geographic ranges in the state. Several of these broods are very small. Brood X, known as the "great eastern brood," is a large brood with heavy concentrations found in the eastern half of the state during late May through early July of the years they emerge. This brood will next emerge in 2021.

Periodical cicada adults are about one-and-a-half inches long and have eyes and wing veins that are reddish orange. They are smaller than their cousin, the annual or dog-day cicada. The dog-day cicadas, *Tibicen* spp., are mostly large, blackish insects, usually with lime green wing veins, and they appear every year during the hot summer months of July and August.

After 17 years of living in the soil from depths of 2 to 24 inches, mature nymphs of the periodical cicada start burrowing upward. In April they burrow to about an inch beneath the soil surface where they stop and await the proper time to emerge. If the ground is too damp, the nymph builds a protective earthen turret. Their bodies undergo major changes in muscle structure at this time. When the undetermined signal for emergence occurs, nymphs exit from about a one-half-inch diameter hole in the ground. Nymphs crawl a foot or more up tree trunks, weeds, or other upright objects where adults emerge leaving their nymphal skins behind. The process of shedding a nymphal skin is completed in an hour or less. The periodical cicada is now an adult, but it is soft and white. In time its exoskeleton hardens and becomes darker. During some years, practically all of the population in a brood from a forest may emerge on the same night or on two or three different nights.

Adults are clumsy fliers and often collide into objects during flight, including the surface of a river, lake, or stream. Soon after emerging, males begin their constant "singing" while females remain mostly silent. The sound made by adult males is sometimes haunting and eerie. Adult periodical cicadas do not or seldom feed. If they feed at all, it is by sucking plant fluid from young twigs. About 10 days after emergence, females will mate and begin depositing eggs in twigs and branches of nearly 80 different preferred species of trees and woody shrubs. They usually do not deposit eggs in coniferous trees. Generally, one female will deposit 400 to 600 eggs in the twigs of their preferred plant species. Using the blades of a saw-like, egg-laying device at the end of the abdomen, the female punctures the bark of the twig and makes a pocket in the wood. A female may deposit from 24 to 28 eggs in two rows in one of these pockets. She then moves forward, cuts another pocket, and lays more eggs. The pockets are placed close together in a straight row sometimes forming a continuous slit for two to three inches. Adults live for approximately three to four weeks above ground. Most are usually gone by the beginning of July.

Hatching occurs six to seven weeks after egg laying, and the white, antlike nymphs work their way out of the slits and drop to the ground where they enter the soil. Here they insert their piercing-sucking mouthparts and draw plant fluid from roots of plants for the next 17 years. The effect of root feeding by the nymph is considered inconsequential to most trees. The number of nymphal instars (growth phases) is still uncertain, although some studies indicate that there are only five instars.

Since adult periodical cicadas are more active from mid-morning through mid-afternoon, I would suggest that fly rod anglers target these times to be on the water. The adults are clumsy fliers and do thrash around on the surface of rivers and lakes with forested edges. One effective tactic would be to present your cicada pattern with a "twitching" or "skating" motion. Another deadly method is to drive a cicada pattern hard onto the water surface beneath overhanging cover. This method of presentation often generates vicious rises.

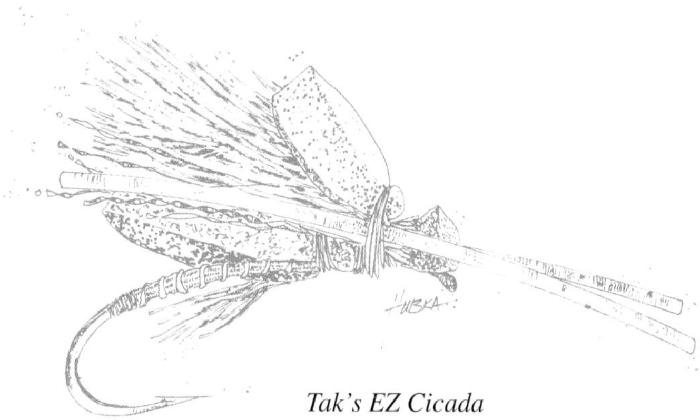

Tak's EZ Cicada

PART I

Tying Terrestrials

Tak's Foam Head Hot Hopper

Common Materials

FOAM CUTTERS AND CUTTING TOOLS

Foam cutters, such as those available from River Road Creations, allow you to quickly tie realistic grasshopper, beetle, ant, and other terrestrial patterns. You can use these cutters with many different materials such as sheet foam, winging materials, or any other type of material that is not too dense or tough. We also use rotary fabric cutters and a metal ruler to cut straight sections of foam sheeting and other materials. Tip: rotary cutters with larger diameter wheels track along the straight edge easier.
MARK TRACY

FOAM BODIES

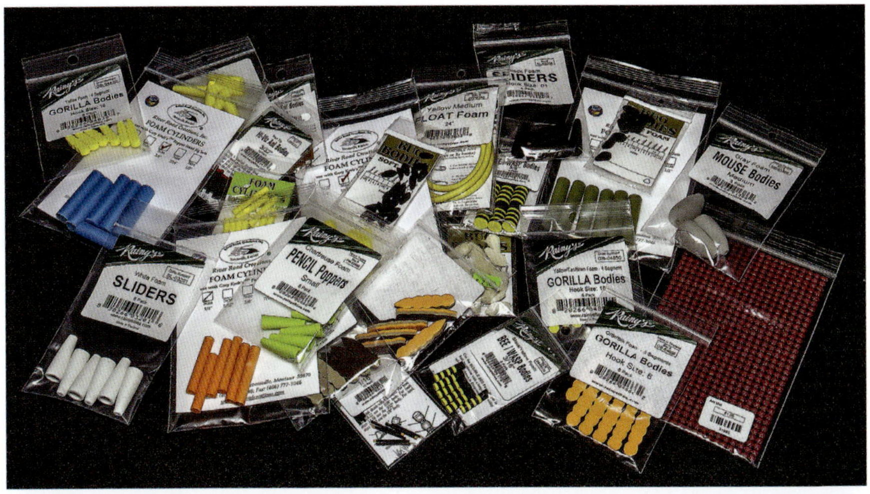

Foam cylinders, ant bodies, pre-cut hopper bodies, foam legs, and other precut foam shapes allow tiers to easily create all manner of terrestrial flies. You can cut them up to meet your needs or use the precut shapes right out of the package. MARK TRACY

FOAM SHEETS

Foam sheets come in a wide range of colors and thicknesses, from super thin (Razor Foam) to thick foam blocks. You can layer sheets of foam together using super strong spray glues, such as Scotch's Super 77 spray glue or double-faced carpet tape. In addition to using a rotary cutter, you can also easily cut strips of foam using a small lever-type paper cutter. MARK TRACY

RUBBER LEGS

Rubber legs come in several sizes and with flat, square, or round cross sections. Several companies make precut hopper legs. MARK TRACY

UV RESINS

Loon's UV Knot Sense was one of the first producers of a UV light sensitive resin that was liquid in application but quickly if not instantaneous became hard when introduced to sunlight. UV resins, now available from several manufacturers, such as Clear Cure Goo, Deer Creek, Bug Bond, and Solarez, are designed to be cured with a handheld light and allow tiers to cover their patterns with a clear and hard covering that sets within seconds when the resins are introduced to a UV light. Tuffleye is a light-cured acrylic that sets when it is exposed to blue light, which is different than UV light. MARK TRACY

WING MATERIALS

Many companies have realistic wing materials that come in a wide range of colors. MARK TRACY

Tying Ants

Fur Bodied Ant

Originator: Unknown
Tier: Rick Takahashi

Hook: #10-20 Tiemco 100
Thread: Black 70-denier UTC
Rear Gaster: Black Super Fine Dubbing
Waist: Tying thread
Legs: Grizzly Whiting Farms saddle hackle
Thorax: Black Super Fine Dubbing

TYING THE FUR BODIED ANT

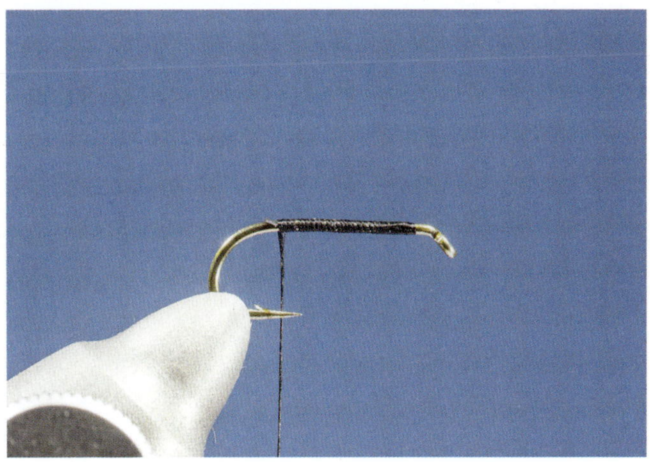

1. Attach the tying thread to the hook approximately one eye width back from the hook eye. Wrap the thread back to the hook bend to a point opposite the barb and trim the excess thread.

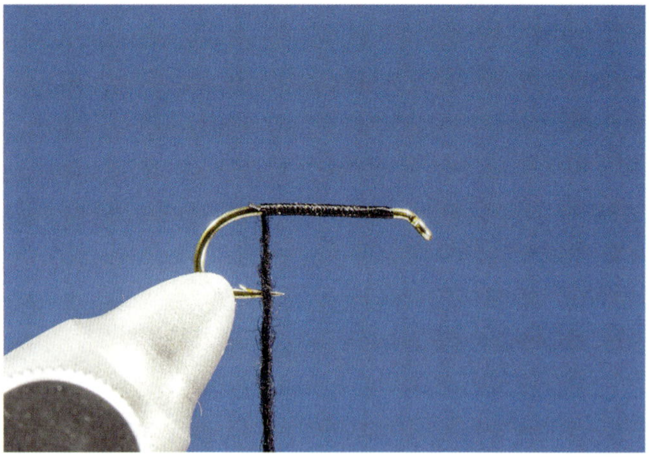

2. Twist a slim two-inch noodle of dubbing onto the thread. You can use any color to match the naturals in your area.

3. Wrap the dubbing forward to form a small ball.

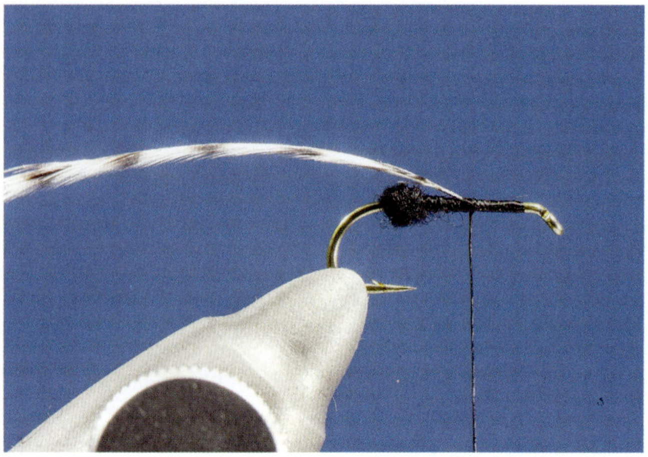

4. Wrap the thread to the midpoint of the hook to form a waist. Tie in the hackle with the shiny side forward.

5. Take several wraps of the hackle at the midpoint of the hook. Tie off the hackle and trim the excess.

6. Wrap the tying thread toward the hook eye.

7. Dub the tying thread, forming a slim two-inch noodle of dubbing.

8. Wrap the dubbing to form a small thorax.

9. Whip-finish and trim the excess thread.

10. Completed Fur Bodied Ant.

Glass Bead Ant

Originator: Unknown
Tier: Rick Takahashi

Hook: #10-20 Tiemco 100
Thread: Black 70-denier UTC
Rear Gaster: Cinnamon colored 10/0 glass seed bead
Waist: Tying thread
Legs: Black bristles from a cleaning brush
Thorax: Black 10/0 glass seed bead
Note: *Cover gaster and thorax with CCG Thin.*

TYING THE GLASS BEAD ANT

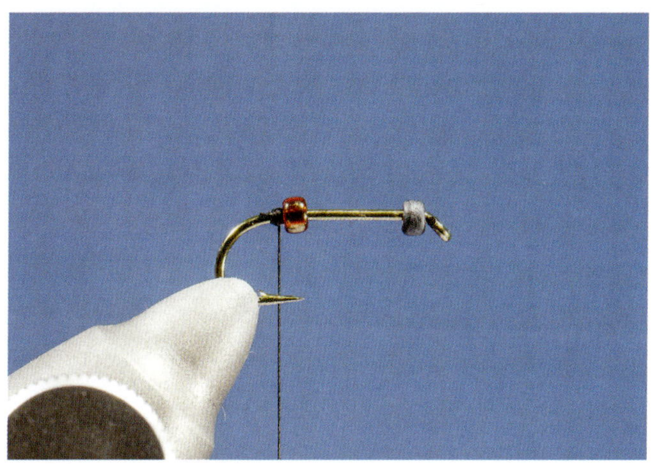

1. Slide a black glass bead followed by a cinnamon colored clear bead onto the hook shank. Slide the bead to the hook eye. Wrap the tying thread at the hook bend and form a small dam of thread to prevent the glass bead from sliding back. Whip-finish the thread and trim it. Slide the bead back to the thread dam.

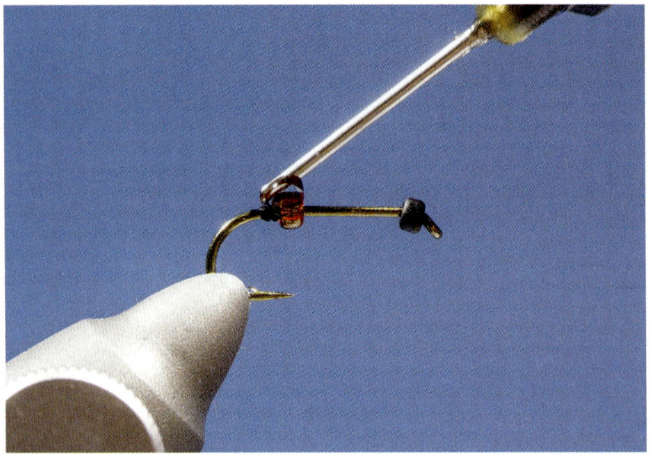

2. Cover the glass bead with Clear Cure Goo (CCG) Hydro to set it in place.

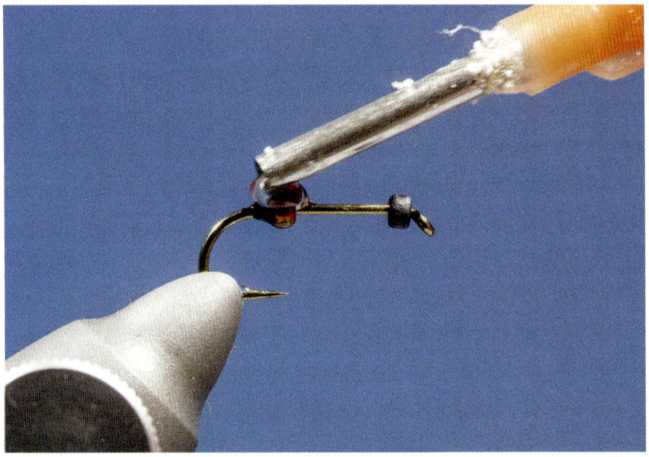

3. Cover the glass bead with CCG Thin to form the gaster.

4. Set the UV resin with a UV light.

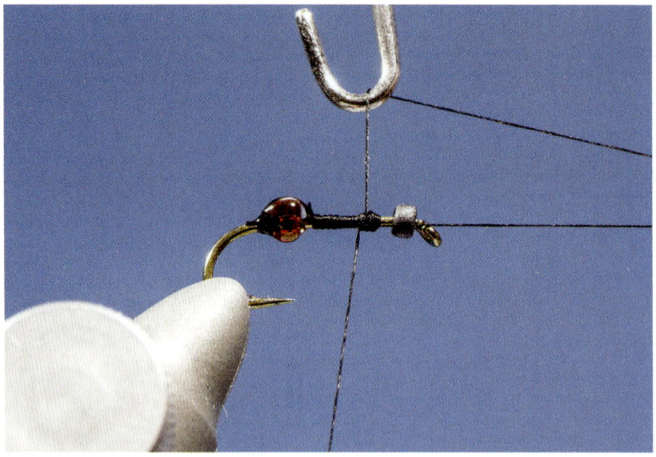

5. Attach the tying thread in front of the gaster and wrap to the midpoint of the hook. Form a small dam of thread to prevent the glass bead from sliding back. Position the bead at the midpoint of the remaining space. Whip-finish and trim the tying thread.

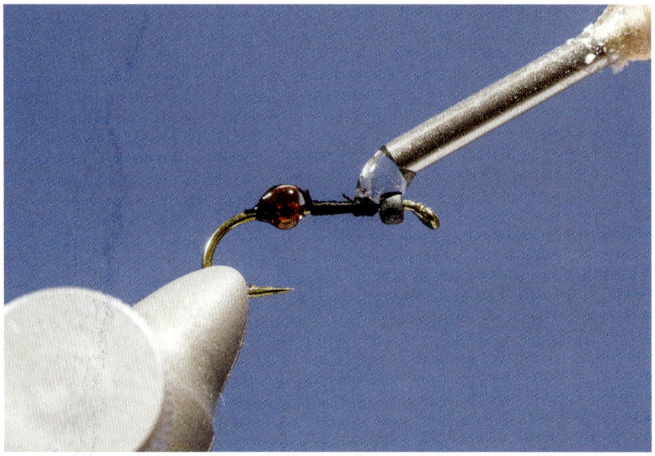

6. Slide the bead back and apply CCG Thin to set the bead and to form the front thorax.

7. Set the CCG with UV light.

8. Attach the tying thread at the midpoint of the hook and tie in one strand of the leg material in the middle of the strand with figure-eight wraps. Fold the strands to the rear of the hook.

9. Attach the second pair of leg material using a figure-eight wrap.

10. Attach the third pair of leg material with figure-eight wraps and bend forward.

11. Slightly warm a bodkin with a match or lighter, then position it to form the leg joint and gently bend the material toward the rear.

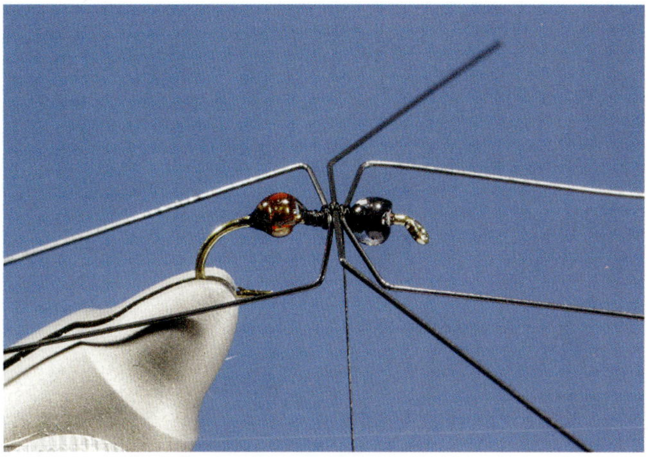

12. Form each of the legs as shown above.

13. Position the thread in between the legs.

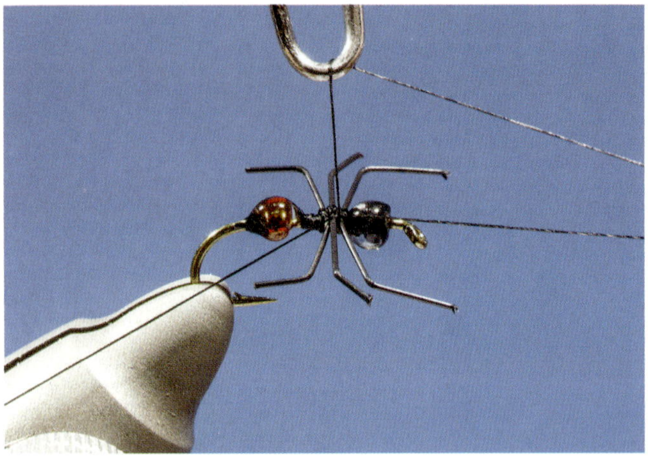

14. Make several wraps overlapping the legs to strengthen them. Whip-finish and trim thread.

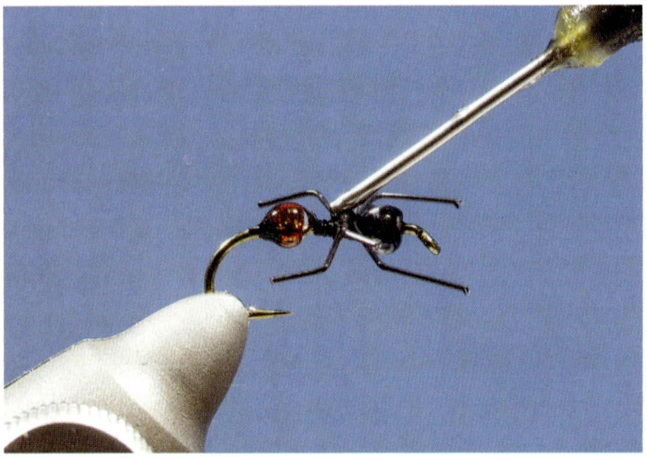

15. Apply CCG Hydro to seal the leg joints.

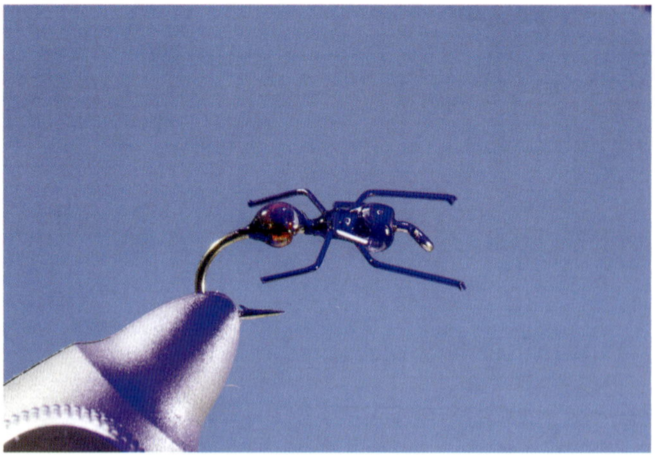

16. Set the CCG with UV light.

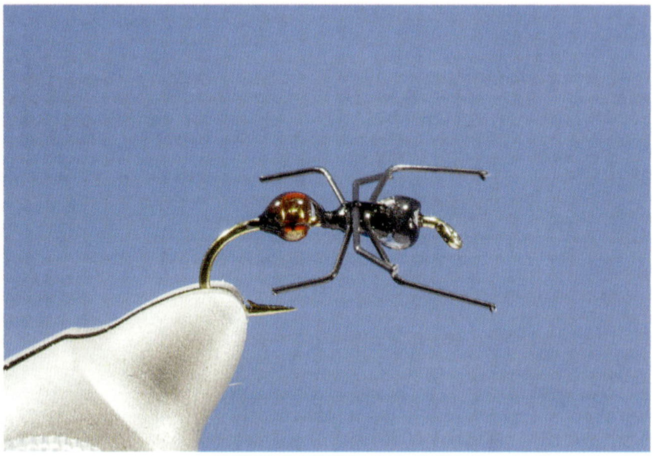

17. Completed Glass Bead Ant.

San Juan Carpenter Ant

Originator: Rick Takahashi
Tier: Rick Takahashi

Hook: #10-20 Tiemco 2302
Thread: Black 70-denier UTC
Rear Gaster: Black Rainy's Float Foam
Waist: Tying thread and brown Whiting Farms saddle hackle
Wing: Clear Medallion Sheeting
Legs: Brown round rubber legs (medium)
Thorax: Black Rainy's Float Foam
Head: Black Rainy's Float Foam

TYING THE SAN JUAN CARPENTER ANT

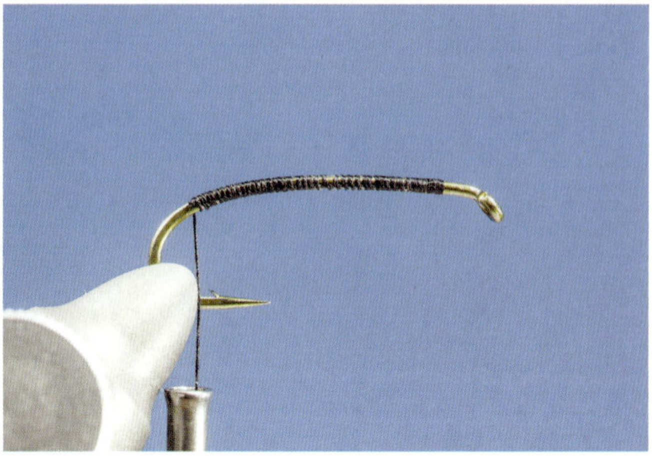

1. Attach the tying thread three eye widths back from the hook eye. Wrap the thread in touching wraps back to the point on the hook bend opposite the barb.

2. Cut a three-inch-long piece of Rainy's Float Foam, then cut it in half, lengthwise. Cut a small section from the end of the inside edge, creating a small divot.

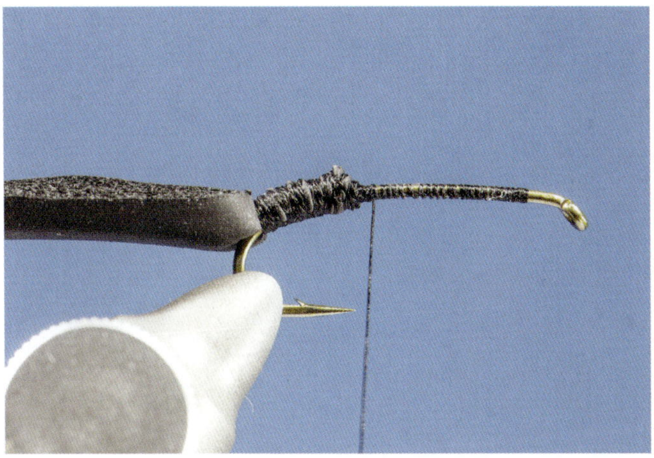

3. Turn the foam upside down so that the shiny side is facing down with the divot positioned over the end of the hook. The entire length of foam should extend beyond the hook bend. Attach the foam to the hook securely. The divot will help the foam collapse and make it easier to attach to the hook. Wrap the thread forward to the midpoint of the hook.

4. Fold the foam over to the midpoint and attach it with several wraps of thread to form the rear gaster.

5. Stretch the foam toward the front of the hook and take several wraps of thread over the foam to compress it and create the ant's waist. Twist the middle of a piece of Medallion Sheeting that is the same width as the body.

6. Tie in the wing material and fold it back and over the rear of the pattern.

7. Trim the ends of the wing.

8. Tie in the round rubber legs so that they are in the midsection of the waist of the ant on both sides of the hook.

9. Attach the hackle with the shiny side facing toward the hook eye.

10. Take several wraps of the hackle, tie it off, and trim the excess.

11. Lift the remaining foam and wrap the thread forward to a point one eye width behind the hook eye.

12. Fold the remaining foam over the hook shank and tie it in. Make several wraps to secure the foam to the hook and whip-finish.

13. Trim the head of the ant as shown and trim the excess thread.

14. Completed San Juan Carpenter Ant.

Ant Patterns

CDC Foam Ant

Originator: Unknown
Tier: Spirit River

Hook: #12-18 Spear-It D100 or Daiichi 1180
Thread: Black 6/0 Uni-Thread
Body: Black Spirit River Fly Foam (2mm)
Indicator: Yellow Fly Foam (2mm)
Throat: Black CDC
Legs/Antennae: Black Crystal Splash

Fishy's Epoxy Ant

Originator: Jay "Fishy" Fullum
Tier: Spirit River

Hook: #12 Spear-It D100
Thread: Black 6/0 Uni-Thread
Body: Black Fly Foam (2mm)
Legs: Black Spirit River Flex Floss
Adhesive: Epoxy

Mr. Bill's Flying Ant (Black)

Originator: Bill Black
Tier: Spirit River

Hook: #10-18 Spear-It D100
Thread: Black 6/0 Uni-Thread
Body: Black Antron dubbing
Wing: Mottled silver/black Spirit River Wings and Things
Legs/Antennae: Black Crystal Splash

Mr. Bill's Flying Ant (Red)

Originator: Bill Black
Tier: Spirit River

Hook:	#10-18 Spear-It D100
Thread:	Orange 6/0 Uni-Thread
Body:	Ginger Antron dubbing
Wing:	Mottled tan Spirit River Wings and Things
Legs:	Orange Crystal Splash

Snake River Angler's Chernobyl Bug (Tan)

Originator: Unknown
Tier: Spirit River

Hook:	#6-12 Maruto 7008
Thread:	Tan 3/0 Uni-Thread
Body:	Two layers of tan Spirit River Fly Foam (2mm)
Underbody:	Brown Spirit River angora goat dubbing
Legs:	Tan/black barred Tarantu-Leggs (medium)
Indicator:	White Spirit River Fly Foam (2mm)

Rainy's Red Butt Carpenter Ant

Originator: Rainy Riding
Tier: Rainy's Flies

Hook:	#12-18 Tiemco 100
Thread:	Black 6/0 Uni-Thread
Body:	Red/black Rainy's Cross-Link Sheet Foam
Thorax:	Black Super Fine Dubbing
Indicator:	Fluorescent orange poly yarn
Legs:	Black Rainy's Bug Eye Stick (fine)

Rainy's Black Ant

Originator: Rainy Riding
Tier: Rainy's Flies

Hook:	#12-18 Tiemco 100
Thread:	Black 6/0 Uni-Thread
Body:	Black Rainy's Float Foam (small)
Underbody:	Tying thread
Indicator:	Red Rainy's Evazote Sheet Foam (1/8")
Legs:	Black Rainy's Rubber Legs (fine)

Rainy's Red Ant

Originator: Rainy Riding
Tier: Rainy's Flies

Hook:	#12-18 Tiemco 100
Thread:	Red 8/0 Uni-Thread
Body:	Red Rainy's Cross-Link Sheet Foam (2mm)
Underbody:	Tying thread
Indicator:	White Rainy's Cross-Link Sheet Foam (2mm)
Legs:	Black Rainy's Rubber Legs (fine)

Rainy's Cinnamon Ant

Originator: Rainy Riding
Tier: Rainy's Flies

Hook:	#12-18 Tiemco 100
Thread:	Tan 8/0 Uni-Thread
Body:	Cinnamon Rainy's Cross-Link Sheet Foam (2mm)
Underbody:	Tying thread
Indicator:	Chartreuse Rainy's Evazote Sheet Foam (1/8")
Legs:	Tan Rainy's Rubber Legs (fine)

Rainy's Orange Tip Hi-Viz Ant

Originator: Rainy Riding
Tier: Rainy's Flies

Hook: #14-20 Tiemco 100
Thread: Black 6/0 Uni-Thread
Body: Rainy's Hi-Viz Ant Body Foam
Hackle: Black Whiting Farms dry fly saddle

Rainy's Chernobyl Ant

Originator: Rainy Riding
Tier: Rainy's Flies

Hook: #6-10 Tiemco 5263
Thread: Black 6/0 Uni-Thread
Body: Black Rainy's Float Foam (L/XL)
Underbody: Black/peacock Crystal Chenille
Indicator: Red Rainy's Evazote Sheet Foam (1/8")
Legs: Black Rainy's Rubber Legs (medium)

J's Obe-Wan-Chernobe Ant

Originator: Jesse Riding
Tier: Rainy's Flies

Hook: #6-12 Tiemco 5230
Thread: Tan 6/0 Uni-Thread
Body: Brown Rainy's Gorilla Body
Underbody: Tan Rainy's Gorilla Body (thin)
Indicator: Chartreuse Rainy's Cross-Link Sheet Foam (2mm)
Wing: Light elk hair
Underwing: Pearl Krystal Flash
Legs: Tan Rainy's barred Rubber Legs (medium)

Johnston's Cottonwood Winged Carpenter Ant

Originator: Ray Johnston
Tier: Ray Johnston

Hook: #16 Tiemco 900 BL
Thread: Black 8/0 Uni-Thread
Body: Black foam cylinder (1/8")
Wing: Pearl Mylar Strip
Indicator: Yellow 3D fabric paint
Hackle: Brown Whiting Farms dry fly

Johnston's Cottonwood Black Carpenter Ant

Originator: Ray Johnston
Tier: Ray Johnston

Hook: #16 Tiemco 900 BL
Thread: Black 8/0 Uni-Thread
Body: Black foam cylinder (1/8")
Indicator: Chartreuse 3D fabric paint
Hackle: Black Whiting Farms dry fly

Haddix's Hard Body Ant

Originator: Jason Haddix
Tier: Jason Haddix

Hook: #16-20 Daiichi 1110
Thread: Black 6/0 Danville's
Body: Red 6/0 Danville's
Thorax: Black Whiting Farms dry fly saddle
Wing: White Spirit River CDC and pearl Krystal Flash
Legs: Black MFC Tentacles (medium)
Head: Black 6/0 Danville's
Adhesive: Coat body with Sally Hansen Hard As Nails

Haddix's CDC Para-Ant

Originator: Jason Haddix
Tier: Jason Haddix

Hook: #16-20 Daiichi 1130
Thread: Black 14/0 Gordon Griffiths
Head: Black 14/0 Gordon Griffiths
Body: Black Super Fine Dubbing
Thorax: Black Super Fine Dubbing
Wing: Whiting Farms grizzly dry fly hackle
Post: Three chartreuse Nature's Spirit select CDC feathers
Legs: Black Spirit River Sea Hair

Haddix's Semi-Real Ant

Originator: Jason Haddix
Tier: Jason Haddix

Hook: #18-20 Tiemco 900 BL
Thread: Trico white 17/0 Uni-Thread
Head: Tying thread
Body: Tying thread
Thorax: Tying thread
Eyes: Deep Blue Mono
Legs: RIO mono (4X)
Antennae: Clear paintbrush fibers
Adhesive: Sally Hansen Hard As Nails
Marker: Black Copic permanent
Note: *Form the underbody with one piece of 20-pound-test and two pieces of 10-pound-test. For the eyes, use 15-pound-test.*

Psycho Ant

Originator: Bubba Smith
Tier: Orvis

Hook: #6-10 Tiemco 200R
Thread: Black 6/0 Uni-Thread
Overbody: Black foam (3mm)
Underbody: Peacock Ice Dub
Wing: White Orvis poly yarn
Underwing: Pearl Krystal Flash
Legs: Red/black and chartreuse/black Rainy's round rubber (medium)
Hackle: Brown Whiting Farms dry fly

San Juan Ant

Originator: Bubba Smith
Tier: Orvis

Hook: #8-10 Tiemco 5212
Thread: Black 6/0 Uni-Thread
Body: Black foam (2mm)
Wing: White Orvis poly yarn
Legs: White and black Centipede Legs (small)
Hackle: Black Whiting Farms dry fly

Splitsville Flying Ant

Originator: Jonny King
Tier: Jonny King

Hook: #14-18 Tiemco 2487 or 206 BL
Thread: Black 6/0 Uni-Thread
Rear Body: Mahogany Harrop Pro Dry Fly Dubbing
Front Body: Black Harrop Pro Dry Fly Dubbing
Wing: White Niche Products siliconized poly yarn
Hackle: Grizzly dry fly
Note: *This pattern was inspired by Bob Quigley. Tie poly yarn as a split down wing and tie grizzly feather hackle stacker style and pull hackle forward over the top of the split down wing.*

Berg's Cinnamon Ant

Originator: Ed Berg
Tier: Ed Berg

Hook: #14-18 Daiichi 1182
Thread: Light brown 8/0 Gudebrod
Abdomen: Medium red brown and amber Targus SST Dubbing
Head: Medium red brown and dark brown Targus SST Dubbing
Legs: Furnace or brown Whiting Coq de Leon hen

Berg's Fire Ant

Originator: Ed Berg
Tier: Ed Berg

Hook: #14-18 Daiichi 1182
Thread: Red 8/0 Gudebrod
Body: Blood red and amber Targus SST Dubbing
Legs: Red Whiting Coq de Leon hen

Berg's Black Ant

Originator: Ed Berg
Tier: Ed Berg

Hook: #14-18 Daiichi 1182
Thread: Black 8/0 Gudebrod
Body: Targus SST Dubbing
Legs: Starling
Note: *Dubbing mix is 80% black, 10% brilliant purple, and 10% spring green.*

Dunnigan's Rocky Mountain Ant

Originator: Casey Dunnigan
Tier: Casey Dunnigan

Hook: #16-18 Tiemco 101
Thread: Black 8/0 MFC
Body: Black Wapsi Fly Foam ($\frac{1}{8}$")
Hackle: Brown Whiting Farms dry fly
Wing: Yellow Widow's Web

Ghetto Booty Ant

Originator: Jake Ruthven
Tier: Jake Ruthven

Hook: #14-18 Tiemco 2499 SPBL
Thread: Black 70-denier UTC
Body: Black glass beads secured with CCG Hydro
Legs: Hot orange Centipede Legs
Hackle: Dun or black Whiting Farms dry fly saddle
Adhesive: CCG Hydro

Cupboard Ant

Originator: Mike Kruise
Tier: Jake Ruthven

Hook: #14-18 Tiemco 101
Thread: Black 70-denier UTC
Body: Foam shelf liner sheet
Underbody: Tying thread
Legs: Black Whiting Farms dry fly saddle
Adhesive: CCG Hydro
Note: *Grasp two squares of shelf foam and pull sharply off of sheet.*

Foam Ant

Originator: Unknown
Tier: Tim Jacobs

Hook: #18 Tiemco 100
Thread: Black 70-denier UTC
Underbody: Waxed tying thread
Body: Black foam cylinder ($^1/_{16}$")
Legs: Black Whiting Farms dry fly hackle

Red Fur Ant

Originator: Ken Miyata
Tier: Tim Jacobs

Hook: #10-18 Tiemco 100
Thread: Tan 70-denier UTC
Body/Head: Cinnamon Hareline Micro Fine Dry Fly Dubbing
Legs: Brown Whiting Farms dry fly hackle

Black and Red Fur Ant

Originator: Ken Miyata
Tier: Tim Jacobs

Hook: #10-18 Tiemco 100
Thread: Black 70-denier UTC
Body: Black Hareline Micro Fine Dry Fly Dubbing
Head: Cinnamon Hareline Micro Fine Dry Fly Dubbing
Legs: Black Whiting Farms dry fly hackle

Black Fur Ant

Originator: Ken Miyata
Tier: Tim Jacobs

Hook: #10-18 Tiemco 100
Thread: Black 70-denier UTC
Body: Black Hareline Micro Fine Dry Fly Dubbing
Legs: Black Whiting Farms dry fly hackle

CDC Winged Ant (Red)

Originator: Unknown
Tier: Tim Jacobs

Hook: #10-18 Tiemco 100
Thread: Tan 70-denier UTC
Body: Cinnamon Hareline Micro Fine Dry Fly Dubbing
Wing: Ginger CDC
Legs: Brown Whiting Farms High and Dry hackle

CDC Winged Ant (Black)

Originator: Variation of Harrop's Winged Ant
Tier: Tim Jacobs

Hook: #10-18 Tiemco 100
Thread: Black 70-denier UTC
Body: Black Hareline Micro Fine Dry Fly Dubbing
Wing: Natural CDC
Legs: Black Whiting Farms hackle

Deer Hair Ant (Black)

Originator: Unknown
Tier: Tim Jacobs

Hook: #10-14 Tiemco 100
Thread: Black 140-denier UTC
Legs: Black Wapsi deer hair
Body: Black Wapsi deer hair

Chernobyl Ant (Green)

Originator: Unknown
Tier: Vic Loiselle

Hook: #6-8 Dai-Riki 700
Thread: Olive 6/0 Uni-Thread
Body: Yellow and green foam (2mm)
Underbody: Tying thread
Indicator: Orange foam (2mm)
Legs: Green/black Tarantu-Leggs (medium)

Vic's Chernobyl Ant (Black)

Originator: Vic Loiselle
Tier: Vic Loiselle

Hook: #6-8 Dai-Riki 700
Thread: Black 6/0 Uni-Thread
Body: Black closed-cell foam (2mm)
Underbody: Red Danville's Uni-Floss and peacock Hareline Ice Dub
Indicator: Red craft foam (2mm)
Legs: Black Rainy's round rubber
Adhesive: Griff's Thin Multi-Coat

Half n Half Ant (Legs)

Originator: Tim Mack
Tier: Tim Mack

Hook: #14-18 Tiemco 100
Thread: Black 6/0 Uni-Thread
Body: Black/white Wapsi Foam Ant Body
Underbody: Black Super Fine Dubbing
Legs: Black Spirit River Rubber Legs (mini)
Hackle: Black Whiting Farms saddle
Adhesive: Fish Pimp Hard Headed
Note: *A version without the rubber legs is also effective.*

Bead Butt Flying Ant (Black)

Originator: Tim Mack
Tier: Tim Mack

Hook: #14-18 Tiemco 101
Thread: Black 70-denier UTC
Body: Red Czech bead and tying thread
Wing: White Whiting Farms hen cape
Legs: Black Spirit River Rubber Legs (mini)
Hackle: Black Whiting Farms saddle, trimmed
Adhesive: Fish Pimp Hard Headed

Bead Butt Ant (Black/White)

Originator: Tim Mack
Tier: Tim Mack

Hook: #14-18 Tiemco 101
Thread: Black 70-denier UTC
Body: Red Czech bead and tying thread
Legs: White/black Hareline Rubber Legs (mini)
Hackle: Whiting Farms grizzly saddle, trimmed
Adhesive: Fish Pimp Hard Headed

Bead Butt Ant (Black with Legs)

Originator: Tim Mack
Tier: Tim Mack

Hook: #14-18 Tiemco 101
Thread: Black 70-denier UTC
Body: Red Czech bead and tying thread
Legs: Black Spirit River Rubber Legs (mini)
Hackle: Black Whiting Farms saddle
Adhesive: Fish Pimp Hard Headed

Bead Butt Ant (Black)

Originator: Tim Mack
Tier: Tim Mack

Hook: #14-18 Tiemco 101
Thread: Black 70-denier UTC
Body: Red Czech bead and tying thread
Hackle: Black Whiting Farms saddle, trimmed
Adhesive: Fish Pimp Hard Headed

Bead Butt Flying Ant (Brown)

Originator: Tim Mack
Tier: Tim Mack

Hook: #14-18 Tiemco 101
Thread: Brown 70-denier UTC
Body: Hareline Tyer's Bead (midge) and tying thread
Legs: White/black barred Spirit River Rubber Legs (mini)
Hackle: Brown Whiting Farms saddle
Adhesive: Fish Pimp Hard Headed

Bead Butt Ant (Brown with Legs)

Originator: Tim Mack
Tier: Tim Mack

Hook: #14-18 Tiemco 101
Thread: Brown 70-denier UTC
Body: Brown Hareline Tyer's Bead (midge) and tying thread
Legs: White/black barred Hareline Rubber Legs (mini)
Hackle: Brown Whiting Farms saddle, trimmed
Wing: White Whiting Farms hen cape
Adhesive: Fish Pimp Hard Headed

Half n Half Ant (Brown with Legs)

Originator: Tim Mack
Tier: Tim Mack

Hook: #14-18 Tiemco 100
Thread: Brown 8/0 Uni-Thread
Body/Head: Brown/white Wapsi Foam Ant Body
Underbody: Brown Super Fine Dubbing
Legs: Brown Spirit River Rubber Legs (mini)
Hackle: Brown Whiting Farms saddle
Adhesive: Fish Pimp Hard Headed

Fuzzy Ant (Black)

Originator: Tim Mack
Tier: Tim Mack

Hook: #8-12 Tiemco 512
Thread: Black 8/0 Uni-Thread
Body: Black Wapsi Furry Foam
Underbody: Tying thread
Indicator: Chartreuse Wapsi Antron Yarn
Legs: Black Spirit River round rubber (small)
Hackle: Black Whiting Farms saddle
Adhesive: Brush on Super Glue

Fuzzy Ant (Brown)

Originator: Tim Mack
Tier: Tim Mack

Hook: #8-12 Tiemco 512
Thread: Brown 8/0 Uni-Thread
Body: Brown Wapsi Furry Foam
Underbody: Tying thread
Indicator: Chartreuse Wapsi Antron Yarn
Legs: Brown Spirit River round rubber (small)
Hackle: Cree Whiting Farms saddle
Adhesive: Brush on Super Glue

Wired Red Ant

Originator: Ron Donahue
Tier: Ron Donahue

Hook: #16 Tiemco Daiichi 1273
Thread: Red 6/0 Uni-Thread
Body: Red Ultra Wire (large)
Thorax: Red Ultra Wire (brassie)
Hackle: White Whiting Farms saddle
Adhesive: Coat body and head with Loon UV Knot Sense
Marker: Crimson red Prismacolor

Bicolor Ant (Black/Red)

Originator: Ron Donahue
Tier: Ron Donahue

Hook: #16 Tiemco 2488
Thread: Black 70-denier UTC
Body: Black 1X Uni-Floss
Head: Chinese red Uni-Stretch
Legs: Black Whiting Farms hackle

Black-n-Brown Floater

Originator: Ron Donahue
Tier: Ron Donahue

Hook: #16 Dai-Riki 135 or Tiemco 2487
Thread: Black 70-denier UTC
Body: Black Super Fine Dubbing
Head: Mahogany and brown Super Fine Dubbing (50% of each)
Legs: Whiting Farms grizzly hackle

UV Termite

Originator: Ron Donahue
Tier: Ron Donahue

Hook: #12 Tiemco 100
Thread: White 150-denier Lagartun
Body: Dun Super Fine Dubbing
Legs: Whiting Farms grizzly hackle
Note: *Body and head coated with UV Knot Sense.*

High Life Ant

Originator: Connor Murphy
Tier: Connor Murphy

Hook: #18 Dai-Riki 320
Thread: Black 6/0 Uni-Thread
Body: Black Easy Liner shelf liner
Underbody: Tying thread
Indicator: Orange Wapsi Fly Foam (3mm)
Legs: Black MFC Tentacles
Adhesive: Loctite Super Glue

CDC Flying Ant (Black)

Originator: Henry Ramsay
Tier: Henry Ramsay

Hook: #14-20 Daiichi 1100
Thread: Black 6/0 Uni-Thread
Body: Black Super Fine Dubbing
Wing: Dun CDC feather
Legs: Black Wapsi Midge Flash

Parachute Black Ant

Originator: Henry Ramsay
Tier: Henry Ramsay

Hook: #14-22 Daiichi 1100
Thread: Black 6/0 Uni-Thread
Body: Black Super Fine Dubbing
Post: Fluorescent orange Antron Yarn
Legs: Black Whiting Farms hackle

Parachute Red Headed Ant

Originator: Henry Ramsay
Tier: Henry Ramsay

Hook: #14-22 Daiichi 1100
Thread: Black 6/0 Uni-Thread
Body: Black Super Fine Dubbing
Head: Midge red Super Fine Dubbing
Post: Fluorescent orange Antron Yarn
Legs: Dark dun Whiting Farms hackle

CDC Flying Red Headed Ant

Originator: Henry Ramsay
Tier: Henry Ramsay

Hook: #14-20 Daiichi 1100
Thread: Black 6/0 Uni-Thread
Body: Black Super Fine Dubbing
Head: Midge red Super Fine Dubbing
Wing: Dun CDC feather
Legs: Black Wapsi Midge Flash

CDC Flying Cinnamon Ant

Originator: Henry Ramsay
Tier: Henry Ramsay

Hook: #14-20 Daiichi 1100
Thread: Rusty brown 8/0 Uni-Thread
Body/Head: Cinnamon caddis Super Fine Dubbing
Wing: Dun CDC feather
Legs: Root beer Wapsi Midge Flash

Parachute Cinnamon Ant

Originator: Henry Ramsay
Tier: Henry Ramsay

Hook: #18-22 Daiichi 1100
Thread: Rusty brown 8/0 Uni-Thread
Body: Cinnamon caddis Wapsi Super Fine Dubbing
Post: Fluorescent orange Antron Yarn
Legs: Brown Whiting Farms hackle

Parachute Red Ant

Originator: Henry Ramsay
Tier: Henry Ramsay

Hook: #14-20 Daiichi 1100
Thread: Red 8/0 Uni-Thread
Body: Midge red Super Fine Dubbing
Post: Fluorescent orange Antron Yarn
Legs: Dark dun Whiting Farms hackle

Parachute Carpenter Ant

Originator: Henry Ramsay
Tier: Henry Ramsay

Hook: #10-14 Daiichi 1100
Thread: Black 6/0 Uni-Thread
Body: Black Super Fine Dubbing
Head: Mahogany Super Fine Dubbing
Post: Fluorescent orange Antron Yarn
Legs: Dark dun Whiting Farms hackle

CDC Flying Red Ant

Originator: Henry Ramsay
Tier: Henry Ramsay

Hook: #18-22 Daiichi 1100
Thread: Red 8/0 Uni-Thread
Body: Midge red Super Fine Dubbing
Wing: Dun CDC feather
Legs: Root beer Wapsi Midge Flash

CDC Flying Carpenter Ant

Originator: Henry Ramsay
Tier: Henry Ramsay

Hook: #10-14 Daiichi 1100
Thread: Black 6/0 Uni-Thread
Body: Black Super Fine Dubbing
Head: Mahogany Super Fine Dubbing
Wing: Dun CDC feather
Legs: Black Wapsi Midge Flash

Bionic Ant

Originator: Lance Egan
Tier: Lance Egan

Hook: #12 Tiemco 900 BL
Thread: Black 70-denier UTC
Body: Black Wapsi Foam Ant Body (large)
Wing: Brown caddis Hareline Para Post Wing
Legs: Black MFC Tentacles (medium)
Hackle: Brown Whiting Farms

JR's Lady Carpenter

Originator: John Rohmer
Tier: John Rohmer

Hook: #14 Daiichi 1560
Thread: Black 6/0 Uni-Thread
Body: Black Rainy's Round Ant Foam Body
Underbody: Tying thread
Wing: Orange Raffia
Indicator: Orange foam (2mm)
Legs: Black Whiting Farms dry fly hackle
Adhesive: Zap-A-Gap

Hang-On Ant

Originator: Jay Zimmerman
Tier: Jay Zimmerman

Hook: #14 Tiemco 2487
Thread: Black 6/0 Uni-Thread
Body: Tying thread
Thorax: Black Super Fine Dubbing
Wing: White CDC Feather
Hackle: Black Whiting Farms saddle
Adhesive: Loon UV Knot Sense

Ava's Red Ant

Originator: Ryan Keyes
Tier: Ryan Keyes

Hook: #10-14 Tiemco 2312
Thread: Rusty brown 70-denier UTC
Body: Red quill Micro Fine Dubbing
Wing: Mottled brown Web Wing
Legs: Orange/black Tarantu-Leggs
Indicator: Orange McFlylon
Hackle: Brown rooster saddle

Ken's Foam Ant (Black)

Originator: Ken Iwamasa
Tier: Ken Iwamasa

Hook: #14-18 Mustad 94842
Thread: Black 6/0 Uni-Thread
Body: Black craft foam (2mm)
Legs: Black Whiting Farms dry fly saddle

Fall River Flying Ant

Originator: Dennis Collier
Tier: Dennis Collier

Hook: #12-16 Tiemco 100 SPBL
Thread: Dark brown 16/0 Tiemco
Body: Mahogany and black Trout Hunter Dry Fly Dubbing
Wing: Pearl Krystal Flash (micro)
Post: White Wapsi Polypropylene Floating Yarn
Hackle: Dark-brown Metz saddle
Adhesive: Loctite Super Glue

Foam Ant (Black)

Originator: Inspired by Jack Dennis
Tier: Jimbo Busse

Hook: #16-20 Dai-Riki 300
Thread: Black 6/0 Uni-Thread
Body: Black foam (2mm)
Underbody: Tying thread
Wing: Tan Bett's Zing Wing or Swiss Straw
Legs: Grizzly Whiting Farms hackle

Brown Deer Hair Ant

Originator: Chauncy Lively
Tier: Jimbo Busse

Hook: #16-18 Dai-Riki 300
Thread: Brown 8/0 Uni-Thread
Underbody: Brown rabbit dubbing
Body/Head: Brown deer hair
Legs: Copper Krystal Flash

CDC Cinnamon Ant

Originator: Unknown
Tier: Russell Ellis

Hook: #16-18 Tiemco 2488
Thread: Rusty brown 8/0 Uni-Thread
Body: Rusty spinner Trout Hunter Dubbing
Wing: Brown or tan Spirit River CDC feather
Legs: Furnace Whiting Farms dry fly hackle

Crazy Ant (Brown)

Originator: Ken Walrath
Tier: Ken Walrath

Hook: #16 Mustad 94840
Thread: Brown 8/0 Uni-Thread
Body: Brown Mainstay Shelf Liner
Wing: White poly yarn
Legs: Brown Whiting Farms dry fly hackle
Adhesive: Super Glue

Ken's Gorilla Ant (Red/Black)

Originator: Ken Walrath
Tier: Ken Walrath

Hook: #16 Mustad 94840
Thread: Black 6/0 Uni-Thread
Body: Gorilla Glue
Head: Gorilla Glue
Wing: White Antron Yarn
Legs: Black Whiting Farms dry fly hackle
Marker: Red and black Sharpie
Note: *Allow body glue to dry at least one hour before coloring.*

Red Butt Ant

Originator: Ken Walrath
Tier: Ken Walrath

Hook: #18 Mustad 94840
Thread: Black 6/0 Uni-Thread
Body: Black Super Fine Dubbing
Wing: White Antron Yarn
Tail: Red 70-denier UTC Thread
Legs: Black Whiting Farms dry fly hackle

Scott's Flying Ant

Originator: Scott Stisser
Tier: Scott Stisser

Hook: #14 Tiemco 100
Thread: Black 6/0 Danville's
Underbody: Tying thread
Overbody: Black Razor Foam
Head: Black Razor Foam
Wings: Medium dun hackle tips
Post: White poly yarn
Hackle: Dark dun Whiting Farms hackle

Ken's Gorilla Ant (Red)

Originator: Ken Walrath
Tier: Ken Walrath

Hook: #16 Mustad 94840
Thread: Red 8/0 Uni-Thread
Body: Gorilla Glue
Head: Gorilla Glue
Wing: White Antron Yarn
Legs: Black Whiting Farms dry fly hackle
Marker: Red Sharpie
Note: *Allow body glue to dry at least one hour before coloring.*

Crazy Ant (Red/Black)

Originator: Ken Walrath
Tier: Ken Walrath

Hook: #16 Mustad 94840
Thread: Black 6/0 Uni-Thread
Body: Red Mainstay Shelf Liner
Head: Black Mainstay Shelf Liner
Wing: White poly yarn
Legs: Black Whiting Farms dry fly hackle
Antenna: Body foam
Adhesive: Super Glue

Real Hip Ant

Originator: Yukihiro Ishikawa
Tier: Yukihiro Ishikawa

Hook: #12 Varivas 2200 BL
Thread: Black 6/0 Uni-Thread
Underbody: Black Super Fine Dubbing
Body: Stripped peacock herl
Post: Pink Tiemco Aero Dry Wing
Hackle: Black Whiting Farms saddle
Adhesive: Coat body with CCG Hydro or clear nail polish

Multi Bug

Originator: Yukihiro Ishikawa
Tier: Yukihiro Ishikawa

Hook: #13 Tiemco 102Y
Thread: Black 6/0 Uni-Thread
Body: Black Real Foam
Indicator: Pink Tiemco Aero Dry Wing
Legs: Black round rubber (small)
Eyes: Red EZ-Shape Sparkle Body

Hot Glue Ant

Originator: Katsuhito Saito
Tier: Katsuhito Saito

Hook: #12-16 Tiemco 5210
Thread: Black 6/0 Uni-Thread
Body: Black hot glue
Thorax: Black Fine Dry Fly Dubbing
Post: Pink Tiemco Aero Dry Wing
Hackle: Black Whiting dry fly hackle

Micro Flying Ant

Originator: Masahiko Ohnishi
Tier: Masahiko Ohnishi

Hook: #20-24 Tiemco 2488
Thread: Brown 8/0 Uni-Thread
Body: Black mono thread
Thorax/Head: Tying thread
Wing: Clear Z-Lon melted at ends

Foam Buck Ant

Originator: Takashi Nakajima
Tier: Takashi Nakajima

Hook: #10-18 Tiemco 2487
Thread: Black 6/0 Uni-Thread
Body: Hareline Peacock Dub
Head: Umpqua Loco Peacock Belly Foam
Wing: White poly yarn
Indicator: Pink TMC Aero Dry Wing
Legs: Coachman brown Whiting Farms dry fly hackle

Stillwater Ant

Originator: Ryo Shimazaki
Tier: Ryo Shimazaki

Hook: #19 Tiemco 212Y
Thread: Black 16/0 Tiemco
Body: Tying thread coated with Super Glue
Indicator: CDC
Adhesive: Super Glue

CDC Spent Ant

Originator: Noritaka Osada
Tier: Noritaka Osada

Hook: #22 Tiemco 2488
Thread: Black 16/0 Tiemco
Body: Tying thread
Thorax: Tying thread
Head: Natural medium brown CDC folded over wing
Wing: Natural medium brown CDC with glued tips
Rib: Copper Lagartun wire (x-fine)
Adhesive: UV Knot Sense

Traditional Chernobyl Ant

Originator: Emmett Heath
Tier: Montana Fly Company

Hook: #8 MFC 7022
Thread: Black 6/0 MFC
Body: Black foam (3mm)
Indicator: Yellow foam (2mm)
Legs: Black Centipede Legs

Wilson's Winged Chernobyl (Red)

Originator: Scott Wilson
Tier: Montana Fly Company

Hook: #8 MFC 7026
Thread: Black 6/0 MFC
Underbody: Red Furry Foam
Body: Black foam (3mm)
Legs: Brown Centipede Legs
Indicator: Blue Widow's Web

MFC Foam Ant

Originator: Unknown
Tier: Montana Fly Company

Hook: #12 MFC 7000
Thread: Black 6/0 MFC
Body: Black foam (2mm)
Hackle: Black hackle

MFC Parachute Ant

Originator: Unknown
Tier: Montana Fly Company

Hook: #14 MFC 7000
Thread: Black 6/0 MFC
Body: Black MFC Frog Hair
Hackle: Grizzly hackle
Indicator: White Widow's Web

Black Flying Ant

Originator: Unknown
Tier: Montana Fly Company

Hook: #12 MFC 7000
Thread: Black 6/0 MFC
Body: Black MFC Frog Hair
Hackle: Brown hackle
Wing: Golden stone Widow's Web

Oswald's Parachute Ant

Originator: Duncan Oswald
Tier: Duncan Oswald

Hook: #12 MFC 7000
Thread: Black 6/0 MFC
Body: Black foam (2mm)
Hackle: Brown hackle
Indicator: Yellow foam (2mm)

Nyman's Foam Flying Ant

Originator: Rowan Nyman
Tier: Montana Fly Company

Hook: #12 MFC 7000
Thread: Red and black 6/0 MFC
Body: Red and black foam (2mm)
Wing: White Z-Lon
Legs: Brown MFC Tentacles

Green River Flying Ant

Originator: J. D. Magee
Tier: Montana Fly Company

Hook: #12 MFC 7027
Thread: Black 6/0 MFC
Body: Black foam (2mm)
Wing: Clear MFC Skinny Skin
Indicator: White foam (2mm)
Legs: Black MFC Tentacles
Hackle: Brown saddle

Silverman's Sparkle Ant (Cinnamon)

Originator: Joel Silverman
Tier: Montana Fly Company

Hook: #14 MFC 7000
Thread: Rusty brown 6/0 MFC
Body: Orange and copper Wing N' Flash
Wing: Plain web MFC Etha Wing
Indicator: Hot pink Gator Hair
Legs: Red MFC Tentacles
Hackle: Brown saddle

Silverman's Sparkle Flying Ant

Originator: Joel Silverman
Tier: Montana Fly Company

Hook: #12 MFC 7000
Thread: Black 6/0 MFC
Body: Black Wing N' Flash
Wing: Dun MFC Etha Wing
Indicator: Hot pink Gator Hair
Legs: Black MFC Tentacles
Hackle: Black saddle

Wiese's Glass Head Ant (Red/Black)

Originator: Walter Wiese
Tier: Montana Fly Company

Hook: #14 MFC 7048
Thread: Rusty brown 6/0 MFC
Body: Black and rust MFC Frog Hair
Head: Root beer (#11) glass seed bead
Waist: Tying thread
Legs: Brown hackle

Wilson's Winged Chernobyl (Black)

Originator: Scott Wilson
Tier: Montana Fly Company

Hook: #8 MFC 7026
Thread: Yellow 6/0 MFC
Body: Brown/ black Furry Foam (3mm)
Wing: Plain web MFC Wing Material
Indicator: Ocean blue Widow's Web
Legs: Brown Centipede Legs

Trina's Noble Chernobyl (Red)

Originator: Adam Trina
Tier: Montana Fly Company

Hook: #12 MFC 7026
Thread: Black 6/0 MFC
Underbody: Red foam (2mm)
Body: Black foam (2mm)
Wing: Cow elk flank hair
Indicator: Yellow foam (2mm)
Indicator: White Widow's Web
Hackle: Grizzly saddle
Legs: White Centipede Legs

Willy's Ant

Originator: Will Dornan
Tier: Montana Fly Company

Hook: #8 MFC 7008
Thread: Red 6/0 MFC
Body: Red MFC Wabbit Dubbing and red and pearl Wings N' Flash
Overbody: Black foam (4mm)
Wing: White Widow's Web
Legs: Black Centipede Legs

Swisher's Chernobyl (Black)

Originator: Doug Swisher
Tier: Montana Fly Company

Hook: #8 MFC 7026
Thread: Brown 6/0 MFC
Overwing: Smoke Widow's Web
Body: Black foam (3mm)
Underbody: Peacock herl
Indicator: White foam (2mm)
Wing: Plain MFC Web Wing
Legs: Tan/brown LSS 24mm
Hackle: Brown saddle

MFC Chernobyl Ant (Black/Chartreuse)

Originator: MFC
Tier: Montana Fly Company

Hook: #8 MFC 7026
Thread: Black 6/0 MFC
Underbody: Chartreuse Wings N' Flash
Body: Black and chartreuse foam (2mm)
Indicator: Yellow foam (2mm)
Legs: Olive black barred Sili Legs
Hackle: Brown saddle

MFC Chernobyl Ant (Brown/Yellow)

Originator: MFC
Tier: Montana Fly Company

Hook: #8 MFC 7026
Thread: Brown 6/0 MFC
Overbody: Pre-cut Chernobyl (large) brown foam (2mm)
Body: Pre-cut Chernobyl (medium) yellow foam (2mm)
Underbody: Gold Wing N' Flash
Legs: Gold/black barred Sili Legs
Hackle: Brown neck

Kingfisher Foam Para Grasshopper (Yellow)

Originator: Kingfisher Fly Shop
Tier: Montana Fly Company

Hook: #8 MFC 7026
Thread: Yellow 6/0 MFC
Body: Yellow foam (2mm)
Wing: Mottled brown MFC Wing Material
Underwing: Tan Widow's Web
Post: White Widow's Web
Legs: Red/black barred Sili Legs
Hackle: Grizzly

Gould's Half Drowned Ant

Originator: John Gould
Tier: Montana Fly Company

Hook: #16 MFC 7048
Thread: Black 8/0 MFC
Body: Black MFC Swisher's Rub-a-Dub
Wings: Plain web MFC Wing Material
Indicator: White Widow's Web
Hackle: Black saddle

Bloom's Parachute Flying Ant (Rust)

Originator: Dave Bloom
Tier: Dave Bloom

Hook: #12-18 Dai-Riki 305
Thread: Rusty brown 8/0 Uni-Thread
Back: Caddis amber Blue Ribbon Crinkled Zelon
Body: Rusty spinner Harrop's Pro Dubbing
Thorax: Tying thread
Head: Rusty spinner Harrop's Pro Dubbing
Wing: Caddis gold Blue Ribbon Crinkled Zelon
Indicator: Pink McFlylon
Hackle: Brown Whiting Farms saddle
Adhesive: Trout Hunter tying cement

Bloom's Parachute Ant (Purple)

Originator: Dave Bloom
Tier: Dave Bloom

Hook: #12-18 Dai-Riki 305
Thread: Purple 8/0 Uni-Thread
Rear Back: Purple Wapsi Antron Yarn
Body: Purple Hareline STS Trilobal Dub
Thorax: Tying thread
Head: Purple Hareline STS Trilobal Dub
Indicator: Pink McFlylon
Hackle: Dark dun Whiting Farms saddle
Adhesive: Trout Hunter tying cement

Sandy Ant

Originator: Franz Potts
Tier: Sue Armstrong

Hook: #8-14 Mustad 3906
Thread: Orange rod wrapping thread, size A
Body: Sandy ox hair over orange wrapping thread, woven
Thorax: Tying thread
Head: Black 70-denier UTC
Legs/Hackle: Sandy ox hair woven
Note: *Body is the Mite body weave method. This pattern is fished as a wet fly.*

Black Ant

Originator: Franz Potts
Tier: Sue Armstrong

Hook: #8-14 Mustad 3906
Thread: Yellow rod wrapping thread, size A
Body: Black horse hair over yellow wrapping thread woven
Thorax: Tying thread
Head: Black 70-denier UTC
Legs: Black horse hair woven
Note: *Body is the Mite body weave method. This pattern is fished as a wet fly.*

ICU Paintbrush Ant

Originator: Richard Pilatzke
Tier: Richard Pilatzke

Hook: #12 Dai-Riki 305
Thread: Black 6/0 Uni-Thread
Underbody: Tying thread
Body: Black Evazote foam (1/8")
Indicator: Yellow Evazote foam (1/8")
Legs: Black nylon paintbrush bristles
Adhesive: Krazy Glue

Jungle Ant

Originator: Dron Lee
Tier: Dron Lee

Hook: #8 Tiemco 100
Thread: Brown 140-denier UTC
Body: Brown foam (3mm)
Thorax: Brown Wapsi foam (3mm)
Head: Brown Wapsi foam (3mm)
Eyes: Black Loon Hard Head
Legs: Brown Centipede Legs (mini)
Antennae: Dark brown pheasant tail fibers
Adhesive: Flexament
Marker: Burnt sienna Promarker

Kaufmann's Drowned Carpenter Ant

Originator: Randall Kaufmann
Tier: Umpqua Feather Merchants

Hook: #8-14 Mustad 94845
Thread: Black 6/0 Uni-Thread
Abdomen: Black floss and epoxy
Head: Black floss and epoxy
Wing: Dark dun hackle tips
Legs: Black soft hackle

Parachute Glue Ant

Originator: Hiroyuki Maki
Tier: Hiroyuki Maki

Hook: #10-16 Tiemco 2487 BL
Thread: Black 8/0 Uni-Thread
Rear Body: Black hot glue
Waist: Tying thread
Head: Black RH Professional Dubbing
Indicator: Orange poly yarn
Hackle: Black cock neck

Mill's Red Cow Killer Ant

Originator: Mark Mills
Tier: Mark Mills

Hook: #12-16 Tiemco 101
Thread: Black 70-denier UTC
Gaster: Red deer hair over black Antron
Thorax: Black deer hair over black Antron Dubbing
Head: Black dyed deer hair
Indicator: White Para Post
Hackle: Black saddle
Antennae: Black deer hair

Mill's Cinnamon Cow Killer Ant

Originator: Mark Mills
Tier: Mark Mills

Hook: #12-16 Tiemco 101
Thread: Black 70-denier UTC
Gaster: Cinnamon deer hair over black Antron
Thorax: Black deer hair over cinnamon Antron Dubbing
Head: Black dyed deer hair
Indicator: White Para Post
Hackle: Black saddle
Antennae: Black deer hair

Mill's Flying Cow Killer Ant

Originator: Mark Mills
Tier: Mark Mills

Hook: #12-16 Tiemco 200R
Thread: Black 70-denier UTC
Gaster: Yellow deer hair over yellow Antron
Thorax: Black deer hair over black Antron Dubbing
Head: Black dyed deer hair
Wing: Natural tan CDC
Hackle: Black saddle
Antennae: Black deer hair

Bloody Ant Wet Fly

Originator: Eric A. Pettine
Tier: Eric A. Pettine

Hook: #18-22 Tiemco 101
Thread: Black 16/0 Tiemco
Body: Rusty brown Hare E Ice Dub
Thorax: Black $\frac{3}{32}$" tungsten bead
Head: Bloody black Ice Dub
Hackle: Black saddle

Bloody Ant Dry

Originator: Eric A. Pettine
Tier: Eric A. Pettine

Hook: #18-22 Tiemco 101
Thread: Black 16/0 Tiemco
Body: Black hackle and rusty orange Hareline Hare'E Ice Dub
Head: Bloody black Hareline Hare'E Ice Dub and black hackle
Waist: Red Krystal Flash

Hi Viz Tootsie Roll Ant

Originator: Unknown
Tier: George Daniel

Hook: #12 Tiemco 100
Thread: Black 6/0 Uni-Thread
Body: Black Wapsi Ant Body (medium)
Underbody: Tying thread
Indicator: Fluorescent pink Hi Viz Darlon
Legs: Black Wapsi Spanflex (medium)

Tak's Foam San Juan Flying Ant

Originator: Rick Takahashi
Tier: Rick Takahashi

Hook: #10-16 Daiichi 1270
Thread: Black 16/0 Veevus
Body: Black Evazote foam
Hackle: Brown Whiting Farms saddle
Wing: Clear Swiss Straw
Legs: Brown speckled MFC Sexi-Floss

Tak's Foam San Juan Ant

Originator: Rick Takahashi
Tier: Rick Takahashi

Hook: #10-16 Daiichi 1270
Thread: Black 16/0 Veevus
Body: Black Evazote foam
Indicator: Red foam (2mm)
Legs: Brown speckled MFC Sexi-Floss

Tak's Rubber Legged Ant

Originator: Rick Takahashi
Tier: Rick Takahashi

Hook: #16-20 Tiemco 9300
Thread: Black 16/0 Veevus
Body: Black Evazote foam
Legs: Black round rubber (small)
Indicator: Red craft foam (1mm)
Note: *Cut body foam with RRC Hopper Body (small).*

Ant Acid Ant (Cinnamon)

Originator: Kelly Galloup
Tier: Kelly Galloup

Hook: #12-18 Daiichi 1180
Thread: Rusty brown UTC GSP 50
Body: Cinnamon brown Super Fine
Underwing: Gold Metallic Braid
Overwing: Deer hair
Legs: Black/orange round rubber (small)

Hackle Winged Ant

Originator: Phil Iwane
Tier: Phil Iwane

Hook: #14 Tiemco 2487
Thread: Rusty brown and black 6/0 Uni-Thread
Body: Tying threads
Thorax: Tying threads
Head: Tying threads
Wing: White hackle tips
Legs: Black hackle
Adhesive: CCG Hydro

Last Gasp Ant

Originator: Phil Iwane
Tier: Phil Iwane

Hook: #14 Tiemco 2487
Thread: Black 6/0 Uni-Thread
Body: Tying thread
Thorax: Tying thread
Post: White Antron Yarn
Hackle: Black saddle
Adhesive: CCG Hydro

Peek-a-Boo Black Ant

Originator: Phil Iwane
Tier: Phil Iwane

Hook: #14 Tiemco 101
Thread: Black 6/0 Uni-Thread
Body: Tying thread
Thorax: Tying thread
Head: Tying thread
Hackle: Black saddle
Overbody: Glow in the Dark Flashabou
Adhesive: CCG Hydro

CDC Winged Red Ant

Originator: Phil Iwane
Tier: Phil Iwane

Hook: #14 Tiemco 2488
Thread: Rust 6/0 Uni-Thread
Body: Tying thread
Thorax: Tying thread
Head: Tying thread
Hackle: Brown saddle
Wing: White CDC
Adhesive: CCG Hydro

Calf Tail Red Ant

Originator: Phil Iwane
Tier: Phil Iwane

Hook: #14 Tiemco 2488
Thread: Rust 6/0 Uni-Thread
Body: Tying thread
Head: Tying thread
Hackle: Brown saddle
Wing: White calf tail
Adhesive: CCG Hydro

Space Ant (Black)

Originator: Spirit River Mr. Bill's Flying Ant
Tier: Marty Staab

Hook: #14 Dai-Riki 070
Thread: Black 6/0 Danville's
Body: Black Super Fine Dubbing
Thorax: Tying thread
Head: Black Super Fine Dubbing
Wing: Clear Spirit River Wings and Things
Legs: Rainbow Krystal Flash
Antennae: Rainbow Krystal Flash

Marty's Ant

Originator: Marty Staab
Tier: Marty Staab

Hook: #14 Dai-Riki 730
Thread: Black 8/0 Uni-Thread
Gaster: Black Super Fine Dubbing
Head: Red Walmart Cupboard Mat
Wing: White Widow's Web
Legs: Brown saddle hackle

Hub's Down Under Ant (Blue)

Originator: Jerry Hubka
Tier: Jerry Hubka

Hook: #14-16 Daiichi 1150
Thread: Black 70-denier UTC
Body: One rainbow black/blue 11/0 glass seed bead and one blue silver lined 8/0 glass seed bead
Thorax: Tying thread
Head: Rainbow black/blue 11/0 glass seed bead
Legs: Black/blue flake Sili Legs
Antennae: Black Krystal Flash
Adhesive: CCG Thin coat body beads and thorax
Note: *This ant pattern is fished "Down-Under" the surface.*

Hub's Down Under Ant (Black/Red)

Originator: Jerry Hubka
Tier: Jerry Hubka

Hook: #14-16 Daiichi 1150
Thread: Black 70-denier UTC
Body: One black 11/0 and one black 8/0 glass seed beads
Thorax: Tying thread
Head: Black 11/0 glass seed bead
Legs: Black/red tipped Hareline Crazy Legs
Antennae: Black Krystal Flash
Adhesive: CCG Thin
Note: *This ant pattern is fished "Down-Under" the surface.*

Hub's Down Under Ant (Red)

Originator: Jerry Hubka
Tier: Jerry Hubka

Hook: #14-16 Daiichi 1150
Thread: Red 70-denier UTC
Body: One pearl red 11/0 and one red 8/0 silver lined glass seed beads
Thorax: Tying thread
Head: Pearl red 11/0 glass seed bead
Legs: Black/red tipped Hareline Crazy Legs
Antennae: Copper Krystal Flash
Adhesive: CCG Thin
Note: *This pattern is fished "Down-Under" the surface.*

Hub's Down Under Ant (Black/Yellow)

Originator: Jerry Hubka
Tier: Jerry Hubka

Hook: #14-16 Daiichi 1150
Thread: Black 70-denier UTC
Body: One black 11/0 and one 8/0 glass seed beads
Thorax: Tying thread
Head: Black 11/0 glass seed bead
Legs: Black/yellow chartreuse tipped Hareline Crazy Legs
Antennae: Black Krystal Flash
Adhesive: CCG Thin
Note: *This pattern is fished "Down-Under" the surface.*

High Float Ant

Originator: Eric Ishiwata
Tier: Eric Ishiwata

Hook: #12-16 Gamakatsu S10
Thread: Black 8/0 Uni-Thread
Back: Black foam
Body: Peacock herl
Spotter: Fluorescent green TMC Aero Dry Wing
Legs: Brown Whiting Farms dry fly hackle
Thorax: Peacock herl
Treatment: Watershed

Sunken Ant

Originator: Eric Ishiwata
Tier: Eric Ishiwata

Hook: #12-16 Gamakatsu S10
Thread: Black 8/0 Uni-Thread
Weight: Red seed beads
Body: Peacock herl
Thorax: Peacock herl
Post: Fluorescent orange TMC Aero Dry Wing
Hackle: Grizzly variant Whiting Farms saddle

Drowned Ant

Originator: Eric Ishiwata
Tier: Eric Ishiwata

Hook: #12-16 Gamakatsu S10
Thread: Black 8/0 Uni-Thread
Weight: Pearl seed beads
Body: Peacock herl

Feighny's Ant

Originator: Mike Feighny
Tier: Mike Feighny

Hook: #14-16 Dai-Riki 270
Thread: Black 8/0 Uni-Thread
Underbody: Black Super Fine Dubbing
Legs: Black 140-denier UTC
Note: *Coat with CCG Thin.*

Feighny's Flying Ant

Originator: Mike Feighny
Tier: Mike Feighny

Hook: #14-16 Dai-Riki 270
Thread: Black 8/0 Uni-Thread
Underbody: Black Super Fine Dubbing
Wing: Cellophane bag with ridges created by serrated hemostat
Legs: Black 140-denier UTC thread
Antennae: Brown 70-denier UTC thread
Note: *Coat body, antennae, legs with CCG Thin.*

Monsoon Flying Ant

Originator: John Larson
Tier: John Larson

Hook: #24 Tiemco 2487
Thread: Brown 12/0 Orvis
Body: Buckskin Hareline Midge Tubing
Underwing: Tan CDC oiler puffs
Overwing: Amber Medallion Sheeting
Legs: Black Microfibetts
Markers: Red and brown permanent

Two Tone Ant

Originator: Gary Okizaki
Tier: Gary Okizaki

Hook: #6-10 Daiichi 1770
Thread: Black 70-denier UTC
Gaster: Black Super Fine Dubbing
Thorax: Rusty dun Super Fine Dubbing
Hackle: Grizzly
Post: White McFlylon

Two Tone Ant/Black Beetle

Originator: Gary Okizaki
Tier: Gary Okizaki

Hook: #6-10 Daiichi 1770
Thread: Black 70-denier UTC
Beetle: Black Glitter Foam (2mm) and peacock Estaz
Ant: Black and rusty dun Super Fine Dubbing
Hackle: Grizzly
Post: White McFlylon

Black Ant

Originator: Gary Okizaki
Tier: Gary Okizaki

Hook: #14-16 Tiemco 3761
Thread: Black 70-denier UTC
Body: Black latex strip cover with Loon's Knot Sense
Legs: Brown Whisk Broom fibers

Two Tone Ant/Red Beetle

Originator: Gary Okizaki
Tier: Gary Okizaki

Hook: #6-10 Daiichi 1770
Thread: Black 70-denier UTC
Beetle: Red Glitter Foam (2mm) and peacock Estaz
Ant: Black and rusty dun Super Fine Dubbing
Hackle: Grizzly
Post: White McFlylon

Amy's Ant (Black)

Originator: Jack Dennis
Tier: Jack Dennis

Hook: #6-12 Tiemco 5262 or 5263
Thread: Red 3/0 Danville's Monocord
Underbody: Peach Fly Foam (2mm); red Estaz
Overbody: Black Fly Foam (2mm)
Legs: Black round rubber (medium)
Hackle: Grizzly rooster neck or saddle, trimmed short
Underwing: Rainbow and gold Krystal Flash
Overwing: Cow or yearling elk hair
Thorax: Red Arizona Synthetic Peacock Dubbing

Tak's S. J. Carpenter Ant

Originator: Rick Takahashi
Tier: Rick Takahashi

Hook: #16 Dai-Riki 280
Thread: Black 16/0 Veevus
Gaster: Brown Rainy's Ant Bodies
Waist: Rio bendable wire
Thorax: Black foam (2mm)
Legs: Brush bristle
Wing: Clear Medallion Sheeting cut out with RRC Mayfly Body Cutter
Antennae: Polyester tapered paintbrush fibers
Note: *Underside covered with CCG Hydro.*

Tak's Cinnamon Ant

Originator: Rick Takahashi
Tier: Rick Takahashi

Hook: #16 Dai-Riki 280
Thread: Black 16/0 Veevus
Gaster: Brown Rainy's Ant Bodies
Waist: Rio bendable wire
Thorax: Black foam (2mm)
Legs: Brush bristle
Antennae: Polyester tapered paintbrush fibers
Note: *Underside covered with CCG Hydro.*

Harder's Ant

Originator: John Harder
Tier: Rick Takahashi

Hook: #10 Tiemco 9300
Thread: Black 70-denier UTC
Body: Black Evazote foam
Legs: Black small round rubber
Indicator: Red foam (2mm)
Note: *Harder's version of Allan Wooley's Chernobyl Ant.*

Wooley's Chernobyl Ant

Originator: Allan Wooley
Tier: Allan Wooley

Hook: #10 Tiemco 9300
Thread: Black 70-denier UTC
Body: Black foam (2mm)
Legs: Black small round rubber
Indicator: White foam strip folded (2mm)

Note: *Allan Wooley is one of the originators of the Chernobyl Ant.*

KLH Hackle Stacker Ant

Originator: Kenneth Held
Tier: Kenneth Held

Hook: #12-18 Tiemco 200R
Thread: Black 70-denier UTC
Body: Black and medium tan RRC River Foam (.5mm) cut 1mm wide
Hackle: Dark dun
Adhesive: CCG Hydro
Marker: Chrome orange Chartpak

Note: *Color tan foam with marker; coat the body with CCG Hydro.*

Tying Beetles

Foam Beetle

Originator: Unknown
Tier: Rick Takahashi

Hook: #8-14 Tiemco 2302
Thread: Black 6/0 UNI-Thread
Shell: Black craft foam (2mm)
Underbody: Peacock herl
Legs: Black Senyo's Shaggy Dub
Indicator: Fluorescent pink foam strip (2mm)

TYING THE FOAM BEETLE

1. Attach the thread at the hook eye and wrap it to the hook bend (opposite the barb). Wrap the thread forward to the mid-section of the hook. Cut a body from 2mm black foam using a River Road Creations Beetle Body Cutter sized for the hook.

2. Place the foam on top of the hook shank with the small tapered tag end facing the hook eye. Position the foam so the beginning of the rear part of the body is at the hook bend. Bind the foam to the hook shank.

3. Select the peacock herl and trim the tips.

4. Tie in the peacock herls and wrap them around the tying thread.

5. Wrap them forward to the front third of the hook.

6. Tie them off and trim the excess.

7. Select a small bundle of Senyo's Shaggy Dub.

8. Tie in the dubbing in the middle of the bundle directly in front of the peacock herl body using figure-eight wraps.

9. Fold the foam over the underbody and legs and tie in one eye width back from the hook eye.

10. Trim the front end of the foam body to create the head and trim the legs to the desired length.

11. Take a small strip of brightly colored 2mm foam and tie it in.

12. Trim the rear of the foam as shown. Whip-finish, trim the excess thread, and trim the indicator to desired length.

Rodgers' Beetle

Originator: Kevin Rodgers
Tier: Rick Takahashi

Hook: #8-14 Tiemco 2302
Thread: Black 6/0 UNI-Thread
Shell: Black Rainy's Float Foam
Underbody: Mixed peacock and claret Ice Dub
Legs: Black bristles from a cleaning brush
Indicator: Fluorescent red McFlylon

TYING RODGERS' BEETLE

1. Attach the thread at the hook eye and wrap it to the hook bend (opposite the barb). Wrap the thread forward to the midsection of the hook shank.

2. Cut a length of Rainy's Float Foam $1\frac{1}{4}$ times longer than the hook shank. Cut the foam in half lengthwise, creating two long equal portions. Cut a small divot at the end of the foam on the dull side.

3. Attach the foam to the hook with the shiny side down. Tie in the end with the divot at the midpoint of the hook.

4. Wrap the tying thread over the foam to the hook bend (opposite the barb).

5. Twist a slim noodle of dubbing onto the thread.

6. Wrap the dubbing to the midpoint of the hook.

7. Tie in the leg material in front of the dubbed body and bend it toward the rear using figure-eight wraps.

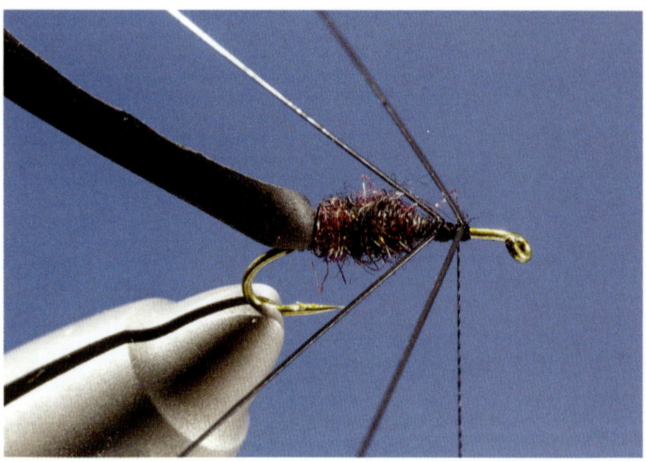

8. Tie in the second pair of leg materials.

9. Tie in the third pair of legs and bend toward the hook eye.

10. Very briefly heat the tip of a bodkin and bend the legs as indicated.

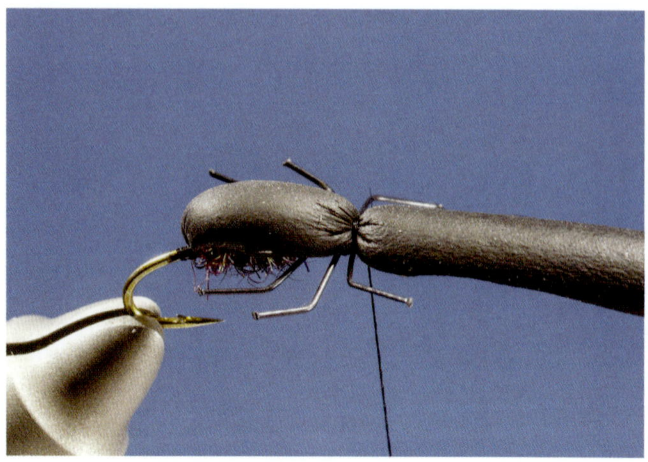

11. Trim the legs to the desired length. Fold the foam forward and tie it down at a point two eye widths behind the hook eye.

12. Fold the foam back and wrap the tying thread to the hook eye.

13. Fold the foam forward over the eye and tie it in directly behind the hook eye.

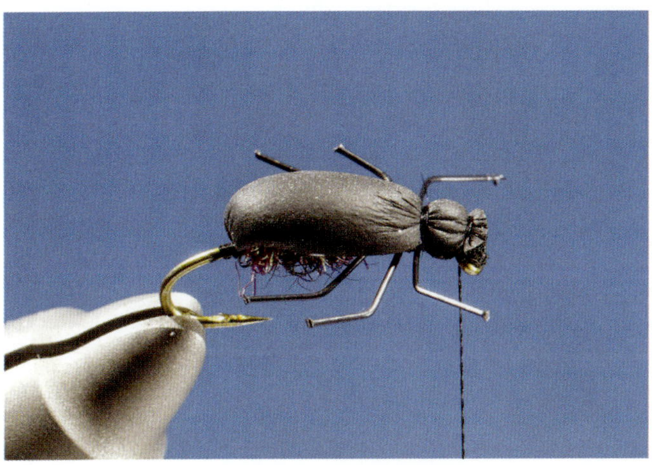

14. Trim the foam to create a small head.

15. Place the wrap underneath the head of the fly to the first segment and tie in a small 2-inch length of McFlylon (about half the diameter of a pencil) in the middle of the yarn.

16. Take several wraps to secure the foam. Take both ends of the yarn, pull up and trim close to the body of the fly to create a small indicator.

17. Whip-finish behind the indicator and trim excess thread.

Hubka's Green Bow Tie Beetle

Originator: Jerry Hubka
Tier: Rick Takahashi

Hook: #8-14 Tiemco 2302
Thread: Black 6/0 UNI-Thread
Shell: Green metallic Hareline foam
Underbody: Olive brown Ice Dub
Legs: Black Wapsi Sili Legs
Flared Wing: Orange Krystal Flash
Antennae: Black Krystal Flash
Indicator: Red/orange craft foam strip (2mm)
Adhesive: CCG Hydro

TYING THE GREEN BOW TIE BEETLE

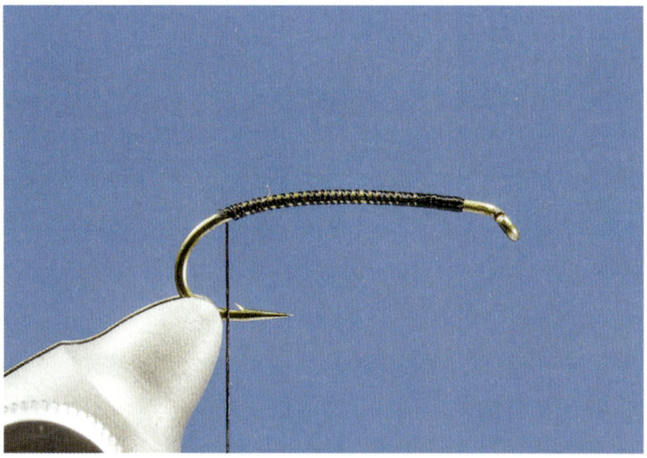

1. Attach the thread at the hook eye and wrap it to the hook bend (opposite the barb).

2. Tie in a tag of copper wire at the hook bend, secure it with thread, and trim excess wire.

3. Cut out a beetle shape using a River Road Creations Beetle Body Cutter. At the waist of the fly, cut two small notches on each side of the foam. These notches will form the head. Attach the foam body by the tag.

4. Twist a small noodle of dubbing onto the thread. Wrap the dubbing to the midpoint of the hook.

5. Tie in the square rubber legs on each side of the body.

6. Tie in the orange Krystal Flash between the legs.

7. Turn the flash perpendicular to the hook (spent-wing style) using figure-eight wraps.

8. Trim the flash. Tie in the black Krystal Flash for the antennae.

9. Fold over the foam and attach it to the hook. Tie in the waist and then in front of the notch. Tie down the head.

10. Tie in the indicator foam strip at the position shown and trim to desired length.

11. Trim the antennae.

Coch-a-bon-ddu

Originator: Unknown
Tier: Tom Logan

Hook: #10-16 Daiichi 1550
Thread: Black 6/0 Danville's or 8/0 Gudebrod
Body: Peacock herl
Hackle: Furnace Indian rooster neck
Rib: Gold wire (fine)
Tag: Gold tinsel (small)

Splitsville Beetle

Originator: Jonny King
Tier: Jonny King

Hook: #12-16 Tiemco 206 BL
Thread: Black 6/0 Uni-Thread
Body: Black foam (2mm)
Underbody: Peacock Hareline Hare'E Ice Dub
Thorax: Peacock Hareline Hare'E Ice Dub
Wing: Niche Products siliconized dun poly yarn or divided CDC feathers
Hackle: Grizzly dry fly
Note: *This pattern was inspired by Bob Quigley. Tie poly yarn or CDC feathers as a split downwing and tie grizzly feather hackle-stacker style; pull hackle forward over the top of the split wing.*

Dickster Beetle

Originator: Dick Shinton
Tier: Dick Shinton

Hook: #14-18 Umpqua U100
Thread: Black 70-denier UTC
Body: Black closed-cell foam (2mm)
Underbody: Peacock herl
Indicator: Yellow closed-cell foam (1mm x 2mm)
Legs: Black Hareline round rubber (fine)

Foam Beetle

Originator: Unknown
Tier: Tim Jacobs

Hook: #10-16 Tiemco 100
Thread: Black 140-denier UTC
Body: Black Rainy's Evazote Sheet Foam (2 or 3mm)
Underbody: Tying thread
Legs: Black deer hair

Ice Dub Beetle

Originator: Vic Loiselle
Tier: Vic Loiselle

Hook: #10-14 Dai-Riki 320
Thread: Black 6/0 Uni-Thread
Body: Peacock black Hareline Ice Dub
Indicator: Red Spirit River Antron
Eyes: Melted 40-pound monofilament
Legs: Black Krystal Flash
Back: Mottled black Wings and Things
Adhesive: Griff's Thin Multi-Coat

CM Beetle

Originator: Tim Mack
Tier: Tim Mack

Hook: #12-16 Tiemco 100
Thread: Black 70-denier UTC
Underbody: Black Super Fine Dubbing
Body: Black Rainy's Foam Ant Body
Head: Black/white Rainy's Foam Ant Body
Wing: White McFlylon
Legs: Black Spirit River Rubber Legs (small)
Hackle: Black Whiting Farms saddle, trimmed
Adhesive: Fish Pimp Hard Headed

High Viz Foam Beetle

Originator: Variation of Wapsi's Foam Beetle
Tier: Tim Mack

Hook: #14 Tiemco 100
Thread: Black 6/0 Uni-Thread
Body: Wapsi foam (2mm)
Underbody: Peacock herl
Indicator: Charereuse foam (2mm)
Legs: Black Spirit River Flex Floss
Adhesive: Fish Pimp Hard Headed

Ben's Beetle

Originator: Ben Nillso
Tier: Ron Donahue

Hook: #14 Umpqua 103
Thread: Black 70-denier UTC
Body: Black Hareline Evazote foam (1/8")
Underbody: Black Ice Dub
Wing: White CDC
Legs: Peacock herl

Black and Orange Beetle

Originator: Ron Donahue
Tier: Ron Donahue

Hook: #12 Tiemco 100
Thread: Black 70-denier UTC
Body: Orange and black craft foam
Underbody: Orange Ice Dub
Legs: Red Spirit River Tarantu-Leggs (mini)

Sunburst Beetle

Originator: Ron Donahue
Tier: Ron Donahue

Hook: #14 Umpqua U103
Thread: Black 70-denier UTC
Body: Black Hareline Evazote foam (1/8")
Underbody: Black Ice Dub
Wing: Chartreuse Wapsi Egg Yarn
Legs: Yellow MFC Tentacles

Park Special

Originator: Ron Donahue
Tier: Ron Donahue

Hook: #15 Tiemco 102Y
Thread: Fluorescent green 70-denier UTC
Body: Green Sparkle Craft Foam (1mm)
Underbody: Chartreuse Ice Dub
Legs: Black Krystal Flash
Adhesive: Loctite Super Glue

Hot Spot Beetle (Black)

Originator: Ron Donahue
Tier: Ron Donahue

Hook: #14 MFC 7000
Thread: Black 70-denier UTC
Body: Black craft foam (2mm)
Underbody: Tying thread
Indicator: Pink craft foam (2mm)
Legs: Black round rubber
Adhesive: Zap-A-Gap

Green Sparkle Beetle

Originator: Ron Donahue
Tier: Ron Donahue

Hook: #14 MFC 7000
Thread: Fluorescent green 70-denier UTC
Body: Green Sparkle Craft Foam (1mm)
Underbody: Tying thread
Wing: Green Lite-Brite
Legs: Fluorescent green round rubber
Adhesive: Zap-A-Gap

Silver Lake Special

Originator: Ryan Keyes
Tier: Ryan Keyes

Hook: #12-16 Tiemco 2488
Thread: Black 6/0 Uni-Thread
Body: Black foam (2mm)
Underbody: Peacock Ice Dub
Indicator: Bright green foam (2mm)
Legs: Black round rubber (small)
Post: Orange McFlylon
Hackle: Golden badger rooster cape

Beetle Bailey

Originator: Ken Iwamasa
Tier: Ken Iwamasa

Hook: #12 Tiemco 5210
Thread: Black 6/0 Uni-Thread
Underbody: Black Ice Dub
Body: Black craft foam (2mm)
Legs: Black/yellow round rubber (small)
Indicator: Green fluorescent lacquer

DC's Snowball Beetle

Originator: Dennis Collier
Tier: Dennis Collier

Hook: #8-16 Tiemco 3769
Thread: Black 3/0 Danville's Waxed Monocord
Body: Black Spirit River Fly Foam (3mm)
Underbody: Tying thread
Indicator: White deer hair belly
Legs: Black Wapsi round rubber (small)
Adhesive: Loctite Super Glue

DC's Snowball Laminate Beetle

Originator: Dennis Collier
Tier: Dennis Collier

Hook: #8-16 Tiemco 3769
Thread: Black 3/0 Danville's Waxed Monocord
Body: Black and red Spirit River Fly Foam (3mm)
Underbody: Tying thread
Indicator: White deer hair belly
Legs: Black Wapsi round rubber (small)
Adhesive: Loctite Super Glue foam to hook; laminate foam with Barge's contact cement

DC's Flying Snowball Beetle

Originator: Dennis Collier
Tier: Dennis Collier

Hook: #8-14 Tiemco 3769
Thread: Black 3/0 Danville's Waxed Monocord
Body: Black Spirit River Fly Foam (3mm)
Underbody: Tying thread
Wing: Pearl Krystal Flash under white deer hair
Legs: Black Wapsi round rubber (small)
Adhesive: Loctite Super Glue

Jimbo's Foam Beetle

Originator: Unknown
Tier: Jimbo Busse

Hook: #14-18 Tiemco 100 or 101
Thread: Black 6/0 Uni-Thread
Underbody: Peacock herl
Back: Black foam (2mm)
Indicator: White Antron Yarn

Red Belly Foam Beetle

Originator: Unknown
Tier: Jimbo Busse

Hook: #14-18 Tiemco 2487
Thread: Black 6/0 Uni-Thread
Underbody: Red Metallic Braid
Back: Black foam (2mm)
Legs: Black round rubber (small)

Holo Micro Beetle

Originator: Curtis Fry
Tier: Curtis Fry

Hook: #18-22 Tiemco 101
Thread: Black 70-denier UTC
Body: Beetle green Wapsi Loco Foam
Underbody: Black UTC Holo Tinsel (medium)
Thorax: UV black Ice Dub
Indicator: Bright orange McFlylon
Legs: Black Krystal Flash

Black High Floater Beetle

Originator: Frank Whispell
Tier: Frank Whispell

Hook: #8-14 Tiemco 2499 SPBL
Thread: Black 140-denier UTC
Body: Black craft foam (2mm)
Underbody: Chartreuse craft foam (2mm)
Side Body: Two 1/8" strips of black craft foam (2mm)
Indicator: Orange foam (1/8" strip)
Legs: Brown/black Centipede Legs
Adhesive: Super Glue
Note: *Cut body with RRC Beetle Cutters. Poke hook through underbody foam and glue.*

Big Ugly (Black)

Originator: John Gribb
Tier: John Gribb

Hook: #8 Mustad 3366
Thread: Black #3 Orvis Braided
Body: Black craft foam (2mm)
Head: Body foam
Wing: Deer hair
Eyes: Red foam
Legs: Black Stretch Magic
Adhesive: Super Glue

Big Ugly (Tan)

Originator: John Gribb
Tier: John Gribb

Hook: #8 Mustad 3366
Thread: Olive #3 Orvis Braided
Body: Tan craft foam (2mm)
Head: Body foam
Wing: Deer hair
Eyes: Red foam
Legs: Red Stretch Magic
Adhesive: Super Glue

Crowe Beetle

Originator: MFC
Tier: Montana Fly Company

Hook: #12 MFC 7000
Thread: Black 6/0 MFC
Underbody: Peacock herl
Head/Body/Legs: Black dyed deer hair
Indicator: Pink foam (2mm)

Foam Beetle

Originator: MFC
Tier: Montana Fly Company

Hook: #14 MFC 7000
Thread: Black 6/0 MFC
Underbody: Peacock herl
Body: Black foam (2mm)
Indicator: Yellow foam (2mm)
Legs: Black Flashabou Accent

Fire Beetle

Originator: MFC
Tier: Montana Fly Company

Hook: #12 MFC 7000
Thread: Black 6/0 MFC
Body: Black foam (2mm)
Underbody: Red Wings N' Flash
Legs: Black Centipede Legs
Indicator: Yellow foam (2mm)
Adhesive: Zap-A-Gap

Quick Sight Beetle

Originator: MFC
Tier: Montana Fly Company

Hook: #12 MFC 7000
Thread: Black 6/0 MFC
Underbody: Black monofilament
Body: Black foam (2mm)
Indicator: Orange fluorescent paint
Legs: Black Centipede Legs

Taylor's Beetle

Originator: Brent Taylor
Tier: Montana Fly Company

Hook: #8 MFC 7077
Thread: Black 6/0 MFC
Underbody: Peacock Wings N' Flash
Body: Black foam (5mm)
Indicator: Orange (1mm) and white foam (2mm)
Legs: Black Centipede Legs

Nyman's Tiger Beetle

Originator: Rowan Nyman
Tier: Montana Fly Company

Hook: #12 MFC 7077
Thread: Black 6/0 MFC
Underbody: Black MFC Wabbit Dubbing
Body: Black/orange/black foam (2mm)
Legs: Black #3 MFC Tentacles

Pinkeye Beetle

Originator: Andrew Grillos
Tier: Idylwilde Flies

Hook: #12-16 Tiemco 3761
Thread: Black UTC GSP 100
Underbody: Peacock Ice Dub
Back: Black foam (2mm)
Wing: Neon pink McFlylon
Eyes: Neon pink round rubber leg (medium)
Legs: Black round rubber (fine)

Cantaria Beetle

Originator: Andrew Grillos
Tier: Idylwilde Flies

Hook: #1 Tiemco 811
Thread: Black UTC GSP 100
Underbody: Peacock Cactus Chenille
Back: Black foam (2mm)
Indicator: Lime green foam (2mm)
Antennae: Black round rubber legs (medium)
Legs: Tan and black barred round rubber (medium)
Adhesive: Super Glue

Xtra Terrestrial

Originator: Justin Karnopp
Tier: Justin Karnopp

Hook: #12 Daiichi 1170
Thread: Black 8/0 Uni-Thread
Underbody: Black Hareline Ice Dub
Thorax: Olive Hareline Ice Dub
Legs: Black round rubber (mini)
Indicator: White poly yarn
Back: Black and bright green foam (1mm)
Tail: Pearl Krystal Flash

Godzilla Beetle

Originator: Richard Pilatzke
Tier: Richard Pilatzke

Hook: #4 Mustad 94840
Thread: Black 6/0 Uni-Thread
Underbody: Brown and gold speckled Hareline Chenille
Body: Black Evazote foam (1/8")
Indicator: Yellow Evazote foam (1/8")
Legs: Black Blue Ribbon Flies Flutter Legs

Heavy Metal Beetle

Originator: Richard Pilatzke
Tier: Richard Pilatzke

Hook: #12 Dai-Riki 305
Thread: Black 6/0 Uni-Thread
Underbody: Lime and black Hareline Speckled Chenille
Body: Black self-adhesive foam (2mm) covered with green Staedtler Hot Foil Pen
Indicator: Yellow Evazote foam (1/8")
Legs: Black Wapsi Krystal Flash
Note: *Apply pen to Mylar sheet and press onto self-adhesive foam then peel off Mylar.*

Frosty

Originator: Ron Donahue
Tier: Ron Donahue

Hook: #14 Tiemco 2302
Thread: Black 70-denier UTC
Underbody: Black Ice Dub
Body: Black foam (2mm)
Wing: White Spirit River Arctic Aire
Legs: Clear/pearl Wapsi Sili Legs
Adhesive: Loctite Super Glue

Sunburned Peach

Originator: Ron Donahue
Tier: Ron Donahue

Hook: #14 Tiemco 2302
Thread: Tan 70-denier UTC
Underbody: Tan Super Fine Dubbing
Body: Tan foam (1mm)
Overbody: Orange Wapsi Mottled Thin Skin
Wing: Orange Egg Yarn
Legs: Orange black flake Crazy Legs
Adhesive: Loctite Super Glue

Pheasant Wing Beetle

Originator: Ron Donahue
Tier: Ron Donahue

Hook: #14 Tiemco 2302
Thread: Brown 70-denier UTC
Underbody: Wine Super Fine Dubbing
Body: Rusty red foam (2mm)
Wing: Dark breast pheasant feather
Legs: Orange Tarantu-Leggs (medium)
Adhesive: Loctite Super Glue

Dress Brown Beetle

Originator: Ron Donahue
Tier: Ron Donahue

Hook: #14 Tiemco 2302
Thread: Brown 70-denier UTC
Underbody: Brown Super Fine Dubbing
Body: Brown foam (2mm)
Legs: Speckled yellow/black/red Centipede Legs
Adhesive: Loctite Super Glue

Greenie Beetle

Originator: Ron Donahue
Tier: Ron Donahue

Hook: #14 Tiemco 2302
Thread: Lime green 70-denier UTC
Underbody: Chartreuse Ice Dub
Body: Green Sparkle Foam (2mm)
Wing: White Spirit River Arctic Aire
Legs: Chartreuse black flake Crazy Legs
Adhesive: Loctite Super Glue

Marmalade Beetle

Originator: Ron Donahue
Tier: Ron Donahue

Hook: #14 Tiemco 2302
Thread: White 70-denier UTC
Underbody: Orange Ice Dub
Body: Orange foam (2mm)
Legs: Orange black flake Crazy Legs
Adhesive: Loctite Super Glue
Marker: Orange permanent

Red Cloud Beetle

Originator: Ron Donahue
Tier: Ron Donahue

Hook: #14 Tiemco 2302
Thread: Black 70-denier UTC
Underbody: Black Ice Dub
Body: Black foam (2mm) coated with CCG Hydro
Wing: Red Egg Yarn
Legs: Clear black Grizzly Legs
Adhesive: Loctite Super Glue

Sparkle Red Beetle

Originator: Ron Donahue
Tier: Ron Donahue

Hook: #14 Tiemco 2302
Thread: Red 70-denier UTC
Underbody: Red Ice Dub and wine Super Fine Dubbing
Body: Red Sparkle Foam (2mm) coated with CCG Hydro
Legs: Orange brown Tarantu-Leggs (small)
Adhesive: Loctite Super Glue

Apricot Beetle

Originator: Ron Donahue
Tier: Ron Donahue

Hook: #14 Tiemco 2302
Thread: Tan 70-denier UTC
Underbody: Peach Super Fine Dubbing
Body: Tan foam (2mm)
Wing: Peach Egg Yarn
Legs: Orange black flake Crazy Legs
Adhesive: Loctite Super Glue

Bever's Black Beetle

Originator: Jeff Bever
Tier: Jeff Bever

Hook: #16-18 Tiemco 200R
Thread: Black 70-denier UTC
Body: Black Sparkle Dub
Thorax: Peacock herl and olive green goose biots
Wing Case: Black goose biots
Legs: Black Japanese Nymph Legs
Antennae: Black Microfibetts
Note: *Coat thorax and wing case with CCG Hydro.*

Bever's Brown Beetle

Originator: Jeff Bever
Tier: Jeff Bever

Hook: #16-18 Tiemco 200R
Thread: Brown 70-denier UTC
Body: Tan foam (2mm) covered with tan Sparkle Dub
Thorax: Brown ostrich herl
Wing Case: Black goose biots
Legs: Clear 17-pound-test mono colored with brown marker
Note: *Coat thorax and wing case with CCG Hydro.*

Harlequin Beetle

Originator: Ron Donahue
Tier: Ron Donahue

Hook: #16 Dai-Riki 301
Thread: Black 70-denier UTC
Underbody: Tying thread
Body: Black foam (2mm)
Indicator: Yellow foam (2mm)
Legs: Yellow/black/red Centipede Legs

Propper Beetle

Originator: Hiroyuki Maki
Tier: Hiroyuki Maki

Hook: #8-12 Tiemco 2487 BL
Thread: Brown 8/0 Uni-Thread
Body: Copper Metallic Foam
Underbody: Tying thread
Legs: Black round rubber (small)
Note: *Use brown permanent marker for side stripe.*

Limeade Beetle

Originator: Ron Donahue
Tier: Ron Donahue

Hook:	#14 Tiemco 2302
Thread:	Fluorescent chartreuse 70-denier UTC
Underbody:	Lime dubbing and tying thread
Body:	Black foam (2mm)
Tag:	Tying thread
Overbody:	Green foam (2mm)
Indicator:	Chartreuse Egg Yarn
Legs:	Chartreuse Centipede Legs

Little Lady

Originator: Mark Mills
Tier: Mark Mills

Hook:	#16 Tiemco 206 BL
Thread:	Black 70-denier UTC
Body:	Black Antron Dubbing
Head:	Black Antron and thread
Wing Case:	Red deer hair and black Holographic Flashabou
Legs:	Black saddle hackle
Marker:	Black Sharpie

EZ2C Beetle

Originator: Eric A. Pettine
Tier: Eric A. Pettine

Hook:	#12 Mustad 94833
Thread:	Black 70-denier Danville's
Body:	Orange and black foam (2mm)
Head:	Orange and black foam (2mm)
Tail:	Black Krystal Flash
Legs:	Black Krystal Flash
Adhesive:	Super Glue

CW's Electric Beetle

Originator: Chris Williams
Tier: Chris Williams

Hook:	#13-15 Tiemco 102Y
Thread:	Black 16/0 Tiemco
Underbody:	Peacock herl twisted with olive Whiting Farms Midge grizzly hackle
Overbody:	Black Evazote foam (2mm) with electrical tape pulled over the back
Thorax:	Same as overbody
Head:	Same as overbody
Wing:	Electrical tape back divided with blue metallic thread
Legs:	Black hackle stems

GD's Fat Head Beetle

Originator: George Daniel
Tier: George Daniel

Hook:	#12 Tiemco 921
Thread:	Black 6/0 Uni-Thread
Underbody:	Peacock Ice Dub
Body:	Black Hareline Evazote foam (1/8")
Indicator:	Yellow foam (2mm)
Legs:	Black Wapsi Spanflex (medium)

Tak's EZ Foam Beetle

Originator: Rick Takahashi
Tier: Rick Takahashi

Hook:	#16-20 Tiemco 9300
Thread:	Black 16/0 Veevus
Body:	Black Evazote foam
Indicator:	Red craft foam (1mm)
Legs:	Black round rubber (small)

Tak's Foam Beetle

Originator: Rick Takahashi
Tier: Rick Takahashi

Hook: #16-20 Tiemco 9300
Thread: Black 16/0 Veevus
Body: Black Evazote foam
Underbody: Brown Whiting Farms saddle
Indicator: Fluorescent red McFlylon
Legs: Black round rubber (small)
Note: *Cut body foam with RRC Beetle Body Cutter (#16).*

Tak's Jumbo EZ Beetle

Originator: Rick Takahashi
Tier: Rick Takahashi

Hook: #12-16 Tiemco 9300
Thread: Black 16/0 Veevus
Body: Black Evazote foam
Underbody: Brown Whiting Farms Midge saddle
Indicator: Red foam (2mm)
Legs: Brown speckled MFC Sexi-Floss
Note: *Cut body foam with RRC Beetle Body cutter (#18).*

Tak's Crystal Legged Beetle

Originator: Rick Takahashi
Tier: Rick Takahashi

Hook: #16-20 Tiemco 9300
Thread: Black 16/0 Veevus
Body: Black Evazote foam
Indicator: Red Evazote foam (1mm)
Legs: Black Krystal Flash
Note: *Cut body foam with RRC Beetle Body Cutter (#16).*

Furimsky's Green Bottle Fly

Originator: Ben Furimsky
Tier: Ben Furimsky

Hook: #12-10 Tiemco 900 BL
Thread: Black 6/0 Uni-Thread
Body: Black foam (2mm)
Underbody: Green Bill's Bodi-Braid
Wing: White poly yarn
Legs: Black hackle

Furimsky's Wing Tip Beetle

Originator: Ben Furimsky
Tier: Ben Furimsky

Hook: #14-18 Tiemco 100
Thread: Black 6/0 Uni-Thread
Body: Black foam (2mm)
Wing: Off-white hackle tips
Indicator: Orange foam (2mm)
Legs: Black Wapsi Spanflex
Adhesive: Glitter Hard As Nails over foam body

Jamaican Beetle

Originator: Marty Staab
Tier: Marty Staab

Hook: #12 Dai-Riki 070
Thread: Black 70-denier UTC
Body: Black craft foam (2mm)
Thorax: Peacock herl
Underbody: Peacock herl
Legs: Black Senyo's Shaggy Dub
Indicator: Red craft foam (2mm)
Note: *Cut body with RRC Beetle Body cutter.*

RRC Beetle

Originator: Tony Tomsu
Tier: Tony Tomsu

Hook: #12-18 Tiemco 100
Thread: Black 8/0 Danville's
Underbody: Medium olive and ginger variant Antron dubbing
Body: Black RRC Foam (2mm)
Legs: Black Spanflex leg material (fine)
Indicator: Orange foam (1mm)
Note: *Body cut using RRC Foam Beetle cutter.*

Loco Green Beetle

Originator: Unknown
Tier: Marty Staab

Hook: #14 Dai-Riki 320
Thread: White 8/0 Uni-Thread
ShellBack: Beetle green Wapsi Loco Foam
Abdomen: UV pearl Spirit River Diamond Brite
Head: Black foam shelf line
Indicator: Fluorescent orange Gator Hair
Legs: Black Flexi Floss
Note: *Cut foam with RRC Beetle Body Cutter (#14).*

Patriot Beetle

Originator: Unknown
Tier: Marty Staab

Hook: #14 Dai-Riki 320
Thread: Red 140-denier UTC
Shell: Royal blue craft foam (2mm)
Shell Stripe: Wapsi opaque Razor Foam (.5mm)
Abdomen: Strung peacock
Indicator: Fluorescent orange Gator Hair
Legs: Black Senyo Shaggy Dub
Note: *Cut foam with RRC Beetle Body Cutter (#14).*

Marty's Beetle

Originator: Marty Staab
Tier: Marty Staab

Hook: #14 Dai-Riki 320
Thread: Black 140-denier UTC
Shell: Black craft foam (2mm)
Hackle: Black Whiting Farms saddle
Abdomen: Strung peacock
Indicator: Pink McFlylon
Legs: Pearl Krystal Flash
Note: *Cut foam with RRC Beetle Body Cutter (#14).*

M.S.U. Beetle

Originator: Gary Barnes
Tier: Gary Barnes

Hook: #14-18 Daiichi 1270
Thread: Black 70-denier UTC
Underbody: Black fine dubbing
Body: Black deer hair
Head: Black fine dubbing
Legs: Black deer hair
Tail: Pearl Mylar
Covering: Bug Bond Light UV Resin

Manuka Beetle

Originator: Unknown
Tier: Gene Decker

Hook: #10 Tiemco 9300
Thread: Black 8/0 Uni-Thread
Tail: Dun hackle fibers
Body: Peacock Ice Dub
Wing: Peacock swords
Hackle: Brown furnace

Matuka Beetle

Originator: Unknown
Tier: Gene Decker

Hook: #10 Tiemco 9300
Thread: Black 8/0 Uni-Thread
Tail: Black hackle fibers
Body: Olive deer hair
Wing: White poly yarn
Hackle: Brown furnace

Hub's Split Back Beetle

Originator: Jerry Hubka
Tier: Jerry Hubka

Hook: #12 Daiichi 1250
Thread: Black 140-denier UTC
Underbody: Red peacock herl
Rib: Blue Ultra Wire (small)
Underwing: Black Krystal Flash
Head/Back: Northern Lights Wapsi Loco Foam (2mm)
Tag: Blue Ultra Wire (small)
Legs: Rainbow shimmer/black Hareline Legs
Antennae: Black Krystal Flash
Adhesive: CCG Hydro and Zap-a-Gap
Note: *Split wing cut with RRC #6 Hopper Wing cutter.*

Hub's Chewee Blue Beetle

Originator: Jerry Hubka
Tier: Jerry Hubka

Hook: #14 Tiemco 2312 or 2302
Thread: Peacock blue 140-denier UTC
Underbody: Tying thread
Body: Royal blue craft foam (2mm)
Overbody: Black UV D's Flies Chewee Skin
Indicator: Opaque yellow Razor Foam (.5mm)
Legs: Black/blue flake Sili Legs
Antennae: Black Krystal Flash
Adhesive: Zap-A-Gap (Brush On) and CCG Hydro
Note: *Foam body and Chewee Skin are cut with RRC Beetle cutters (#16).*

Hub's Borealis Beetle

Originator: Jerry Hubka
Tier: Jerry Hubka

Hook: #12 Daiichi 1250
Thread: Black 140-denier UTC
Underbody: Red peacock herl
Rib: Blue Ultra Wire (small)
Underwing: Black Krystal Flash
Head/Back: Northern lights Wapsi Loco Foam (2mm)
Tag: Blue Ultra Wire (small)
Legs: Rainbow shimmer/black Hareline Legs
Antennae: Black Krystal Flash
Adhesive: Zap-A-Gap and CCG Hydro
Note: *Shell back cut with RRC #6 Hopper Wing cutter.*

Hub's Bow Tie Beetle (Pearl)

Originator: Jerry Hubka
Tier: Jerry Hubka

Hook: #14 Tiemco 2312 or 2302
Thread: Black 140-denier UTC
Underbody: Peacock Ice Dub
Rib: Red Ultra Wire (small)
Head/Back: Northern lights Wapsi Loco Foam (2mm)
Wings: Pearl Krystal Flash
Tag: Red Ultra Wire (small)
Thorax: Rusty brown Ice Dub
Legs: Black Hareline Flex Floss
Antennae: Black Krystal Flash
Adhesive: Zap-A-Gap and CCG Hydro
Note: *Shell back is cut with RRC #16 Beetle Body cutter.*

Hub's Bright Bottom Beetle

Originator: Jerry Hubka
Tier: Jerry Hubka

Hook: #14 Tiemco 2302 or 2312
Thread: Black 140-denier UTC
Body: Beetle green Loco Foam Wapsi
Indicator Stripe: Opaque chartreuse Wapsi Foam (.5mm)
Legs: Black/yellow chartreuse tipped Hareline Crazy Legs
Antennae: Peacock Krystal Flash
Adhesive: Loctite Super Glue Gel and CCG Hydro
Note: *Cut body foam with RRC #16 Beetle Cutter; Loco Foam body is bright side down.*

Drunken Beetle

Originator: Eric Ishiwata
Tier: Eric Ishiwata

Hook: #10-14 Gamakatsu S10
Thread: Black 8/0 Uni-Thread
Tag: Pearl seed bead or Mirage Tinsel
Head: Gunmetal bead (2.8mm)
Weight: .020" round lead free wire
Body: Dark Stone Nymph SLF Dubbing
Rib: Amber Ultra Wire (small)
Underwing: Peacock swords
Wing: Black ringneck pheasant rump feather
Head: Dark Stone Nymph SLF Dubbing

Lady Luck Beetle

Originator: John Larson
Tier: John Larson

Hook: #16 Gamakatsu C12
Thread: Black 8/0 Uni-Thread
Body: White foam
Spots: Black Prismacolor marker
Underbody: Black UV Ice Dub
Legs: Pheasant tail fibers
Note: *Color body with white and orange Wet and Wild nail polish. Color head with black Prismacolor marker, white paint.*

Cape Crusader

Originator: Gary Okizaki
Tier: Gary Okizaki

Hook: #14-18 Tiemco 3761
Thread: Black 70-denier UTC
Underbody: Peacock herl
Thorax: Silver lined red glass bead (small)
Shell: Black Glitter Foam (2mm)
Wing: Ringneck pheasant rump feather
Legs: Brown Spirit River Flex Floss
Note: *Glitter side down on the shell.*

Double Beetle

Originator: Gary Okizaki
Tier: Gary Okizaki

Hook: #6-10 Daiichi 1770
Thread: Black 70-denier UTC
Beetle: Red and chartreuse Glitter Foam (2mm) over peacock Estaz

Lady You

Originator: Mark Tracy
Tier: Mark Tracy

Hook: #14 Tiemco 2457
Thread: Black 8/0 Uni-Thread
Legs: Strand of black poly-rope
Underbody: Black 1mm foam (3/16")
Shell case: Red/orange Razor Foam (.5mm)
Dots: Black marker coated with CCG Thin
Eyes: White Rainy's Foam Parachute Post (1/16")

Ringo

Originator: Inspired by Cathy Beck's Super Beetle
Tier: Stephen Johnson

Hook: #16 Tiemco 100
Thread: Black 6/0 Danville's
Body: Black Wapsi Fly Foam (2mm)
Underbody: Peacock Krystal Flash
Wing: White SAAP Float-Viz
Legs: Peacock Krystal Flash
Adhesive: Gloss coat

Tying Hoppers and Crickets

Takahopper

Originator: Ed Shenk
Tier: Rick Takahashi

Hook: #10-18 Tiemco 2312
Thread: Yellow 3/0 Danville's Monocord
Abdomen: Yellow Super Fine Dubbing
Wing: Mottled dark brown RRC River Wing
Collar: Natural deer hair
Adhesive: CCG Hydro
Note: *This is my version of Ed Shenk's Letort Hopper and the first dry fly I fished. I've been fishing it over 45 years, and I can't tell you how many fish I have caught with it.*

TYING THE TAKAHOPPER

1. Attach the tying thread to the hook approximately one eye width back from the hook eye, trim the tag, and wrap the thread to the hook bend (opposite the barb).

2. Twist a two-inch noodle of dubbing onto the thread. Wrap the dubbing in touching wraps to a point two eye widths behind the hook eye.

3. Cut a wing from the winging material with River Road Creations Hopper Wing Cutters.

4. Tie in the wing directly in front of the abdomen, secure with several wraps, and trim the excess wing material in front of the tie-in point. Wrap the tying thread to the eye and then back to the front edge of the trimmed wing.

5. Select a bunch of deer hair about half the size of a pencil and stack it. Measure the deer hair so that the tips are slightly shorter that the length of the wing. Use your index finger and thumb to mark the desired length of deer hair.

6. Grasp the measured deer hair in your left hand immediately next to your index finger and thumb of your right hand. Trim the butt section of the deer hair approximately ¼ of an inch in front of your fingers perpendicular to the hair.

7. Place the deer hair over the hook eye so that it is even with the end of the front edge of the eye. Take several wraps of thread over the hook eye and then draw the thread tight to flare the butt ends. Do not let go of the hair until the wing is secured or it will spin around the shank.

8. Take several snug wraps forward through the hair.

9. Place several half hitches in front of the deer hair.

10. Trim the thread and the deer hair under the hook parallel to the hook shank.

11. Turn the fly over and place a small dab of CCG Hydro at the tie-in point of the wing. Cure the resin with a UV light.

12. The completed Takahopper.

Hubka's Simple Foam Hopper

Originator: Jerry Hubka
Tier: Rick Takahashi

Hook: #8-12 Tiemco 2302
Thread: Yellow 3/0 Danville's Monocord
Abdomen: Yellow Rainy's Evazote Foam
Underwing: Mottled brown RRC River Wing (2mm)
Wing: White MFC Widow's Web
Legs: Black and yellow speckled MFC Centipede Legs
Adhesive: CCG Hydro

TYING HUBKA'S SIMPLE FOAM HOPPER

1. Attach the tying thread to the hook approximately one eye width back from the hook eye, trim the tag, and wrap the thread to the hook bend (opposite the barb). Wrap the thread back to the tie-in point.

2. Cut a hopper body shape from the foam with a River Road Creations Hopper Body Cutter sized for the hook you are using. I usually like to make the body slightly longer than the hook shank.

3. Tie in the foam so that the square end is positioned over, or slightly longer than, the hook eye. Take several wraps back and forth over the tie-in point to form a small waist.

4. Trim the head as shown. Place wing material (cut with a River Road Creations Wing Cutter) over the body so that the rounded end of the wing is slightly longer than the end of the body. Secure it with several wraps of thread and trim the butt end if it is too long.

5. Attach one rubber leg on each side of the wing. Tie in the legs at their midpoints.

6. Tie in the Widows Web wing material.

7. Place the wing over the waist of the pattern, allowing a small portion of the wing material to extend forward even with the hook eye. Take several wraps to secure and trim the wing.

8. Trim the rear of the wing as shown. Whip-finish.

9. Turn the fly upside down, apply CCG Hydro, and cure with UV light. This reinforces all of the material to the hook.

10. The completed Simple Foam Hopper.

Bullethead Hopper

Originator: Tim England
Tier: Rick Takahashi

Hook: #10-14 Tiemco 2302
Thread: Yellow 3/0 Danville's Monocord
Tail: Red Whiting Farms hen hackle fibers
Abdomen: Yellow craft wool yarn
Tail: Red hackle fibers
Rib: Copper UTC Wire (small)
Hackle: Brown Whiting Farms saddle hackle
Wing: MFC mottled brown Etha Wing
Rear Legs: Knotted pheasant tail
Front Legs: Black and tan speckled MFC Centipede Legs
Head/Wing: Deer hair
Adhesive: CCG Hydro
Note: *This is my version of Tim England's hopper.*

TYING THE BULLETHEAD HOPPER

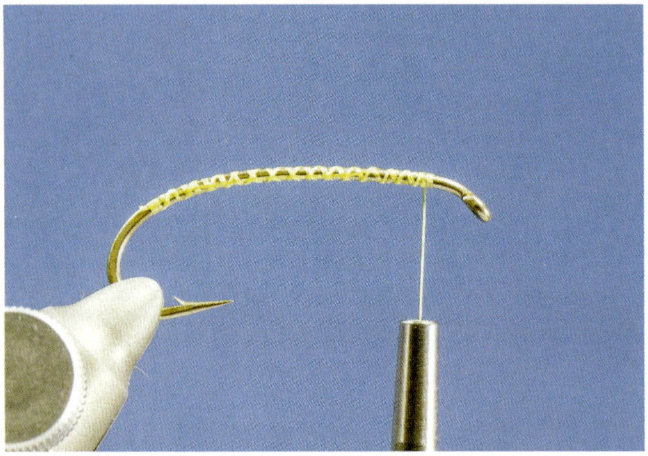

1. Attach the tying thread to the hook approximately one eye width back from the hook eye. Take about six wraps, trim the tag, and wrap the thread back to the hook bend (opposite the barb). Then, wrap the thread forward to the original tie-in point.

2. Attach the red hackle fibers so that they extend approximately one-quarter the length of the abdomen.

3. Wrap the tying thread over the hackle fibers to the point on the shank opposite the barb.

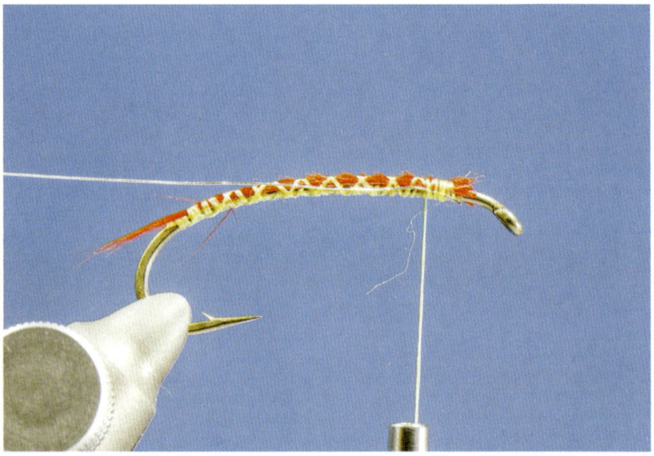

4. Wrap the tying thread forward and tie in the wire for the rib. Wrap the thread back to the point on the shank opposite the barb.

5. Attach the tag end of the yarn.

6. Wrap the yarn toward the hook eye to the two-thirds position of the hook. Secure the yarn and trim excess.

7. Trim the tag end of the yarn. Tie in the saddle hackle with the shiny side facing to the front of the body.

8. Reverse palmer wrap the hackle toward the hook bend, taking evenly spaced wraps. Take a wrap of the wire at the hook bend to secure the hackle.

9. Counter wrap the wire with evenly spaced wraps toward the two-thirds position of the fly body.

10. Tie off the wire and trim it. Cut the top of the hackle along the hook shank.

11. Cut out a wing using the River Road Creations Hopper Wing Cutters and tie it in. Continue to wrap the thread to the hook eye and back to the front edge of the wing. Wings can be cut from materials such as Pellon 808, MFC mottled brown Wing Material, MFC Lucent Wing material, MFC mottled brown Etha Wing, section of mottled turkey wing, or River Road Creations River Wing foam.

12. Attach one of the hopper legs to each side of the hook so that they are symmetrical. The tips of the legs should be even with the abdomen or slightly shorter.

13. Wrap the tying thread in touching wraps over the butt ends of the leg material.

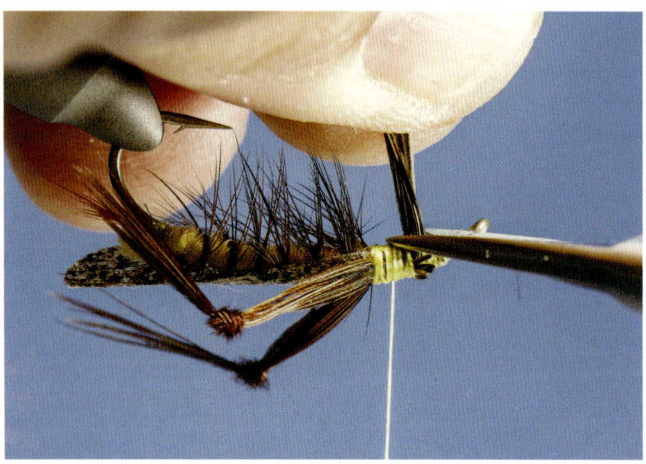

14. Trim the butt ends of the leg material.

15. Select a bunch of deer hair about the size of a pencil and stack it. Take the evened hair and grasp the butt ends with your right hand; the tips of the deer hair should face toward the rear of the hook. Measure the deer hair so that the tips of the deer hair do not exceed the length of the wing. Use your index finger and thumb of your left hand to mark the desired length of deer hair. Trim the butt section of the deer hair approximately one-quarter inch in front of your fingers perpendicular to the hair. Place the deer hair back into the stacker and stack the hair.

16. Take the base of the stacker and rotate it to rear of the hook so the tips of hair are facing forward. Place the deer hair over the hook eye so that the hair tips are even with the end of front edge of the wing.

17. Take several wraps of thread over the deer hair directly behind the hook eye and draw the thread tight, flaring the butt ends. Release the hair and allow the hair to spin around the hook shank. Take several wraps back through the hair toward the rear making sure each wrap is tight.

18. Trim the butts of the deer hair.

19. Gently start to fold the hair back toward the wing and spread out the hair so that no hair covers the hook eye.

20. Take a Bic Classic pen with the ball point and the ink reservoir removed or a plastic tube slightly smaller in diameter than the diameter of the deer hair and use it to gently start to push the deer hair and form the bullet head. If the diameter of the deer hair is larger than the pen opening, try using a soda straw or hollow plastic tubing that will accommodate the amount of hair. This compression will result in a very compact and tight bullet head. Take the tying thread and wrap around the end of the hair with enough wraps to secure the head. I try and tie the head just in front of the wing. This will flare out the deer hair tips.

21. Slide the tube off of the head and take several more wraps to secure the head.

22. Attach the rubber legs, whip-finish, and trim the thread.

23. Apply thinned out head cement or use Pliobond, and allow to dry. Trim underside of the flared deer hair if desired and trim the round rubber leg material.

24. Apply CCG Hydro to the junction of bullethead and legs.

25. Cure the resin with UV light.

26. The completed Bullethead Hopper.

Grasshopper Patterns

Parachute Grasshopper

Originator: Unknown
Tier: Spirit River

Hook: #6-16 Maruto 7522 or Tiemco 5212
Thread: Olive 6/0 Uni-Thread
Body: Dark olive Spirit River Fine and Dry Dubbing
Hackle: Grizzly dry fly
Down Wing: Turkey feather
Post Wing: White calf body hair
Legs: Pheasant tail
Adhesive: Super Glue
Note: *Glue base of post wing before wrapping hackle.*

Fishy's Foam Grasshopper (Yellow)

Originator: Jay "Fishy" Fullum
Tier: Spirit River

Hook: #6-8 Maruto 7526 or Spear-It N062
Thread: Chartreuse 3/0 Uni-Thread
Body: Special Yellow PVC Forex Soft Foam
Underbody: Light green fingernail polish
Wing: Black woven interface fabric
Head: Brown fingernail polish
Legs: Olive/black Spirit River Silicone Leggs
Eyes: Black fingernail polish
Marker: Gray, walnut, and black permanent
Note: *The foam used for the body should be (3/16" square; 1 1/4" long). Coat head and body sides where legs enter the foam with clear fingernail polish.*

Thunder Grasshopper

Originator: Unknown
Tier: Spirit River

Hook: #6-8 Daiichi 1720
Thread: Brown 6/0 Uni-Thread
Body: Gray, yellow, and tan Spirit River Fly Foam (2mm)
Indicator: Yellow Fly Foam (2mm)
Flash: Pearl Crystal Splash
Wing: Olive calf tail
Head: Elk hair
Legs: Gray round rubber
Note: *Other hook models include Daiichi N063 or Tiemco 5263.*

Dave's Hopper

Originator: Dave Whitlock
Tier: Rainy's Flies

Hook: #4-14 Tiemco 5263
Thread: Pale yellow 6/0 Uni-Thread
Body: Yellow poly yarn
Underwing: Yellow calf tail
Rib: Grizzly Whiting Farms dry fly hackle
Wing: Turkey tail feather
Overwing: Natural and yellow deer hair
Head: Natural and yellow deer hair
Legs: Ringneck pheasant tail
Tag: Red calf tail
Adhesive: Dave's Flexament

Dave's Whit Hopper

Originator: Dave Whitlock
Tier: Rainy's Flies

Hook: #8-14 Tiemco 2302
Thread: Yellow 6/0 Uni-Thread
Body: Deer hair dyed yellow
Rib: Tying thread
Wing: Turkey tail feather
Head: Natural and yellow deer hair
Legs: Pheasant tail
Indicator: Fluorescent orange deer hair
Antennae: Dry fly hackle
Adhesive: Dave's Flexament

Rainy's Grand Hopper

Originator: Rainy Riding
Tier: Rainy's Flies

Hook: #4-16 Tiemco 5263
Thread: Tan 6/0 Uni-Thread
Body: Camel Rainy's Evazote Sheet Foam (2mm)
Thorax: Golden tan Wapsi Antron Sparkle Dubbing
Underwing: Pearl Krystal Flash
Wing: Brown hen saddle
Legs: Tan Rainy's round rubber (medium)
Adhesive: Super Glue Gel
Marker: Yellow and black Sharpie

Furimsky's Hot Legs Hopper

Originator: Chuck Furimsky
Tier: Rainy's Flies

Hook: #8-12 Daiichi 1180
Thread: Tan 6/0 Uni-Thread
Body: Chartreuse Rainy's Cross-Link Sheet Foam (4mm)
Indicator: Orange poly yarn
Wing: Mottled brown Bug Skin
Legs: Wapsi TNT Hopper Legs colored with olive and red
Front Legs: Yellow Rainy's barred rubber legs (medium)
Eyes: Black Sharpie
Antennae: Tan Rainy's barred rubber legs (fine)
Adhesive: Super Glue Gel underwing
Marker: Red, olive, and black Sharpie
Note: *Burn the tips of the rubber legs to form the antennae.*

Rainy's Red Legged Hi-Viz Hopper

Originator: Rainy Riding
Tier: Rainy's Flies

Hook: #6-12 Tiemco 5263
Thread: Tan 6/0 Uni-Thread
Body: Tan Rainy's Gorilla Body
Wing: Mottled brown Whiting Farms hen saddle
Underwing: Pearl Krystal Flash
Indicator: Orange and chartreuse Rainy's 2-Tone Indicator Strip
Eyes: Black Rainy's Bug-Eye Stick (medium)
Legs: Red Rainy's barred round rubber (medium and small)
Antennae: Red Rainy's barred round rubber (small)

J's Saddle Back Hopper

Originator: Jesse Riding
Tier: Rainy's Flies

Hook: #8-12 Tiemco 5263
Thread: Brown 6/0 Uni-Thread
Body: Tan Rainy's Gorilla Body
Underbelly: Yellow Rainy's Cross-Link Sheet Foam (1mm)
Wing: Elk hair
Underwing: Pearl Krystal Flash
Indicator Saddle: Orange and chartreuse Rainy's 2-Tone Indicator Strip
Front Legs: Yellow Rainy's barred round rubber (small)
Rear Legs: Tan/yellow Rainy's 2-Tone Foam Hopper Legs

Rainy's Red Gorilla Hopper

Originator: Rainy Riding
Tier: Rainy's Flies

Hook: #6-12 Tiemco 5263
Thread: Red 6/0 Uni-Thread
Body: Rainy's black/tan/red Gorilla Body
Underbody: Tying thread
Wing: Turkey tail feather
Underwing: Pearl Krystal Flash
Eyes: Black Rainy's Bug Eye Stick
Legs: Tan Rainy's barred round rubber (medium)

Rainy's Marshmallow Hopper

Originator: Rainy Riding
Tier: Rainy's Flies

Hook: #6-12 Tiemco 5263
Thread: Brown 6/0 Uni-Thread
Body: Tan Rainy's Cross-Link Sheet Foam
Head: Tan Rainy's Sparkle Dub
Wing: Whiting Farms hen saddle
Underwing: Pearl Krystal Flash
Post: White Rainy's Parachute Post (3/16" or 1/8")
Legs: Tan Rainy's barred round rubber
Hackle: Bleached grizzly dyed tan Whiting dry fly
Rib: Tying thread

Ted's Fire Tiger Hopper

Originator: Ted Kraimer
Tier: Rainy's Flies

Hook: #6-12 Tiemco 200R
Thread: Chartreuse 6/0 Uni-Thread
Body: Chartreuse Rainy's Cross-Link Sheet Foam (2mm)
Wing: Elk hair and polar pearl Lite-Brite
Indicator: Orange Rainy's Cross-Link Sheet Foam (2mm)
Head: Deer hair
Legs: Red and chartreuse/black Wapsi Sili Legs
Marker: Black Sharpie Marker

Schiel's Kicken Hopper

Originator: Chad Schiel
Tier: Rainy's Flies

Hook: #6-12 Tiemco 200R
Thread: Tan 6/0 Uni-Thread
Body: Tan Rainy's Cross-Link Sheet Foam (2mm)
Thorax Cap: Tan Rainy's Cross-Link Sheet Foam (2mm)
Overwing: Root beer Krystal Flash
Wing: Natural Whiting hen saddle feather covered with Glitter Glue
Underwing: Chartreuse deer belly hair
Indicator: White poly yarn
Legs: Rainy's brown round rubber (medium)

Dornan's Hot Rod Hopper

Originator: Will Dornan
Tier: Rainy's Flies

Hook: #6-10 Tiemco 5263
Thread: Yellow 3/0 Uni-Thread
Body: Tan and yellow Rainy's Cross-Link Sheet Foam (2mm)
Thorax: Tan Rainy's Sparkle Dub
Wing: Light elk hair
Underwing: Pearl Krystal Flash
Eyes: Black Rainy's Bug Eye Stick (medium)
Rear Legs: Same as body; one piece split in the middle
Front Legs: Yellow Rainy's barred round rubber
Adhesive: 3M 77 Spray Adhesive

J's Hopper Popper

Originator: Jesse Riding
Tier: Rainy's Flies

Hook: #2-10 Mustad 3366
Thread: Yellow 6/0 Uni-Thread
Body: Yellow Rainy's Cross-Link Sheet Foam (4mm)
Thorax: Yellow Rainy's Sparkle Dub
Wing: Light elk hair
Underwing: Pearl Krystal Flash
Indicator: Orange Rainy's Cross-Link Sheet Foam (2mm)
Eyes: Black Rainy's Bug Eye Stick (medium)
Legs: Fluorescent yellow Rainy's barred round rubber (medium)
Tail: Red Whiting Farms hackle tip
Head: Yellow Rainy's Pee-Wee Pop
Marker: Black Sharpie

Cartoon Hopper (Gray/Pink)

Originator: Bubba Smith
Tier: Orvis

Hook: #6-10 Orvis 122J
Thread: Brown 6/0 Uni-Thread
Overbody: Gray foam (2mm)
Underbody: Pink foam (2mm)
Underwing: Pearl Krystal Flash
Wing: White and orange Orvis poly yarn
Thorax: Peacock Ice Dub
Eyes: Doll eyes (4mm)
Legs: Tan/black barred round rubber (medium)
Hackle: Brown furnace Whiting Farms
Marker: Black permanent

[10

Hog Caller (Yellow)

Originator: Bubba Smith
Tier: Orvis

Hook: #6-10 Tiemco 5212
Thread: Brown 6/0 Uni-Thread
Body: Yellow and tan foam (2mm)
Wing: Moose mane
Underwing: Pearl UV Krystal Flash
Eyes: Doll eyes (2mm)
Front Legs: Yellow with pearl flecks Sili Legs
Rear Legs: Yellow foam (2mm) colored with black marker
Kicker Leg: Orange with black flecks Sili Legs
Post: Fluorescent orange Egg Yarn
Back: Bright yellow foam (2mm)
Hackle: Brown furnace Whiting Farms

Hog Caller (Brown/Tan)

Originator: Bubba Smith
Tier: Orvis

Hook: #6-10 Tiemco 5212
Thread: Brown 6/0 Uni-Thread
Body: Brown and tan foam (2mm)
Wing: Moose mane
Underwing: UV pearl Krystal Flash
Eyes: Doll eyes (2mm)
Front Legs: Yellow with pearl flecks Sili Legs
Rear Legs: Tan foam (2mm) colored with black marker
Kicker Leg: Orange with black flecks Sili Legs
Post: Fluorescent orange Egg Yarn
Back: Bright yellow foam (2mm)
Hackle: Brown furnace Whiting Farms

Hog Caller (Dark Green/Light Green)

Originator: Bubba Smith
Tier: Orvis

Hook: #6-10 Tiemco 5212
Thread: Green 6/0 Uni-Thread
Body: Dark and light green foam (2mm)
Wing: Moose mane
Underwing: UV pearl Krystal Flash
Eyes: Doll eyes (2mm)
Front Legs: Pumpkin with green fleck Sili Legs
Rear Legs: Green foam (2mm) colored with black marker
Kicker Leg: Orange with black fleck Sili Legs
Post: Fluorescent orange Egg Yarn
Back: Bright yellow foam (2mm)
Hackle: Brown furnace Whiting Farms

Ba Donk A Donk (Tan)

Originator: Bubba Smith
Tier: Orvis

Hook: #6-10 Tiemco 200R
Thread: Tan 6/0 Uni-Thread
Body: Tan foam (2mm)
Underbody: Tan foam (2mm)
Wing: White poly yarn
Underwing: Pearl Krystal Flash
Indicator: Fluorescent orange foam (2mm)
Eyes: Doll eyes (4mm)
Legs: Tan/brown Rainy's barred round rubber (medium)
Back: Tan foam (2mm)

Razor Hopper

Originator: Chris Williams
Tier: Chris Williams

Hook: #12-14 Partridge Klinkhammer 15BN
Thread: Yellow Pearsall's Silk Floss
Underbody: Tan Razor Foam
Body: Tan craft foam (2mm) folded at end
Head: Deer hair
Wing: Translucent dun Razor Foam
Legs: Tan/black barred round Sili Legs
Rib: Tying thread
Adhesive: Bondini Super Glue

Dick's EZ Hopper

Originator: Dick Shinton
Tier: Dick Shinton

Hook: #10-14 Tiemco 5212
Thread: Tan 70-denier UTC
Body: Tan foam cylinder
Wing: Deer or elk hair
Underwing: Pearl Wapsi Wing N' Flash
Legs: Pumpkin/black/green flake Wapsi Sili Legs
Adhesive: Zap-A-Gap

Dunnigan's Young Grasshoppa (Chartreuse)

Originator: Casey Dunnigan
Tier: Casey Dunnigan

Hook: #8-12 MFC 7231
Thread: Chartreuse 6/0 MFC
Body: Chartreuse Wapsi Fly Foam (1/8")
Thorax: Chartreuse Superbrite Dubbing
Head: Chartreuse Wapsi Fly Foam (1/8")
Hackle: Light brown Whiting Farms dry fly
Wing: Mottled MFC Flex Wing
Indicator: Chartreuse Wapsi Fly Foam
Eyes: Chartreuse MFC Hoppize
Rear Legs: Chartreuse MFC AK Hopper Legs
Front Legs: Chartreuse MFC Sexi Floss
Adhesive: Loctite Super Glue
Marker: Black Copic

Dunnigan's Young Grasshoppa (Tan)

Originator: Casey Dunnigan
Tier: Casey Dunnigan

Hook: #8-12 MFC 7231
Thread: Sand 6/0 MFC
Body: Tan Wapsi Fly Foam (1/8")
Thorax: Tan Superbrite Dubbing
Head: Tan Wapsi Fly Foam (1/8")
Hackle: Brown Whiting Farms dry fly
Wing: MFC Mottled Flex Wing
Indicator: Tan Wapsi Fly Foam
Eyes: Mottled brown MFC Hoppize (large)
Rear Legs: Tan MFC AK Hopper Legs
Front Legs: Tan MFC Sexi Floss
Adhesive: Loctite Super Glue
Marker: Black Copic

Dave's Hopper

Originator: Dave Whitlock
Tier: Tim Jacobs

Hook: #4-10 Tiemco 5212 or 5263
Body Thread: Hopper yellow 140-denier UTC
Head Thread: White UTC GSP 100
Body: Pale yellow poly yarn
Head: Deer hair over pale yellow deer hair
Wing: Turkey quill
Underwing: Yellow deer hair
Legs: Pheasant tail
Rib: Brown Whiting Farms High and Dry hackle
Tail: Red Hareline Ice Fur
Adhesive: Zap-A-Gap

Letort Hopper

Originator: Ed Shenk
Tier: Tim Jacobs

Hook: #8-12 Tiemco 5212
Body Thread: Hopper yellow 140-denier UTC
Head Thread: White UTC GSP 100
Body: Golden amber Fly Rite Extra Fine Poly Dubbing
Wing: Deer hair
Underwing: Turkey quill
Adhesive: Zap-A-Gap

Simple Foam Hopper

Originator: Tim Jacobs
Tier: Tim Jacobs

Hook: #10 Tiemco 100
Thread: Hopper yellow 140-denier UTC
Body: Camel Rainy's Evazote Foam (1/8")
Head: Camel Rainy's Evazote Foam (1/8")
Wing: Medium tan RRC Speckled River Wing
Underwing: Deer hair
Legs: Tan MFC barred Centipede Legs

Joe's Hopper

Originator: Art Winnie
Tier: Tim Jacobs

Hook: #8-12 Tiemco 5212
Thread: Hopper yellow 140-denier UTC
Body: Yellow Rainy's Float Foam (medium)
Head: Brown and grizzly Whiting Farms rooster
Wing: Turkey quill
Rib: Brown Whiting Farms hackle, trimmed
Tail: Red Hareline Ice Fur
Adhesive: Zap-A-Gap

Chernobyl Hopper (Black/Orange)

Originator: Unknown
Tier: Vic Loiselle

Hook: #4-6 Dai-Riki 700
Thread: Black 6/0 Uni-Thread
Body: Orange and black foam (2mm) strips (1/4" wide)
Underbody: Tying thread
Indicator: Yellow foam (2mm)
Legs: Black Rainy's round rubber (large)
Post: White Antron
Hackle: Whiting Farms grizzly
Rib: Tying thread
Wing: Deer hair
Note: *Body shape with MFC Chernobyl Body Cutter.*

Pink Lady

Originator: Vic Loiselle
Tier: Vic Loiselle

Hook: #4-6 Dai-Riki 730
Thread: Light pink 6/0 Danville's
Body: Pink and white foam (2mm)
Underbody: Tying thread
Wing: Bleached deer hair
Underwing: Pearl Krystal Flash
Indicator: Pink foam (2mm)
Legs: Clear/pearl-silver flake Wapsi Sili Legs
Adhesive: Griff's Thin Multi-Coat

Yellow Hopper

Originator: Vic Loiselle
Tier: Vic Loiselle

Hook: #6-8 Dai-Riki 700
Thread: Yellow 6/0 Uni-Thread
Body: Yellow and gray sheet foam (2mm)
Underbody: Tying thread
Overbody: Yellow foam (2mm)
Wing: Bleached deer hair
Eyes: Black marker
Legs: Yellow Rainy's round rubber

Penasco Foam Hopper (Black)

Originator: Tim Mack
Tier: Tim Mack

Hook: #8 Tiemco 5212
Thread: Black 6/0 Uni-Thread
Body: Black craft foam (2mm)
Underbody: Black Super Fine Dubbing
Wing: Black Wapsi elk hair
Underwing: Red pearl Hareline Krystal Flash
Indicator: Pink craft foam (2mm)
Legs: Red Spirit River Grizzly Legs
Rib: Gold Ultra Wire (small) and black Whiting Farms saddle
Adhesive: Brush on Super Glue

Red Legged Foam Hopper (Tan)

Originator: Tim Mack
Tier: Tim Mack

Hook: #8 Tiemco 5212
Thread: Tan 6/0 Uni-Thread
Body: Tan craft foam (2mm)
Underbody: Tan Super Fine Dubbing
Wing: Spirit River bleached elk hair
Underwing: Pearl Hareline Krystal Flash (midge)
Legs: Red Spirit River Grizzly Legs
Rib: Gold Ultra Wire (small) and brown Whiting Farms saddle
Adhesive: Brush on Super Glue

TWM Foam Hopper (Olive)

Originator: Tim Mack
Tier: Tim Mack

Hook: #10 Tiemco 5212
Thread: Tan 70-denier UTC
Body: Olive brown craft foam (2mm)
Underbody: BWO Super Fine Dubbing
Wing: Olive Hareline deer hair
Underwing: Pearl Hareline Krystal Flash (midge)
Indicator: Chartreuse craft foam (2mm)
Legs: Olive orange tipped Wapsi Sili Legs
Rib: Gold Ultra Wire (small) and brown Whiting Farms saddle
Adhesive: Brush on Super Glue

TWM Foam Hopper (Yellow)

Originator: Tim Mack
Tier: Tim Mack

Hook: #8 Tiemco 5212
Thread: Yellow 8/0 Uni-Thread
Body: Yellow craft foam (2mm)
Underbody: Bright yellow Wapsi Antron Dubbing
Wing: Spirit River bleached elk hair
Underwing: Pearl Hareline Krystal Flash (midge)
Legs: Yellow/fluorescent-orange tipped Hareline Crazy Legs
Rib: Gold Ultra Wire (small) and brown Whiting Farms saddle
Adhesive: Brush on Super Glue

Green Machine Hopper

Originator: K&K Fly Fishers
Tier: Tim Mack

Hook: #8 Tiemco 512
Thread: Black 6/0 Uni-Thread
Overbody: Black 1/4"-wide craft foam (2mm)
Underbody: Forest green 1/4"-wide craft foam (2mm)
Wing: Spirit River bleached elk hair
Underwing: Pearl Hareline Krystal Flash
Legs: Brown Spirit River round rubber (medium)
Adhesive: Loctite Super Glue

Low Rider Hopper

Originator: Ron Donahue
Tier: Ron Donahue

Hook: #12 Umpqua U103
Thread: Brown 74-denier Lagartun
Body: Rainy's Round Foam (medium)
Underwing: Hopper yellow Mottled Web Wing
Overwing: Amber poly yarn
Legs: Tom turkey feather
Eyes: Black Sharpie
Antennae: Tom turkey feather
Marker: Brown and black Sharpie
Adhesive: Loctite Super Glue

Frying Pan Special

Originator: Ron Donahue
Tier: Ron Donahue

Hook: #14 Orvis Big Eye 4641
Thread: Tan 140-denier UTC
Underbody: Tan craft foam (2mm)
Overbody: Pink craft foam (2mm)
Wing: Pink calf tail
Legs: Yellow and red barred black Centipede Legs
Adhesive: Loctite Super Glue

Meadow Master

Originator: Ron Donahue
Tier: Ron Donahue

Hook: #14 Umpqua 7000
Thread: Brown 140-denier UTC
Body: Brown craft foam (2mm)
Underbody: Tying thread
Wing: Brown Web Wing
Overwing: Copper Antron Yarn
Legs: Orange dyed peacock herl orange dyed turkey biot
Adhesive: Loctite Super Glue

Centennial Hopper

Originator: Bruce Staples
Tier: Bruce Staples

Hook: #6-12 Daiichi 1170
Thread: Orange 70-denier UTC
Body: Orange Ice Chenille (fine)
Head: Yellow deer hair
Wing: Ringneck pheasant church window feathers
Underwing: Red Whitlock's SLF Fibers
Collar: Deer hair
Legs: Saddle hackle stems bent to shape

Dry Muddler

Originator: Bruce Staples
Tier: Bruce Staples

Hook: #4-12 Daiichi 2220
Thread: Yellow UTC GSP 75
Body: Gold Danville's Rayon Floss
Head: Deer hair
Wing: Mottled kori bustard quill segments
Underwing: White over brown calf tail
Rib: Gold Lagartun variegated tinsel
Tail: Mottled kori bustard quill segments
Adhesive: Dave's Flexament

Note: *Substitute mottled turkey for wings.*

Red Wing Hopper

Originator: Bruce Staples
Tier: Bruce Staples

Hook: #4-10 Daiichi 2220
Thread: Orange 70-denier UTC
Body: Orange Dan Bailey Antron Yarn
Head: Orange and brown deer hair
Wing: Red tragopan body feather
Underwing: Red Dan Bailey Antron Yarn
Legs: Iridescent blue peacock body feathers
Rib: Brown Whiting Farms saddle hackle

Note: *Substitute red pheasant church window feathers for wings. Coat back of wing feathers with clear nail polish and pull through feathers until dried.*

Sheet Foam Hopper

Originator: Inspired by Dave Whitlock's Hopper
Tier: Jimbo Busse

Hook: #8-14 Tiemco 200R BL
Thread: Brown 8/0 Uni-Thread
Body: Olive sheet foam
Head: Brown deer hair
Wing: Mottled brown Medallion Sheeting
Underwing: White calf tail
Legs: Knotted pheasant tail fibers
Marker: Brown (154M) Pantone

Fred's Hopper

Originator: Fred DuPre
Tier: Fred DuPre

Hook: #6 Mustad 9672
Thread: Yellow 3/0 Uni-Thread
Body: Tan/yellow/tan Blue Ribbon Flies Tiger Strips Foam (2mm)
Thorax: Yellow poly yarn
Wing: Mottled yellow/black Web Wing
Underwing: Deer hair over pearl Krystal Flash
Legs: Brown/black round rubber (medium)
Adhesive: Head cement

Elk and Foam Hopper

Originator: Unknown
Tier: Russell Ellis

Hook: #8-10 Tiemco 2312
Thread: Olive 70-denier UTC
Body: Olive Wapsi Thin Fly Foam (1mm)
Overwing: Nature's Spirit Select bleached cow elk hair
Underwing: Mottled tan Web Wing and black Krystal Flash
Head: Nature's Spirit early season cow elk hair
Legs: Pumpkin barred Wapsi Sili Legs
Note: *Tie body foam on a needle then transfer to hook.*

Scott's Spun Hair Hopper

Originator: Scott Stisser
Tier: Scott Stisser

Hook: #6 Tiemco 5263
Thread: Black 140-denier UTC
Body/Head: Spun deer hair
Wing: Hen pheasant feather
Underwing: Orange bucktail
Legs: Pheasant tail fibers and orange poly yarn
Note: *Leg materials are tied in overhand knot then clip poly yarn at knot. Coat the hen pheasant feather with Dave's Flexament.*

Madam X Hopper (Red)

Originator: Doug Swisher
Tier: Gary Hoag

Hook: #12-14 Tiemco 5262
Thread: Red 140-denier UTC
Body: Tying thread
Head: Elk hair
Wing: Elk hair over copper Krystal Flash
Tail: Elk hair
Legs: Brown barred Hareline round rubber (medium)

Syntho Hopper

Originator: Ken Brink Jr.
Tier: Ken Brink Jr.

Hook: #8-12 Tiemco 2302
Thread: Tan 8/0 Uni-Thread
Body/Thorax: Hexagenia Spirit River Fine and Dry Dubbing
Wing: Mottled yellow Web Wing
Legs: Tan/brown Centipede Legs (medium)
Post: White Hareline McFlylon
Hackle: Grizzly variant Whiting Farms dry fly

Pygmy Hopper

Originator: Ken Hanley
Tier: Ken Hanley

Hook: #6-12 Daiichi 1270
Thread: Gray 8/0 Uni-Thread
Body: Tan, brown, and gray Hareline Antron Dubbing, twisted
Thorax: Light hare's ear dubbing
Head: Gray Fly Foam (3mm) over olive Antron Dubbing
Wing: Tan, brown, and gray Antron Yarn
Legs: Pumpkin with green and black flakes Sili Legs
Marker: Brown and gray Prismacolor

Mini Hopper (Orange)

Originator: Ben Smith
Tier: Ben Smith

Hook: #12 Mustad R50 or 94840
Thread: Black 6/0 Uni-Thread
Body: Black Hare-Tron Dubbing
Head: Orange craft foam (2mm)
Wing: Mule deer hair
Legs: Orange and black barred Wapsi Sili Legs
Adhesive: Super Glue

Mini Hopper (Chartreuse)

Originator: Ben Smith
Tier: Ben Smith

Hook: #12 Mustad R50 or 94840
Thread: Olive 6/0 Uni-Thread
Body: Green Hare-Tron Dubbing
Head: Chartreuse craft foam (2mm)
Wing: Mule deer hair
Legs: Green and black barred Wapsi Sili Legs
Adhesive: Super Glue

Klod Hopper

Originator: Paul Stimpson
Tier: Paul Stimpson

Hook: #8-12 Tiemco 5263
Thread: Brown 210-denier Danville's
Body/Head: Tan foam (3mm) and tan Antron Dubbing
Wing: Bull elk hair
Legs: Red/black Spirit River Grizzly Legs
Rib: Brown Whiting Farms rooster hackle
Note: *Body foam cut with RRC Chernobyl Foam Cutter (medium).*

Batta Batta Bug

Originator: Yukihiro Ishikawa
Tier: Yukihiro Ishikawa

Hook: #1 Daiichi 2461
Thread: Yellow 6/0 Uni-Thread
Belly: Yellow deer hair
Back/Wing: Olive and green mixed deer hair
Eyes: Red plastic
Legs: Hackle Feather dyed green and trimmed
Antennae: Stripped hackle stem
Adhesive: Super Glue Gel for eyes

Hot Tail NS Hopper

Originator: Takashi Nakajima
Tier: Takashi Nakajima

Hook: #4-8 Tiemco 2312
Thread: Black 6/0 Uni-Thread
Underbody: Closed-cell foam
Body: Elk hair
Head: Deer hair
Wing: Elk hair
Underwing: Pearl Krystal Flash
Indicator: Red deer hair
Legs: Tan/black Hareline Grizzly Legs (medium)
Rib: Tying thread
Tail: Orange deer hair
Note: *Body tied with C&F Design's extended body tool.*

Heli-Trrail

Originator: Takashi Nakajima
Tier: Takashi Nakajima

Hook: #4-8 Tiemco 2312
Thread: Black 6/0 Uni-Thread
Underbody: Hareline peacock Dub
Overbody: Northern lights Wapsi Loco Foam
Hackle: Coachman brown and grizzly Whiting Farms dry fly
Indicator: Fluorescent orange and pink Tiemco Aero Dry Wing
Legs: Tan/black Hareline Grizzly Legs (medium)
Tail: Mono loop (20-pound-test) under orange deer hair

Foam Hopper (Green)

Originator: Seiki Taguchi
Tier: Seiki Taguchi

Hook: #6 Daiichi 1270
Thread: Green 6/0 Uni-Thread
Body: Bright green foam cylinder
Head: Green deer hair
Wing: Green deer hair
Underwing: Green TMC Shimazaki Wing
Indicator: Orange foam (2mm)
Legs: Bright green round rubber (medium)
Rib: Tying thread

Twisted Hopper

Originator: Masahiro Kuroishi
Tier: Masahiro Kuroishi

Hook: #8-10 Tiemco 100 SPBL
Thread: White 6/0 Uni-Thread
Body: Fluorescent green Tiemco Aero Dry Wing twisted
Head: Fluorescent green deer hair
Wing: Fluorescent green goose quill
Overwing: Fluorescent green deer hair

Little Green Hopper

Originator: Noritaka Osada
Tier: Noritaka Osada

Hook: #18 Tiemco 200R
Thread: Light cahill 8/0 Uni-Thread
Body: Chartreuse deer hair
Wing: Chartreuse deer hair
Legs: Caddis green goose biots
Rib: Tying thread
Antennae: Hackle stem dyed chartreuse

Taylor's Fat Albert (Yellow)

Originator: Brent Taylor
Tier: Montana Fly Company

Hook: #8 MFC 7037
Thread: Dark brown 6/0 MFC
Overbody: Brown foam (2mm)
Underbody: Yellow foam (2mm)
Wing: White Gator Hair
Underwing: Pearl High Voltage Flash
Indicator: Yellow foam (2mm)
Legs: Speckled tan Centipede Legs

Note: *This basic pattern, as with most hopper patterns, is an excellent cricket imitation in black.*

Taylor's Fat Albert (High Viz Tan)

Originator: Brent Taylor
Tier: Montana Fly Company

Hook: #8 MFC 7037
Thread: Dark brown 6/0 MFC
Overbody: Brown foam (2mm)
Underbody: Tan foam (2mm)
Wing: White Gator Hair
Underwing: Pearl High Voltage Flash
Indicator: Chartreuse Widow's Web
Legs: Speckled tan Centipede Legs

Reiner's Pink Pookie

Originator: Dean Reiner
Tier: Montana Fly Company

Hook: #8 MFC 7026
Thread: Red 6/0 MFC
Body: Pink foam (2mm)
Wing: Bull elk hair
Overwing: Tan foam (2mm)
Indicator: Orange foam (2mm)
Legs: Speckled yellow Centipede Legs

Shanafelt's Mongo Hopper (Peach)

Originator: Pete Shanafelt
Tier: Montana Fly Company

Hook: #10 MFC 7026
Thread: Cream 6/0 MFC
Body: Flesh foam (2mm)
Overbody: Tan foam (2mm)
Indicator: Orange and yellow foam (2mm)
Front Legs: Amber MFC Sexi-Floss
Back Legs: Tan foam (1mm) and copper brown MFC Speckled Sexi-Floss
Marker: Brown magic marker

Gould's Half-Down Hopper

Originator: John Gould
Tier: Montana Fly Company

Hook: #10 MFC 7073 (bent shank)
Thread: Dark brown 6/0 MFC
Body: Tan marabou blood quill
Thorax: Camel MFC Frog Hair
Wing: Cow elk hair
Indicator: White Widow's Web
Legs: Brown Centipede Legs
Hackle: Grizzly dyed brown
Rib: Copper wire (#1)

Simm's Storm Trooper Hopper

Originator: Matt Simms
Tier: Montana Fly Company

Hook: #10 MFC 7027
Thread: Black 6/0 MFC
Body: Yellow and brown foam (2mm)
Head: PMD Frog Hair and yellow foam (2mm)
Overwing: Cow elk hair
Underwing: Red MFC Crystal Flash
Front Legs: Speckled brown Centipede Legs
Back Legs: Brown and speckled gray Centipede Legs
Rib: Tying thread

Kickerleg Parahopper

Originator: Unknown
Tier: Montana Fly Company

Hook: #8 MFC 7026
Thread: Sand 6/0 MFC
Body: Cream elk rump dubbing
Wing: Wild turkey tail
Indicator: White calf tail
Legs: Brown orange polypropylene baling twine
Hackle: Grizzly neck
Rib: Dark brown 6/0 MFC thread

Trina's Noble Chernobyl

Originator: Adam Trina
Tier: Montana Fly Company

Hook: #8 MFC 7026
Thread: Black 6/0 MFC
Underbody: Tan foam (2mm)
Overbody: Black foam (2mm)
Wing: Cow elk flank hair
Indicator: Yellow foam (2mm)
Post: White Widow's Web
Legs: White Centipede Legs
Hackle: Grizzly neck

Kyle's King Kong Hopper

Originator: Kyle Giampaoli
Tier: Montana Fly Company

Hook: #8 MFC 2027
Thread: Brown 6/0 MFC
Underbody: Tan foam (2mm)
Body: Yellow foam (2mm)
Overbody: Brown foam (2mm)
Wings: Cow elk flank hair
Indicator: White foam (2mm)
Legs: Speckled tan Centipede Legs
Tail: Speckled red MFC Centipede Legs

True Parachute Hopper

Originator: Unknown
Tier: Montana Fly Company

Hook: #6 MFC 7077
Thread: Sand 6/0 MFC
Body: Tan True Hopper Body
Wing: Tan True Hopper Wing (medium)
Indicator: White Widow's Web
Legs: Tan True Hopper Legs
Hackle: Brown neck

True Hopper (Green)

Originator: Unknown
Tier: Montana Fly Company

Hook: #8 MFC 7077
Body: Green True Hopper Body
Legs: Green True Hopper Legs

Oswald's Head Turning Hopper (Green)

Originator: Duncan Oswald
Tier: Montana Fly Company

Hook: #8 MFC 7026
Thread: White 6/0 MFC
Body: Chartreuse foam (2mm)
Breast Plate: Chartreuse foam (1mm)
Wing: Brown foam (2mm)
Eyes: Brown or black Hoppize (medium) or black marker
Back Legs: Chartreuse foam (2mm)
Legs: Fluorescent lime Centipede Legs
Rib: Tying thread
Marker: Black Magic Marker
Note: *Body foam is folded over hook.*

Trina's Carnage Hopper (Yellow)

Originator: Adam Trina
Tier: Montana Fly Company

Hook: #10 MFC 7026
Thread: Sand 6/0 MFC
Body: Tan foam (1mm)
Thorax: Golden tan Antron dubbing
Head: Tan foam (5mm)
Wing: Mottled Web MFC Flex Wing
Indicator: White Widow's Web
Eyes: Black MFC Hoppize (medium)
Back Legs: Natural latex and red/black Centipede Legs
Legs: Natural latex Centipede Legs
Marker: Brown and black Magic Marker

JAW

Originator: Ken Iwamasa
Tier: Ken Iwamasa

Hook: #10-12 Tiemco 5210
Thread: Black 6/0 Uni-Thread
Body: Yellow and black Spirit River foam (2mm)
Wing: Calf tail
Hackle: Brown Whiting Farms
Rib: Grizzly dyed yellow Whiting Farms
Tail: Red coastal deer hair

Osteen's Hopper (Gray)

Originator: Drayton Osteen
Tier: Montana Fly Company

Hook: #8 MFC 7231
Thread: Black 6/0 MFC
Body: Gray foam (5mm)
Thorax: Gray drake and light golden stone MFC Wabbit Dubbing
Wing: Mottled brown MFC Wing Material
Overwing: Cow elk flank hair
Underwing: Red Crystal Flash and root beer Flashabou
Indicator: White Widow's Web
Eyes: Red MFC Hoppize (medium)
Back Legs: Red MFC Hopper Legs (large)
Legs: Speckled gray Centipede Legs
Marker: Black Magic Marker
Note: *Body and head cut with RRC Tapered Chernobyl cutter*

Shanafelt's Mongo Hopper (Tan)

Originator: Pete Shanafelt
Tier: Montana Fly Company

Hook: #10 MFC 7026
Thread: Cream 6/0 MFC
Underbody: Tan foam (2mm)
Overbody: Gold foam (2mm)
Indicator: Yellow and orange foam (2mm)
Front Legs: Amber MFC Sexi-Floss
Back Legs: Tan foam (2mm) and copper/brown MFC Sexi-Floss
Legs: Tan speckled MFC Sexi-Floss
Rib: Tying thread
Marker: Brown Magic Marker

PMH Hopper

Originator: Unknown
Tier: Montana Fly Company

Hook: #8 MFC 7022
Thread: Black 6/0 MFC
Body: Golden stone Gator Hair
Thorax: Peacock herl
Wing: Cow elk flank hair
Indicator: White Widow's Web
Back Legs: Tan MFC Hopper Legs (Large)
Legs: White Centipede Legs
Hackle: Grizzly
Marker: Brown Magic Marker

Carleton's Canyon Water Hopper (Tan)

Originator: Scott Carleton
Tier: Montana Fly Company

Hook: #8 MFC 7000
Thread: Sand 6/0 MFC
Body: Tan foam (3mm)
Head: Tan foam (3mm)
Wing: White Widow's Web
Underwing: Pearl MFC High Voltage
Legs: Speckled tan Centipede Legs
Note: *Body cut with Tapered Chernobyl cutter.*

Gould's Western Lady Hopper

Originator: John Gould
Tier: Montana Fly Company

Hook: #10 MFC 7026
Thread: Red 6/0 MFC
Underbody: Fuchsia foam (2mm)
Body: Brown foam (3mm)
Wing: Bull elk flank hair
Indicator: White foam (2mm)
Legs: Speckled tan Centipede Legs
Rib: Brown saddle hackle
Marker: Yellow permanent marker on indicator

Trixie the Hooker Hopper

Originator: Robyn Gianni
Tier: Montana Fly Company

Hook: #8 MFC 7026
Thread: Fluorescent pink 6/0 MFC
Underbody: Pink foam (2mm)
Body: White foam (2mm)
Wing: Cow elk flank hair
Underwing: Pearl MFC Crystal Flash
Indicator: Pink foam (2mm)
Legs: Fleck smoke blue/black Sili Legs

Gould's Western Lady Hopper (Tan)

Originator: John Gould
Tier: Montana Fly Company

Hook: #8 MFC 7026
Thread: Sand 6/0 MFC
Underbody: Tan foam (2mm)
Body: Brown foam (4mm)
Wing: Bull elk flank hair
Indicator: Yellow foam (2mm)
Legs: Speckled tan Centipede Legs
Rib: Brown neck hackle

MFC Chernobyl Hopper

Originator: MFC
Tier: Montana Fly Company

Hook: #8 MFC 7026
Thread: Brown 6/0 MFC
Underbody: Medium brown Wings N' Flash
Body: Black and tan foam (2mm)
Legs: White Centipede Legs (#2)
Indicator: Yellow foam (2mm)
Hackle: Brown

Kingfisher Foam Grasshopper (Tan)

Originator: Kingfisher Fly Shop
Tier: Montana Fly Company

Hook: #8 MFC 7026
Thread: Tan 6/0 MFC
Body: Tan foam (2mm)
Wing: Mottled brown MFC Wing Material
Underwing: Tan Widow's Web
Post: White Widow's Web
Legs: Red/black barred Sili Legs
Hackle: Grizzly

Yeti Hopper (Purple)

Originator: MFC
Tier: Montana Fly Company

Hook: #6 MFC 7026
Thread: Purple 6/0 MFC
Body: Pre-cut tan foam over purple Furry Foam
Underwing: Cream Widow's Web
Indicator: Purple foam (2mm)
Eyes: Black MFC Hoppize (medium)
Legs: Speckled brown/tan Centipede Legs (large)

Sideshow BOB (Yellow)

Originator: Andrew Grillos
Tier: Idylwilde Flies

Hook: #4-10 Tiemco 5263
Thread: Black UTC GSP 100
Body: Yellow under tan foam (2mm)
Underbody: Tying thread
Wing: Elk hair
Underwing: Pearl Krystal Flash
Indicator: Neon orange Corkie and orange foam (2mm)
Legs: Tan/brown barred round rubber (medium)
Hackle: Medium brown Whiting Farms
Rib: Tying thread
Note: *Attach Corkie with 20-pound-test backing.*

Pool Toy (Olive)

Originator: Andrew Grillos
Tier: Idylwilde Flies

Hook: #4-10 Daiichi 1720
Thread: Olive UTC GSP 100
Underbody: Light olive foam (2mm) over olive Ice Dub
Body: Olive foam (2mm)
Top Foam: Light olive foam (2mm)
Underwing: Pearl Midge Krystal Flash
Wing: Olive deer hair
Overwing: Olive poly yarn
Indicator: Neon pink poly yarn
Legs: Tan and black barred round rubber

Bloom's Parachute Hopper (Tan)

Originator: Dave Bloom
Tier: Dave Bloom

Hook: #8-12 Tiemco 5262
Thread: Tan 6/0 Uni-Thread
Body: Natural hare's ear Hare's Ear Plus Dubbing
Overbody: Tan foam (3mm)
Overwing: Brown dyed and lacquered ringneck pheasant saddle
Underwing: Brown Trout Hunter CDC
Indicator: Pink McFlylon
Legs: Brown round rubber (medium)
Hackle: Dark ginger and grizzly Whiting Farms neck
Rib: Brown waxed heavy sewing thread
Adhesive: Trout Hunter tying cement

Hopper Buck

Originator: George Grant
Tier: Sue Armstrong

Hook: #6 Tiemco 2302
Thread: Brown 70-denier UTC
Body: Deer hair
Wing: Pheasant rump feathers coated with acrylic lacquer
Legs: Two knotted elk hairs
Note: *George Grant method of woven hair.*

Kar-hopper

Originator: Justin Karnopp
Tier: Justin Karnopp

Hook: #6 Tiemco 5263
Thread: Olive 6/0 Uni-Thread
Underbody: Olive Acrylic Yarn (mini)
Thorax: Tan Hareline Dubbing
Head: Black foam (2mm) under yellow poly yarn
Wing: Deer hair and olive Krystal Flash
Legs: Tan and olive Flex Floss
Back: Tan foam (2mm)

Hoppin John

Originator: Richard Pilatzke
Tier: Richard Pilatzke

Hook: #10 Dai-Riki 730
Thread: Chartreuse 6/0 Uni-Thread
Underbody: Tying thread
Body: Tan over yellow craft foam (2mm)
Indicator: Orange craft foam (2mm)
Front Legs: Tan and black barred round rubber (medium)
Rear Legs: Tan craft foam (2mm)
Adhesive: Crazy Glue

Foamex Hopper

Originator: Richard Pilatzke
Tier: Richard Pilatzke

Hook: #8 Dai-Riki 070
Thread: Yellow and chartreuse 6/0 Uni-Thread
Underbody: Yellow tying thread
Body: Yellow craft foam (2mm)
Thorax: Chartreuse tying thread
Head/Wings: Whitetail deer hair
Legs: Tan and black barred MFC
Tail: Orange deer hair

Mormon John

Originator: Richard Pilatzke
Tier: Richard Pilatzke

Hook: #8 Dai-Riki 700
Thread: Black 6/0 Uni-Thread
Body: Black over brown craft foam (2mm)
Indicator: Yellow craft foam (2mm)
Front Legs: Black round rubber (medium)
Rear Legs: Black foam (2mm)
Adhesive: Krazy Glue
Note: *Body and legs cut with RRC cutters.*

Hi Vis Hopper X

Originator: Dron Lee
Tier: Dron Lee

Hook: #8 Gamakatsu S114L
Thread: Brown 140-denier UTC
Body: Tan foam (3mm)
Wing: Brown Vinyl Raffia
Underwing: Brown hen saddle and pearl Krystal Flash
Indicator: Yellow foam (1mm)
Eyes: Black Loon Hard Head
Legs: Brown barred Sili Legs
Back Legs: Pheasant tail knotted
Rib: Tying thread
Antennae: Pheasant tail fibers
Adhesive: Flexament
Marker: Brown and orange Promarkers

Jeff's Hopper

Originator: Jeff Bever
Tier: Jeff Bever

Hook: #10-12 Tiemco 2457
Thread: Cream 70-denier UTC
Body: Brown foam (3mm)
Thorax: Body foam covered with Medallion Sheeting
Wing: Artificial Skeleton Leaf colored with marker and covered with clear tape
Legs: Tan Japanese Nymph Legs
Rib: Tying thread
Antennae: Porcupine guard hairs

Valla Hopper

Originator: Mike Valla
Tier: Mike Valla

Hook: #8-12 Tiemco 5212
Thread: Red 6/0 Uni-Thread
Body: Pale yellow dyed seal blended with cream fox fur
Head: Olive deer hair
Wing: Turkey feather dyed yellow
Overwing: Olive deer hair
Throat: Red deer hair flared behind head
Hackle: Grizzly dyed yellow
Tail: Yellow over red deer hair

Western Hopper

Originator: Eric A. Pettine
Tier: Eric A. Pettine

Hook: #8 Dai-Riki 700
Thread: Yellow 140-denier UTC
Body: Yellow closed-cell foam (3mm)
Head: Yellow-green elk hair
Overwing: Rocky Mountain Dubbing Perfect Cut Wing
Underwing: Golden pheasant
Legs: Olive hackle
Antennae: Hackle stems
Marker: Olive marker over body

Western Hopper Wet

Originator: Eric A. Pettine
Tier: Eric A. Pettine

Hook: #8 Dai-Riki 700
Thread: Tan 140-denier UTC
Body: Yellow closed-cell foam (3mm)
Head: Yellow-green elk hair over gold cyclops brass bead (3/16")
Overwing: Rocky Mountain Dubbing Perfect Cut Wing
Underwing: Golden pheasant
Legs: Formed Barred Scarlet and trimmed hen hackle
Marker: Olive

Furimsky's Can-Can Hopper (Light Tan)

Originator: Ben Furimsky
Tier: Ben Furimsky

Hook: #2-6 Tiemco 2312
Thread: Tan 6/0 Uni-Thread
Body: Light tan foam (2mm)
Wing: Mottled tan MFC Flex Wing
Overwing: Elk hair
Underwing: Pearl Krystal Flash
Eyes: Black MFC round foam cylinder
Back Legs: Light tan foam (2mm) and red and black round rubber
Legs: Tan and brown MFC Centipede Legs
Rib: Tying thread
Antennae: Tan MFC Tentacles
Marker: Brown Sharpie

Furimsky's Can-Can Hopper (Green)

Originator: Ben Furimsky
Tier: Ben Furimsky

Hook: #2-6 Tiemco 2312
Thread: Tan 6/0 Uni-Thread
Body: Chartreuse foam (2mm)
Wing: Plain web MFC Flex Wing
Overwing: Chartreuse dyed deer hair
Underwing: Pearl Krystal Flash
Eyes: Black MFC round foam cylinder
Back Legs: Chartreuse foam (2mm) and yellow and olive Centipede Legs
Legs: Yellow and olive MFC Centipede Legs
Rib: Tying thread
Antennae: Olive MFC Tentacles
Marker: Black Sharpie

Bronco Hopper

Originator: Juan Ramirez
Tier: Marty Staab

Hook: #10 Dai-Riki 285
Thread: Orange 140-denier UTC
Body: Light blue craft foam (2mm) cut with RRC Chernobyl Ant cutter (medium)
Wing: Fluorescent orange Hareline deer hair
Legs: Hot orange Tarantu-Leggs (medium)
Note: *Brush on Zap-A-Gap*

Tak's Bullet Head Extended Body Hopper

Originator: Rick Takahashi
Tier: Rick Takahashi

Hook: #8-10 Tiemco 2302
Thread: Hopper yellow 140-denier UTC
Body: Olive deer hair
Collar: Olive deer hair
Wing: Mottled tan MFC Wing
Legs: Umpqua Hopper Legs
Rib: Tying thread

Tak's Foam Hopper

Originator: Rick Takahashi
Tier: Rick Takahashi

Hook: #8-10 Tiemco 2302
Thread: Hopper yellow 140-denier UTC
Body: Tan RRC foam (2mm)
Collar/Head: Olive deer hair
Wing: Brown RRC River Wing
Legs: Umpqua Hopper Legs colored with orange marker
Rib: Tying thread
Marker: Orange permanent

Tomsu's Supreme Hopper (Tan)

Originator: Tony Tomsu
Tier: Tony Tomsu

Hook: #4-12 Tiemco 2302
Thread: Tan 8/0 Danville's
Body: Tan RRC Foam (2mm)
Pronotum: Tan foam (.5mm)
Wing: RRC River Foam
Eyes: Sewing pin heads blackened, cut, glued and inserted in foam
Back Legs: Tan foam (1mm)
Legs: Brown and black speckled rubber legs (medium or small)
Antennae: Brown and black speckled rubber legs (micro)
Marker: Red, brown, and black permanent
Note: *Body, rear legs, wing and pronotum cut using RRC Foam cutters.*

Tomsu's Supreme Hopper (Yellow)

Originator: Tony Tomsu
Tier: Tony Tomsu

Hook: #4-12 Tiemco 2302
Thread: Yellow 8/0 Danville's
Body: Yellow RRC River Foam (2mm)
Pronotum: Yellow foam (.5mm)
Wing: RRC River Wing
Eyes: Sewing pins blackened
Back Legs: Tan foam (1mm)
Legs: Yellow rubber legs (medium or small)
Antennae: Yellow and black speckled rubber legs (micro)
Marker: Black and yellow permanent
Note: *Body, rear legs, wing, and pronotum cut using RRC Foam cutters.*

Morrish Hopper (Olive)

Originator: Ken Morrish
Tier: Ken Morrish

Hook: #6-14 Tiemco 5262
Thread: Brown 6/0 Uni-Thread
Body: Chartreuse and olive foam (2mm)
Wing Indicator: Orange foam (2mm)
Eyes: Black marker
Legs: Olive/black Hareline Grizzly Legs (medium)
Adhesive: 3M spray adhesive to glue layers of foam; Zap-A-Gap glue body to hook
Marker: Black permanent

M.S.U. Hop Stopper

Originator: Gary Barnes
Tier: Gary Barnes

Hook: #8-14 Daiichi 1260
Thread: Olive 70-denier UTC
Body: Golden yellow Antron
Rib: Ginger grizzly Whiting Farms
Wing: Gray EP Fiber
Head: Golden brown deer hair
Legs: Centipede Legs (medium) and Hopper Leg Tubing

Jeff's Green Hopper

Originator: Jeff Goff
Tier: Jeff Goff

Hook: #8-14 Tiemco 100
Thread: Olive 8/0 Uni-Thread
Underbody: Chartreuse deer hair
Wing: Green turkey wing sections
Rear Kickers: Dark green turkey wing section knotted with clipped dyed blue-green hackle stem
Sternum: Dark green turkey wing section
Front Legs: Knotted turkey wing fibers
Pronotum: Green turkey wing sections
Head: Black over green deer hair, clipped

Jeff's Blue Legged Hopper

Originator: Jeff Goff
Tier: Jeff Goff

Hook: #8-14 Tiemco 100
Thread: Rusty dun 8/0 Uni-Thread
Underbody: Deer hair
Body: Olive Antron Dubbing
Wing: Turkey wing sections
Rear Kickers: Turkey wing section knotted with clipped light blue hackle stem
Sternum: Deer hair stacked and clipped
Front Legs: Natural turkey wing fibers
Pronotum: Turkey wing sections
Head: Black over green deer hair, clipped

Jeff's Red Legged Yellow Belly Hopper

Originator: Jeff Goff
Tier: Jeff Goff

Hook: #8-14 Tiemco 100
Thread: Rusty dun 8/0 Uni-Thread
Underbody: Yellow deer hair
Wing: Turkey wing sections
Rear Kickers: Turkey wing section knotted with a clipped red hackle stem
Sternum: Deer hair stacked and clipped
Front Legs: Natural turkey wing fibers
Pronotum: Turkey wing sections
Head: Black over yellow deer hair, clipped

Tak's Monster Hopper

Originator: Rick Takahashi
Tier: Rick Takahashi

Hook: #6-10 Tiemco 2302
Thread: Yellow 70-denier UTC
Underbody: Tan foam (2mm)
Underwing: Pellon 808 colored with light olive permanent marker
Wing: Olive deer hair over pearl Krystal Flash
Thorax: Tan Super Fine Dubbing
Rear Kickers: Metz Hopper Legs
Front Legs: Yellow barred Wapsi Sili Legs
Head: Tan foam (2mm)

Tak's Light Hopper

Originator: Rick Takahashi
Tier: Rick Takahashi

Hook: #6-10 Tiemco 2302
Thread: Yellow 70-denier UTC
Underbody: Tan foam (2mm)
Underwing: Pellon 808 colored with sand permanent marker
Wing: White Spirit River Near Hair
Legs: Speckled yellow/black MFC Centipede Legs
Head: Tan foam (2mm)
Indicator: Red foam (2mm)
Marker: Red permanent

Tak's Silver Lining Hopper

Originator: Rick Takahashi
Tier: Rick Takahashi

Hook: #10-12 Tiemco 2302
Thread: Olive 70-denier UTC
Body: Tan foam (2mm)
Underwing: Rootbeer Krystal Flash
Wing: Pellon 808 colored with olive Pantone markers
Overwing: Olive deer hair
Head: Tan foam (2mm) colored with brown permanent marker
Front Legs: Yellow and black barred Hareline Crazy Legs
Rear Legs: Metz Hopper Legs colored with red permanent marker

Tak's Sunken Hopper

Originator: Rick Takahashi
Tier: Rick Takahashi

Hook: #6-10 Dai-Riki 155
Thread: Olive brown 70-denier UTC
Bead: Black metal
Body: Tan foam (2mm)
Rib: Tying thread
Overwing: Olive Whiting Farms Chickabou
Wing: Mottled brown MFC Wing Material
Collar: Olive Whiting Farms Chickabou
Legs: Metz Hopper Legs

Tak's Drowned Hopper

Originator: Rick Takahashi
Tier: Rick Takahashi

Hook: #6-10 Dai-Riki 155
Thread: Olive brown 70-denier UTC
Bead: Black metal
Tail: Red Whiting Farms saddle hackle fibers
Body: Natural latex colored with sand Chartpak marker
Overwing: Olive Whiting Farms Chickabou and olive brown Ice Dub
Wing: Mottled olive MFC Wing Material
Collar: Olive Whiting Farms Chickabou CDC; olive brown Ice Dub
Legs: Metz Hopper Legs
Head: Olive Rainy's Evazote foam (1mm)

Hub's Peñasco Horse Hopper

Originator: Jerry Hubka
Tier: Jerry Hubka

Hook: #4-6 Daiichi 2220
Thread: Black 140-denier UTC
Underbody: Tying thread
Body/Head: Goldenrod, bright red, and black Foamies Craft Foam (2mm)
Pro Thorax: Opaque yellow Wapsi Foam (.5mm) and black Spirit River Fly Foam (.5mm)
Wing: Black Spirit River Fly Foam (.5mm) glued over mottled medium dun D's Web Wing
Underwing: UV pearl and red Krystal Flash
Eyes: Brown or red MFC Hoppize (medium)
Legs: Yellow/black/red speckled Centipede Legs (medium)
Rib: Tying thread
Antennae: Speckled yellow barred round rubber legs (medium)
Adhesive: Zap-A-Gap and 3M Super 77 Spray Adhesive
Note: *Large, medium, and small RRC Tapered Chernobyl Cutters.*

Hubooka Hopper

Originator: Jerry Hubka
Tier: Jerry Hubka

Hook: #8 Tiemco 5263
Thread: Yellow 140-denier UTC
Body: Goldenrod and peach craft foam (2mm)
Wing: Yellow Mottled Web MFC Etha Wing
Underwing: Brown Krystal Flash
Eyes: Black MFC Hoppize (medium)
Legs: Speckled yellow Centipede Legs (medium)
Adhesive: Zap-A-Gap
Note: *Medium and large RRC Tapered Chernobyl Cutters.*

Hub's North Platte Spey Hopper

Originator: Jerry Hubka
Tier: Jerry Hubka

Hook: #12 Tiemco 8089
Thread: Black 140-denier UTC
Underbody: Tying thread
Body: Black Foamies Glitter Sheet Craft Foam (2mm), Peach Craft Foam (2mm), and yellow mottled Web MFC Etha Wing
Wing: Black Spirit River Super Hair
Indicator: Red craft foam (1.5mm) cut with RRC Tapered Chernobyl Cutter (small)
Legs: Black/red tipped Hareline Crazy Legs
Adhesive: Zap-A-Gap
Note: *Body shapes cut with RRC Tapered Chernobyl Cutter (large).*

Hub's Spey Stinger Hopper

Originator: Jerry Hubka
Tier: Jerry Hubka

Hook Shank: #4 Tiemco 8089, cut off point and barb
Stinger Loop: Red Spectra Power Pro (20-pound-test)
Stinger Hook: #8 red Owner SSW
Mono Loop: Clear 30-pound-test mono
Thread: Yellow 140-denier UTC
Overbody: Peach Spirit River Fly Foam (2mm)
Underbody: Root beer Hareline Cactus Chenille (medium) over yellow Fly Foam
Wing: Black Spirit River Fly Foam (.5mm)
Underwing: Black Krystal Flash
Legs: Yellow/black/red speckled Centipede Legs
Adhesive: Zap-A-Gap
Note: *Body foam cut with RRC Tapered Chernobyl Cutter (large).*

Decker's Aussie Hopper

Originator: Gene Decker
Tier: Gene Decker

Hook: #8 Dai-Riki 280
Thread: Tan 6/0 Uni-Thread
Tail: Dyed rusty brown deer hair
Body: Yellow, brown, yellow poly yarn
Wing: Dyed rusty brown deer hair mixed with fox squirrel tail
Hackle: Brown Whiting Farms saddle

High Float Hop

Originator: Eric Ishiwata
Tier: Eric Ishiwata

Hook: #8-12 Gamakatsu P10-2L1h
Thread: Primrose 6/0 Danville's
Overbody: Tan foam (2mm)
Body: Stone Nymph Gills SLF Whitlock Dubbing
Rib: Copper Ultra Wire (small)
Body Hackle: Grizzly Whiting Farms dry fly
Underwing: Chartreuse lady amherst tippet
Wing: Deer body hair
Spotter: White Hareline Para Post Wing
Legs: Metz Knotted Legs
Thorax: Stone Nymph Gills SLF Whitlock Dubbing
Hackle: Tan or yellow grizzly Whiting Farms dry fly
Treatment: Watershed

Extendo Hopper

Originator: Eric Ishiwata
Tier: Eric Ishiwata

Hook: #8-14 Gamakatsu c12U Caddis
Thread: Primrose 6/0 Danville's
Body: Deer hair coated in varnish
Rib: Chartreuse Danville's 210-denier Flat Waxed Nylon
Underwing: Chartreuse lady amherst tippet
Wing: Deer body hair and chartreuse deer belly hair
Rear Legs: Metz Knotted Legs
Thorax: Stone Nymph Gills SLF Whitlock Dubbing
Head: Deer body hair and chartreuse deer belly hair
Treatment: Watershed

Soggy Hop

Originator: Eric Ishiwata
Tier: Eric Ishiwata

Hook: #8-12 Gamakatsu P10-2LH
Thread: Primrose 6/0 Danville's
Tag: Mirage Tinsel
Weight: Round lead free wire (.020")
Tail: Pheasant tail
Body: Golden Stone Nymph SLF Dubbing
Rib: Copper Ultra Wire (small)
Underwing: Chartreuse lady amherst tippet
Wing: Ringneck pheasant church window feather
Rear Legs: Orange pheasant tail knotted legs
Hackle: Natural hen and straw Brahma Hen Whiting Farms
Head: Peacock herl bleached

Drunken Hopper

Originator: Eric Ishiwata
Tier: Eric Ishiwata

Hook: #8-12 Gamakatsu P10-2LH
Thread: Primrose 6/0 Danville's
Tag: Mirage Tinsel
Weight: Mayfly brown Nymph-Head Heavy Metal (4mm)
Tail: Pheasant tail
Body: Golden Stone Nymph SLF Dubbing
Rib: Copper Ultra Wire (small)
Underwing: Chartreuse lady amherst tippet
Wing: Ringneck pheasant church window feather
Rear Legs: Orange pheasant tail knotted legs
Hackle: Natural hen and straw Brahma Hen Whiting Farms
Thorax: Golden Stone Nymph SLF Dubbing

Charlie Boy Hopper (Yellow)

Originator: Charlie Craven
Tier: Charlie Craven

Hook: #8-10 Tiemco 100 SPBL
Thread: Yellow 3/0 Danville Monocord
Binder Strip: 2mm x 2mm piece of foam
Body: Yellow Thin Fly Foam (2mm)
Wing: Deer hair
Eyes: Black permanent marker
Legs: Yellow round rubber (medium) with red band on the end

Baby Boy Hopper (Black)

Originator: Charlie Craven
Tier: Charlie Craven

Hook: #8-10 Tiemco 2499 SPBL
Thread: Black 3/0 Danville Monocord
Binder Strip: 2mm x 2mm piece of foam
Body: Black Thin Fly Foam (2mm)
Wing: Deer hair
Legs: Black round rubber (small)

Baby Boy Hopper (Chartreuse)

Originator: Charlie Craven
Tier: Charlie Craven

Hook: #8-10 Tiemco 2499 SPBL
Thread: Olive 3/0 Danville Monocord
Binder Strip: 2mm x 2mm piece of foam
Body: Chartreuse Thin Fly Foam (2mm)
Wing: Deer hair
Legs: Chartreuse round rubber (small)

Tak's Ninja Hopper (Tan)

Originator: Rick Takahashi
Tier: Rick Takahashi

Hook: #8 Dai-Riki 280
Thread: Tobacco brown 3/0 Danville's Monocord
Body: Tan foam (2mm)
Underwing: Artificial flower petal dyed yellow
Wing: Deer hair
Legs: Brown Wapsi round rubber legs (medium)

Tak's Ninja Hopper (Yellow)

Originator: Rick Takahashi
Tier: Rick Takahashi

Hook: #8 Dai-Riki 280
Thread: Yellow 3/0 Danville's Monocord
Body: Yellow foam (2mm)
Underwing: Mottled brown RRC River Wing
Wing: Light olive deer hair
Legs: Black/yellow speckled Centipede Legs

Tak's Ninja Hopper (Olive)

Originator: Rick Takahashi
Tier: Rick Takahashi

Hook: #8 Dai-Riki 280
Thread: Olive 3/0 Danville's Monocord
Body: Olive foam (2mm)
Underwing: Mottled brown RRC River Wing
Wing: Light olive deer hair
Legs: Natural Centipede Legs

Suzy's Mini Skirt Hopper (Yellow)

Originator: Rick Takahashi
Tier: Rick Takahashi

Hook: #8 MFC 7022
Thread: Yellow 3/0 Danville's Monocord
Underbody: Golden yellow (#9) Flyrite dubbing
Body: Yellow foam (2mm)
Wing: Yellow artificial flower petal
Hackle: Olive Whiting Farms saddle
Wing: Light olive deer hair
Legs: Speckled yellow and black Centipede Legs

Suzy's Mini Skirt Hopper (Tan)

Originator: Rick Takahashi
Tier: Rick Takahashi

Hook: #8 MFC 7022
Thread: Wood duck 140-denier UTC
Underbody: Golden yellow (#9) Flyrite dubbing
Body: Tan foam (2mm)
Wing: Yellow artificial flower petal
Hackle: Furnace Whiting Farms saddle
Wing: Deer hair
Legs: Tan speckled MFC round rubber (medium)

CDC DH Hopper (Brown/Tan)

Originator: Carl Pennington
Tier: Carl Pennington

Hook: #10 MFC 7000
Thread: Tan 140-denier UTC
Underbody: Tan foam (2mm) with tan MFC Lucent Micro Chenille
Body: Tan (2mm) and orange foam (1mm)
Rib: Brown hackle
Underwing: Rainbow Krystal flash
Wing: Elk hair
Thorax: UV tan Ice Dub between brown and tan foam (2mm)
Legs: Speckled brown MFC round rubber (medium)

Stoned Hippie Hopper (Yellow)

Originator: John Larson
Tier: John Larson

Hook: #8 Daiichi 1720
Thread: Orange 8/0 Uni-Thread
Underbody: Orange UV Ice Dub
Body/Head: Yellow closed-cell foam (2mm)
Rib: Brown grizzly hackle
Wing: Yellow deer hair
Legs: Orange/black barred Hareline Crazy Legs

Deer Creek Plopper Hopper (Tan)

Originator: John Larson
Tier: John Larson

Hook: #8 Daiichi 1720
Thread: Tan 6/0 Uni-Thread
Tail: Orange amherst pheasant tippets
Body/Head: Bleached tan deer hair
Wing: Cream Swiss Straw
Collar: Bleached deer hair
Legs: Tan Wapsi TNT Hopper Legs

Haley Hopper

Originator: Rick Takahashi
Tier: Rick Takahashi

Hook: #8 Tiemco 2302
Thread: Olive brown 70-denier UTC
Tail: Red hackle fiber
Underbody: Cream 70-denier UTC
Rib: Whiting Farms Midge saddle hackle
Wing: Yellow RRC River Wing
Head/Collar: Olive deer hair
Rear Legs: Olive MFC AK Hopper Legs
Legs: Olive MFC Sexi Floss

BC Hopper

Originator: John Barr/Charlie Craven
Tier: John Barr/Charlie Craven

Hook: #4-10 Tiemco 5262
Thread: Tan 3/0 Danville's Monocord
Body: Tan foam (3mm)
Binder Strip: Scrap of foam (3mm)
Adhesive: Zap-A-Gap
Legs: Natural Rainy's round rubber
Underwing: Mottled tan Web Wing
Flash: Root beer Krystal Flash
Overwing: Elk hair
Head: Deer hair
Indicator: Chartreuse McFlylon
Marker: Red permanent

Deer Creek Plopper Hopper

Originator: John Larson
Tier: John Larson

Hook: #8 Daiichi 1720
Thread: Tan 6/0 Uni-Thread
Tail: Golden pheasant tippets
Body: Olive deer hair
Thorax: Olive deer hair
Wings: Olive Swiss Straw
Legs: Yellow Wapsi TNT Hopper Legs
Head: Olive deer hair

Tak's Bopper Hopper (Tan)

Originator: Rick Takahashi
Tier: Rick Takahashi

Hook: #10-16 Dai-Riki 280
Thread: Wood duck 70-denier UTC
Underbody: Tying thread
Body Hackle: Brown Whiting Farms Midge saddle
Tail/Body/Head: Tan foam (2mm)
Underwing: White Widow's Web
Wing: Elk hair
Hackle: Olive grizzly saddle
Legs: Brown/black MFC Sexi Floss

Tak's Bopper Hopper (Chartreuse)

Originator: Rick Takahashi
Tier: Rick Takahashi

Hook: #10-16 Dai-Riki 280
Thread: Chartreuse 140-denier Danville's
Underbody: Tying thread
Body Hackle: Yellow grizzly Whiting Farms Midge saddle
Tail/Body/Head: Chartreuse foam (2mm)
Underwing: White Widow's Web
Wing: Elk hair
Hackle: Yellow grizzly saddle
Legs: Chartreuse round rubber (medium)

Hub's Spey Copper Hopper (Cool)

Originator: Jerry Hubka
Tier: Jerry Hubka

Hook: #12 Tiemco 8089 Special Use
Thread: Olive 140-denier UTC
Underbody: Olive craft foam (2mm)
Middle Body: Dark blue craft foam (2mm)
Top Body: Purple craft foam (2mm)
Wing: Copper Hareline Krystal Flash
Legs: Chartreuse/olive/black Hareline Fly Enhancer Legs
Adhesive: Zap-a-Gap and CCG Hydro
Note: *Body shapes cut with RRC Tapered Chernobyl Cutter (large).*

Hub's Spey Copper Hopper (Warm)

Originator: Jerry Hubka
Tier: Jerry Hubka

Hook: #12 Tiemco 8089
Thread: Tan 140-denier UTC
Underbody: Cocoa Foamies Sheet Craft Foam (2mm)
Middle Body: Goldenrod craft foam (2mm)
Top Body: Orange craft foam (2mm)
Wing: Copper Hareline Krystal Flash
Legs: Gold/amber/black Hareline Fly Enhancer Legs
Adhesive: Zap-a-Gap and CCG Hydro
Note: *Body shapes cut with RRC Tapered Chernobyl Cutter (large).*

DAVID IWANE

Cricket Patterns

Black X Cricket

Originator: Bill Black
Tier: Spirit River

Hook: #6-10 Maruto 7200
Thread: Black 6/0 Uni-Thread
Body: Black Spirit River Fly Foam (2mm)
Thorax: Black Antron dubbing
Underbody: Tying thread
Flash: Three strands of pearl Crystal Splash on each side
Wing: Black calf tail
Head: Black 2mm foam (3/16" wide)
Legs: Black Spirit River round rubber (medium)
Indicator: Yellow Spirit River Fly Foam (2mm)
Adhesive: Thin coat of epoxy along the hook shank on the bottom of the fly
Note: *Other hook models include Spear-It CS200 or Daiichi 1270.*

Rainy's Mormon Cricket

Originator: Rainy Riding
Tier: Rainy's Flies

Hook: #2-4 Maruto 80300
Thread: Black 3/0 Uni-Thread
Body: Black Rainy's Evazote Sheet Foam (1/4")
Underbody: Coffee Danville's Rayon Chenille (medium)
Indicator: Red Rainy's Evazote Sheet Foam
Legs: Black round rubber (medium)
Note: *Other hook models include Mustad 34007 or Tiemco 9395.*

Letort Cricket

Originator: Ed Shenk
Tier: Tim Jacobs

Hook: #10-14 Tiemco 5212
Thread: Black 140-denier UTC
Body: Black Hareline Micro Fine Dry Fly Dubbing
Wing: Black deer hair
Underwing: Black turkey quill
Adhesive: Zap-A-Gap

Simple Foam Cricket

Originator: Tim Jacobs
Tier: Tim Jacobs

Hook: #10 Tiemco 100
Thread: Black 140-denier UTC
Body: Black Rainy's Evazote Foam (1/8")
Head: Black Rainy's Evazote Foam (1/8")
Wing: Medium dun RRC Speckled River Wing
Underwing: Black deer hair
Legs: Black rubber legs (medium)

Curmudgeon Crumpler Cricket

Originator: Erin Block
Tier: Erin Block

Hook: #12-14 Umpqua C300 BL
Thread: Light cahill 6/0 Uni-Thread; brown 3/0 Danville's Waxed Monocord
Body: Tying thread
Thorax: Black Super Fine Dubbing
Wing: Elk hair
Legs: Knotted turkey tail fibers
Overwing: Plain MFC Wing Material
Hackle: Golden badger Whiting Farms dry fly
Adhesive: Coat body with Hard-as-Hull

RK's Black Cricket

Originator: Ryan Keyes
Tier: Ryan Keyes

Hook: #8-12 Tiemco 2312
Thread: Black 140-denier UTC
Thorax: Black Antron Dubbing
Body: Black Hareline standard tubing
Underwing: Black foam (2mm)
Tail: Black Fluoro Fibre
Indicator: Tan McFly Foam
Legs: Black round rubber
Wing: Mottled black Web Wing
Flash: Pearl Krystal Flash
Post: Bug Juice McFlylon
Butt: Black Antron Dubbing

Slurpy Chirpy

Originator: Curtis Fry
Tier: Curtis Fry

Hook: #6 Mustad C49S
Thread: Black 70-denier UTC
Body: Black Rainy's Evazote Foam (3mm)
Underbody: Tan Rainy's Evazote Foam (1mm)
Wing: Speckled dun RRC River Wing
Indicator: Bright orange McFlylon
Pronotum: Black foam sheet (2mm)
Rear Legs: Black foam sheet (2mm)
Front Legs: Black round rubber (medium)
Rib: Tying thread
Tail: Olive brown goose biots
Antennae: Black round rubber (medium)
Adhesive: Super Glue
Note: *Cut foam body with RRC Beaver Cutter. Cut wings with RRC Salmon Fly Wing Cutter. Cut pronotum with RRC Pronotum Cutter. Cut rear legs with RRC Hopper Leg Cutter.*

Big Ugly Cricket

Originator: John Gribb
Tier: John Gribb

Hook: #8-12 Mustad 3366
Thread: Olive #3 Orvis Braided
Body: Black craft foam (2mm)
Underbody: Tying thread
Wing: Deer hair
Eyes: Red foam
Legs: Black Stretch Magic
Adhesive: Super Glue

Flying Cricket

Originator: Norimasa Watanabe
Tier: Norimasa Watanabe

Hook: #10 Tiemco 2488
Thread: Black 6/0 Uni-Thread
Body: Black Super Fine Dubbing
Thorax: Charcoal black Nature's Spirit Emergence Dubbing
Wing: Dark brown Medallion Sheeting
Legs: Brown round rubber (medium)
Note: *Twisted body with C&F Extended Body Twister.*

Taylor's Fat Albert (Black)

Originator: Brent Taylor
Tier: Montana Fly Company

Hook: #8 MFC 7037
Thread: Black 6/0 MFC
Overbody: Black foam (2mm)
Underbody: Black foam (2mm)
Wing: White Gator Hair
Indicator: Red foam (2mm)
Legs: Black Centipede Legs

Osteen's Cricket

Originator: Drayton Osteen
Tier: Montana Fly Company

Hook: #12 MFC 7231
Thread: Black 6/0 MFC
Body/Head: Black foam (5mm)
Thorax: Dark golden stone MFC Wabbit Dubbing
Wing: Mottled brown MFC Wing Material
Overwing: Cow elk flank hair
Underwing: Red and gold Crystal Flash
Indicator: White Widow's Web
Eyes: Black MFC Hoppize (small)
Back Legs: Black MFC Cricket Legs (small)
Legs: Black Centipede Legs
Note: *Body and head cut with RRC Tapered Chernobyl cutter.*

Keller's Cricket

Originator: Kris Keller
Tier: Montana Fly Company

Hook: #10 MFC 7027
Thread: Black 6/0 MFC
Underbody: Black UV Frog Hair Dubbing
Overbody: Black foam (2mm)
Thorax: Black UV Frog Hair Dubbing
Head: Black foam (2mm)
Tail: 40-pound black mono center and 25-pound black mono sides
Overwing: Black foam (2mm)
Underwing: CDC
Indicator: Red foam (2mm)
Back Legs: Black MFC Cricket Legs (medium)
Legs: Black MFC Sexi-Floss
Antennae: Black 25-pound-test mono

MFC Parachute Cricket

Originator: Doug Swisher
Tier: Montana Fly Company

Hook: #8 MFC 1026
Thread: Black 6/0 MFC
Tail: Black cow elk flank
Body: Black cow elk flank
Thorax/Head: Peacock herl
Wing: Black cow elk flank
Post: White Widow's Web
Underwing: Pearl MFC Crystal Flash
Legs: Black Centipede Legs
Hackle: Black

Cricket V3

Originator: Dron Lee
Tier: Dron Lee

Hook: #8 Gamakatsu B10S
Thread: Brown 140-denier UTC
Body/Head: Brown foam (3mm)
Wing: Brown saddle cemented
Eyes: Black Loon Hard Head
Legs: Brown barred Sili Legs
Back Legs: Black dyed pheasant tail, knotted
Rib: Tying thread
Tail: Mahogany brown biots
Antennae: Dark brown pheasant tail fibers

EAP Cricket

Originator: Eric A. Pettine
Tier: Eric A. Pettine

Hook: #10 Mustad 94840
Thread: Black 70-denier UTC
Body: Black closed-cell foam and black hackle clipped
Thorax/Head: Black and brown elk hair
Wing: Black Rocky Mountain Dubbing Wingcase material over black elk hair
Legs: Knotted pheasant tail fibers
Tail: Black stripped hackle
Antennae: Rat tail brush fibers

Tak's Rubber Legged Cricket

Originator: Rick Takahashi
Tier: Rick Takahashi

Hook: #8-10 Tiemco 2302
Thread: Black 6/0 Danville's
Body: Black RRC Foam (2mm)
Collar/Head: Black deer hair
Underwing: Black RRC River Wing
Wing: Black deer hair
Legs: Black round rubber (small)

Tak's Foam Legged Cricket

Originator: Rick Takahashi
Tier: Rick Takahashi

Hook: #8-10 Tiemco 2302
Thread: Black 6/0 Danville's
Body: Black RRC Foam (2mm)
Head: Body Foam
Wing: Black RRC River Wing
Indicator: Fluorescent pink ribbon
Back Legs: Black RRC Hopper Leg Cutter (#10)
Legs: Black round rubber (small)

Tak's Kickin'it Cricket

Originator: Rick Takahashi
Tier: Rick Takahashi

Hook: #8-10 Tiemco 2302
Thread: Black 6/0 Danville's
Underbody: Tying thread
Body: Black RRC Foam (2mm)
Wing: Body foam
Back Legs: Black RRC Hopper Leg Cutter (#10) and black counter brush bristles
Legs: Black round rubber (small)

Kicker Cricket (Black)

Originator: Rod Garren
Tier: Rod Garren

Hook: #4-8 Gamakatsu B10S
Thread: Black 70-denier UTC
Underbody: Black foam (2mm)
Body: Black foam (2mm)
Thorax: Hareline peacock dubbing
Legs: Black round rubber
Rib: Tying thread
Adhesive: Zap-A-Gap

Morrish Roach

Originator: Ken Morrish
Tier: Ken Morrish

Hook: #8 Tiemco 3761
Thread: Black 6/0 Uni-Thread
Body: Black three-ply Hareline foam trimmed to shape
Wing: Hareline Flashback textured with forceps
Indicator: Orange Hareline foam (2mm)
Eyes: 223C Wet-n-Wild Nail Polish
Legs: Black Hareline round rubber (medium)
Tail/Antennae: Black goose biots
Adhesive: Zap-A-Gap

Morrish Cricket

Originator: Ken Morrish
Tier: Ken Morrish

Hook: #6-14 Tiemco 5262
Thread: Black 6/0 Uni-Thread
Body: Black foam (2mm)
Indicator: Orange foam (2mm)
Eyes: Red fingernail polish
Legs: Black round rubber (medium)
Adhesive: 3M Spray adhesive to glue layers of foam; Zap-A-Gap glue body to Hook

Morrish Cricket-Cator

Originator: Ken Morrish
Tier: Ken Morrish

Hook: #6-10 Tiemco 3761
Thread: Black Uni-Thread
Body: Black Hareline foam (2mm)
Head: Black foam (2mm)
Wing: Off-white and yellow poly indicator yarn
Eyes: White Rainy's Float Foam Cylinder (small)
Legs: Black and white round rubber (medium)
Adhesive: 3M 77 Spray Adhesive for gluing layers of foam

Snookie

Originator: Scott Barrus
Tier: Scott Barrus

Hook: #8 Gamakatsu S10
Thread: Black 6/0 Uni-Thread
Underbody: Tying thread
Body: Black foam (3mm)
Overwing: Light pink kip tail
Underwing: Pearl UV Krystal Flash
Legs: Orange/black Hareline Grizzly Legs (small)
Adhesive: Zap-A-Gap

M.S.U. Cricket

Originator: Gary Barnes
Tier: Gary Barnes

Hook: #8-14 Daiichi 1260
Thread: Black 70-denier UTC
Body: Black fine dubbing
Wing: Black EP Fiber
Head: Black deer hair
Legs: Black Hareline Flutter Legs

Jeff's Cricket

Originator: Jeff Goff
Tier: Jeff Goff

Hook: #8-14 Tiemco 100
Thread: Black 8/0 Uni-Thread
Underbody: Black deer hair stacked and clipped
Wing: Turkey wing sections
Rear Kickers: Black turkey wing section knotted with a clipped black stem
Sternum: Black deer hair stacked and clipped
Front Legs: Black turkey wing fibers
Pronotum: Black turkey wing sections
Head: Black deer hair, clipped

Hub's Spey Copper Cricket

Originator: Jerry Hubka
Tier: Jerry Hubka

Hook: #12 Tiemco 8089
Thread: Black 140-denier UTC
Body: Black Glitter Sheet Foam and red craft foam (2mm)
Wing: Copper Krystal Flash
Legs: Black/red tipped Hareline Crazy Legs
Adhesive: Zap-A-Gap
Note: *Body shapes cut with RRC Tapered Chernobyl Cutter (large).*

Deer Creek Plopper Black Cricket

Originator: John Larson
Tier: John Larson

Hook: #8 Daiichi 1720
Thread: Black 6/0 Uni-Thread
Tail: Red amherst pheasant
Underbody: Black UV Ice Dub
Wing: Black Swiss Straw
Collar: Black deer hair
Legs: Black Wapsi TNT Legs

Hubooka Cricket

Originator: Jerry Hubka
Tier: Jerry Hubka

Hook: #8 Tiemco 5263
Thread: Black 140-denier UTC
Body: Black craft foam (2mm)
Wing: Pearl olive Spirit River Crystal Sheetz
Underwing: Black Krystal Flash
Eyes: Black MFC Hoppize (medium)
Tail: Black goose biots
Legs: Black/blue flake Sili Legs
Adhesive: Zap-A-Gap (Brush On)
Note: *RRC Tapered Chernobyl Cutters (small and medium).*

Ba Donk A Donk (Black)

Originator: Bubba Smith
Tier: Orvis

Hook: #6-10 Tiemco 200R
Thread: Black 6/0 Uni-Thread
Body: Black foam (2mm)
Underbody: Black foam (2mm)
Wing: White poly yarn
Underwing: Pearl Krystal Flash
Indicator: Fluorescent orange foam (2mm)
Eyes: Doll eyes (4mm)
Legs: Tan/black Rainy's barred round rubber (medium)
Back: Black foam (2mm)

KLH Stoned Chernobyl Cricket

Originator: Kenneth Held
Tier: Kenneth Held

Hook: #8-10 Dai-Riki 305
Thread: Brown 70-denier UTC
Body: Black RRC foam (2mm)
Rib: Tying thread
Wing: Black Swiss Straw mottled with marker
Back Legs: Black Rainey's knotted hopper legs
Front Legs: Copper brown Speckled Sexi Leggs
Tail: Black Spirit River Tarantu-leggs (mini)
Indicator: Electric Banana Spirit River Polar Aire
Adhesive: Zap-A-Gap and CCG Hydro
Marker: Chartpak delta brown and black
Note: *Cut the body foam with RRC Stonefly (# 4) and Chernobyl cutter.*

KLH Super Natural Cricket

Originator: Kenneth Held
Tier: Kenneth Held

Hook: #10-8 Dai-Riki 305
Thread: Brown 70-denier UTC
Body: Black RRC foam (2mm)
Rib: Brown 70-denier UTC
Wing: Black Swiss Straw mottled
Back Legs: Tan (colored black) MFC AK Hopper Legs (medium)
Front Legs: Brown Hareline round rubber, mottled (medium)
Eyes: Black MFC Hoppize (3.5mm)
Antennae: Black Spirit River Tarantu-Leggs (mini)
Ovipositor: Black hen hackle stem, colored black
Tail: Black hen hackle stem, colored black
Adhesive: Zap-A-Gap and CCG Hydro
Marker: Delta brown and black Chartpak
Note: *Cut the body foam with RRC Stonefly (#4) and Tomsu's Supreme hopper body cutter (#6).*

DAVID IWANE

Tying Cicadas

Hubka's Foam Cicada

Originator: Jerry Hubka
Tier: Rick Takahashi

Hook: #8-14 Tiemco 2312
Thread: Black 140 Denier UTC
Body: Black 3mm craft foam
Underbody: Orange Ice Dub
Wings: White MFC Widow's Web
Legs: Orange round rubber legs
Indicator: Fluorescent pink foam strip (1mm)
Adhesive: CCG Hydro

TYING HUBKA'S FOAM CICADA

1. Attach the thread at the hook eye and wrap it to the hook bend (opposite the barb).

2. Twist orange Ice Dub onto the thread and wrap forward to two eye widths back from the hook eye.

3. Wrap the dubbing forward to two eye widths back from the hook eye.

4. Cut out a body from the foam using River Road Creations Hopper Body Cutters.

5. Tie down the foam, taking several wraps to create a small waist.

6. Attach a clump of Widow's Web (about half the diameter of a pencil) at the same position as the legs. Tie in the yarn at the middle then you will trim the front and back of the yarn.

7. The wing should appear as shown.

8. Tie in the rubber legs on each side of the wing.

9. Trim the legs.

10. Tie in a small strip of fluorescent foam and trim it.

11. Whip-finish and trim the thread.

12. Turn the fly upside down and apply CCG Hydro to the tie-in point.

13. Set the CCG with a UV light.

14. Finished fly.

Tak's Cicada

Originator: Rick Takahashi
Tier: Rick Takahashi

Hook:	#8-14 Tiemco 2312
Thread:	Black 140-denier UTC
Body:	Black foam (2mm)
Underbody:	Tying thread and fluorescent fly line backing
Overbody:	Black foam (2mm)
Rib:	Fluorescent orange fly line backing
Wings:	Bleached deer hair
Indicator:	Orange McFlylon
Legs:	Orange and black round rubber legs
Eyes:	One-inch piece of orange round rubber leg material
Adhesive:	Zap-A-Gap Super Glue

TYING TAK'S CICADA

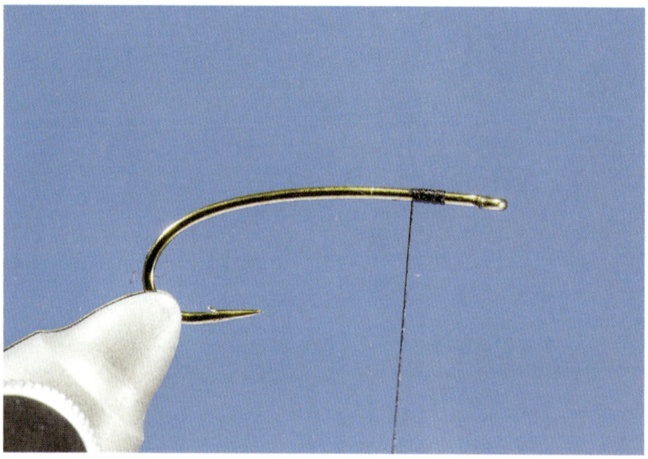

1. Attach the thread one eye width behind the hook eye.

2. Tie in the fly line backing.

3. Wrap the thread over the fly line backing back to the hook bend. Wrap the thread forward to where the backing was tied in.

4. Wrap the backing forward on the hook shank using touching wraps, tie it off, and trim excess.

5. Prepare a 5-inch-long strip of foam equal in width to the hook gap.

6. Tie in the foam by its tip with several secure wraps. Lay the foam flat back over the hook shank to the hook bend.

7. Take cross wraps to form segmentation to a point just above the barb.

8. Turn the fly upside down and wrap the thread to form an alternating pattern of black and orange. Make the final wrap at the front edge of the body segmentation.

9. Apply CCG Hydro to the underside of the body.

10. Set the CCG with a UV light.

11. Pull the remaining foam strip forward over the underbody and tie it in at the one-third position of the hook.

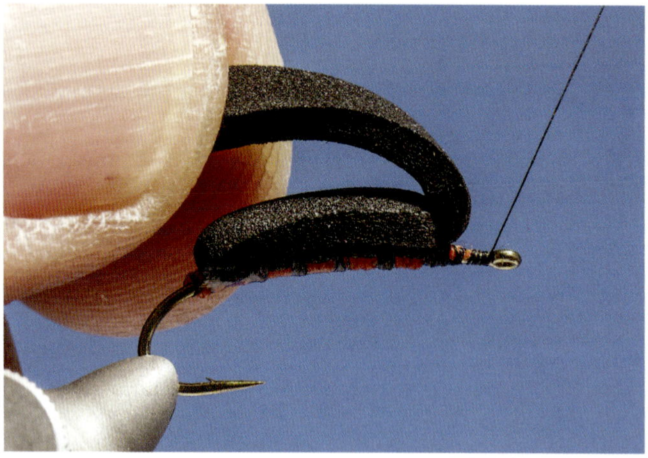

12. Pull the foam back over the body and wrap the thread forward to the hook eye.

13. Make enough wraps to cover the foam completely to the hook eye.

14. Attach the orange round rubber legs using figure-eight wraps (spent-wing style) and wrap the thread in front of the body.

15. Trim the round rubber foam to form the eyes.

16. Tie in the round rubber leg material on each side of the hook.

17. Cut a bunch of bleached deer hair about half the diameter of a pencil and stack it. Measure the hair so that it extends to the halfway point of the body and trim the butts of the hair evenly.

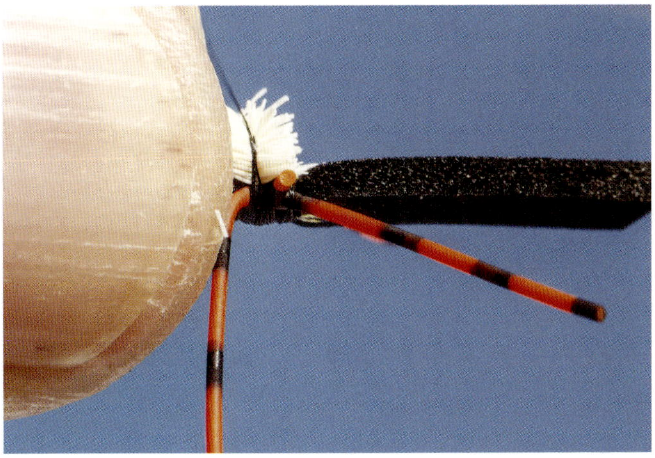

18. Attach the deer hair to the hook with several tight wraps without letting go of the hair.

19. The wing should look like this.

20. Apply superglue to secure the wing.

21. Fold the foam back over the head area and lash it down with several wraps of thread.

22. Trim the foam and whip-finish. Completed Tak's Cicada.

JR's Cicada

Originator: John Rohmer
Tier: John Rohmer

Hook: #8-10 Daiichi 1180
Thread: Black 6/0 Uni-Thread
Body: Black Darice sheet foam (2mm)
Thorax: Rusty brown Super Fine Dubbing
Wing: Bleached deer hair
Underwing: White Raffia
Indicator: Orange sheet foam (2mm)
Legs: Orange/black barred Centipede Legs
Adhesive: Zap-A-Gap

RK's Hi-Vis Cicada

Originator: Ryan Keyes
Tier: Ryan Keyes

Hook: #6-10 Tiemco 5263
Thread: Black 140-denier UTC
Underbody: Hareline black standard tubing
Overbody: Tan and black foam (2mm)
Indicator: McCheese McFly Foam
Legs: Black/gray round rubber
Wing: Black foam (2mm)
Post: White McFlylon

Stalcup's Cicada

Originator: Shane Stalcup
Tier: Jimbo Busse

Hook: #8 Tiemco 5262
Thread: Black 6/0 Uni-Thread
Body: Black sheet foam (2mm)
Head: Black deer hair
Wing: Mottled brown Medallion Sheeting over white calf tail over brown deer hair
Side Wings: Root beer Krystal Flash
Legs: Orange round rubber (medium)
Adhesive: Crazy Glue
Note: *Attach a large needle to vise and wrap foam to create the pointed spiral foam body cone and glue each wrap. Then remove needle and thread spiral foam body onto hook and glue in place.*

Steve Potter's Cicada Indicator Fly

Originator: Inspired by Andre Puyans and John Goddard's caddis
Tier: Steve Potter

Hook: #6-16 Daiichi 2460
Thread: Black 210-denier Danville's Flat Waxed Nylon; black 6/0 Danville's Flymaster
Body: Orange, black, and yellow cow elk belly hair
Thorax: Grizzly dyed yellow Whiting Farms saddle
Legs: Orange, black, and yellow Centipede Legs
Antennae: Stripped grizzly Whiting Farms hackle with black paint on tips

Scott's Cicada

Originator: Scott Stisser
Tier: Scott Stisser

Hook: #2 Tiemco 8089
Thread: Black 140-denier UTC
Abdomen: Black and orange dyed deer hair
Head: Black dyed deer hair
Wing: Rainy's or Hareline Transparent Wing sheeting
Legs: Orange oval rubber legs (medium)

Rubber Leg Cicada

Originator: Yoshihiro Urushihara
Tier: Yoshihiro Urushihara

Hook: #2 Daiichi 2720
Thread: Brown 8/0 Uni-Thread
Body: Black sheet foam (1mm) covered with dark brown seal fur dubbing and peacock Ice Dub
Head: Dark brown seal fur dubbing and peacock Ice Dub
Wing: OOAK Fairy Fantasy Cicada Wing Sheet
Eyes: Burned monofilament colored with brown paint
Legs: Orange and black round rubber
Adhesive: TMC Soft Cement

Spring Cicada (Yellow)

Originator: Miwa Awazaki
Tier: Miwa Awazaki

Hook: #2 Gamakatsu S10
Thread: Olive 6/0 Uni-Thread
Underbody: Soft closed-cell foam
Body: Light olive and orange Salmo Web mixed with UV Ice Dub
Head: Opossum hair dubbing
Wing: Coq de Leon
Indicator: Yellow Antron Yarn

Spring Cicada (Red)

Originator: Miwa Awazaki
Tier: Miwa Awazaki

Hook: #2 Gamakatsu S10
Thread: Olive 6/0 Uni-Thread
Underbody: Soft closed-cell foam
Body: Light olive and orange Salmo Web mixed with UV Ice Dub
Head: Opossum hair dubbing
Wing: Coq de Leon
Indicator: Red Antron Yarn

True Cicada

Originator: MFC
Tier: Montana Fly Company

Hook: #6 MFC 7077
Thread: None
Body: MFC True Cicada Body #8
Legs: True Cicada Legs
Wing: Natural #8 MFC True Cicada Wings
Eyes: Black mono (medium)
Adhesive: Zap-A-Gap

Card's Cicada

Originator: Charles Card
Tier: Montana Fly Company

Hook: #8 MFC 7000
Thread: Black 6/0 MFC
Underbody: Medium brown Wings and Things
Body: Black foam (3mm)
Overwing: White calf tail
Underwing: Rainbow Flashabou Accent
Top Legs: Orange barred Sili legs
Bottom Legs: Black Sexy Floss

Card's Green River Cicada

Originator: Charles Card
Tier: Montana Fly Company

Hook: #8 MFC 7000
Thread: Black 6/0 MFC
Tail: Orange foam (2mm)
Underbody: Burnt orange/black variegated chenille
Body: Black foam (2mm)
Head: Black foam (2mm)
Wing: White Widow's Web
Underwing: Mylar sheet
Indicator: Orange foam (1mm)
Legs: Orange barred Sili Legs
Hackle: Grizzly dyed burnt orange

Foam Para-Cicada

Originator: Unknown
Tier: Montana Fly Company

Hook: #8 MFC 7026
Thread: Black 6/0 MFC
Body: Black foam (2mm)
Wing: Dun MFC Wing Material
Underwing: Black Widow's Web
Indicator: White Widow's Web
Legs: Black Centipede Legs
Hackle: Black saddle

Agee's Knobbler Cicada

Originator: Mike Agee
Tier: Montana Fly Company

Hook: #8 MFC 7027
Thread: Black 6/0 MFC
Underbody: Peacock herl
Body: Black foam (2mm)
Head: Black foam (2mm)
Overwing: Black Supreme Hair
Underwing: UV gray Flashabou
Indicator: White Widow's Web
Legs: Black Centipede Legs

Cicada X

Originator: Dron Lee
Tier: Dron Lee

Hook: #4 Gamakatsu B10S
Thread: Brown 140-denier UTC
Underbody: Any dubbing for shape
Body: Brown foam (3mm)
Thorax: Brown foam (3mm)
Wing: Elk hair and pearl Krystal Flash
Eyes: Black #8 glass bead with melted mono
Legs: Barred brown Sili Legs (small)
Rib: Tying thread
Adhesive: Flexament
Marker: Brown and orange Promarker

Tak's Foam Cicada

Originator: Rick Takahashi
Tier: Rick Takahashi

Hook: #8-10 Tiemco 2302
Thread: Black 6/0 Danville's
Underbody: Tying thread and rib
Body: Black RRC Foam (2mm)
Overwing: Bleached deer hair
Thorax: Fluorescent orange 140-denier thread
Underwing: Pearl Krystal Flash
Indicator: Red foam (2mm)
Back Legs: Orange biot
Legs: Orange round rubber (medium)
Rib: Orange Dacron fly line backing

Tak's Foam Cicada

Originator: Rick Takahashi
Tier: Rick Takahashi

Hook: #8-10 Tiemco 2302
Thread: Black 6/0 Danville's
Underbody: Tying thread and rib
Body: Black RRC foam (2mm)
Overwing: White Spirit River Near Hair
Underwing: Pearl Krystal Flash
Indicator: Fluorescent orange McFlylon
Back Legs: Orange biot
Legs: Fluorescent orange Dacron fly line backing
Rib: Fluorescent orange 140-denier UTC thread

Tak's Orange Eyed Cicada

Originator: Rick Takahashi
Tier: Rick Takahashi

Hook: #8-10 Tiemco 2302
Thread: Black 6/0 Danville's
Underbody: Tying thread and orange foam (2mm)
Body: Black foam (2mm)
Head: Body foam
Overwing: White Spirit River Near Hair
Underwing: Pearl Krystal Flash
Eyes: Hot orange Ultra Chenille
Legs: Orange MFC round rubber (medium)

Tak's Simple Cicada

Originator: Rick Takahashi
Tier: Rick Takahashi

Hook: #8-10 Tiemco 2302
Thread: Black 6/0 Danville's
Underbody: Tying thread
Body: Black foam (2mm) cut with RRC Caddis Wing Cutter
Head: Body foam
Overwing: White Spirit River Near Hair
Underwing: Pearl Krystal Flash
Indicator: Orange RRC Foam (1mm)
Legs: Fluorescent orange Dacron fly line backing
Hackle: Orange dyed Umpqua/Metz neck

Splayed Cicada

Originator: Rod Garren
Tier: Rod Garren

Hook: #6-10 Gamakatsu B10S
Thread: Dark olive 70-denier UTC
Overbody: Tan foam (1mm)
Body: Tan foam (4mm)
Thorax: Olive and copper Ice Dub
Wing: Mirage Krystal Flash and elk hair
Eyes: Mono Damsel Eyes painted red
Legs: Yellow and black Crazy Legs (medium)
Rib: Tying thread
Adhesive: Zap-A-Gap and Head Cement
Marker: Tan and green Prismacolor

Tomsu's Cicada

Originator: Tony Tomsu
Tier: Tony Tomsu

Hook: #4 Daiichi 1550
Thread: Orange 8/0 Danville's
Body: Black RRC Foam (2mm)
Wings: Light dun RRC River Wing
Eyes: Red plastic end sewing pins cut glued and inserted
Legs: Orange and black speckled rubber legs (medium)
Marker: Orange permanent on wings

Note: *Body and wings cut using RRC Foam cutters.*

Tak's Green River Cicada

Originator: Rick Takahashi
Tier: Rick Takahashi

Hook: #8-12 Tiemco 2302
Thread: Black 140-denier UTC
Body: Black foam (2mm)
Underbody: Orange Estaz
Head: Black deer hair Hareline (small)
Wing: White organdy
Overwing: Black deer hair
Legs: Orange round rubber (medium)
Rib: Orange Dacron fly line backing (19-pound-test)
Indicator: Orange McFlylon

Tying Mice, Moths, Caterpillars, and More

Mouse

Originator: Unknown
Tier: Rick Takahashi

Hook:	#8 Tiemco 8089
Thread:	Black 3/0 Danville's Monocord
Tail:	Light brown Vernille
Body:	Deer hair

TYING THE DEERHAIR MOUSE

1. Attach the tying thread to the hook approximately one eye width back from the hook eye, trim the tag, and wrap the thread to the hook bend (opposite the barb). Cut a three-inch section of Vernille and singe the end to form a taper.

2. Attach the Vernille to the hook, and wrap the thread back to the hook bend above the barb.

3. Trim the Vernille.

4. Select a bunch of deer hair about half the size of a pencil and stack it. Take the stacked deer hair and grasp the butt ends with your right hand. The tips should face to the rear of the hook and extend over the hook bend. Trim the butts of the deer hair approximately one quarter of an inch in front of your fingers perpendicular to the hair.

5. Place the deer hair over the hook bend, tie it in with several wraps, and then let it go so that it spins around the hook shank. Take several wraps of thread over the hook eye, then draw the thread tight so the butts flare. Take several wrap forward through the hair making sure each wrap is snug.

6. Repeat the process.

7. Repeat the process until you reach the hook eye.

8. Whip-finish and trim the thread.

9. Trim the underside of the body.

10. The completed Deer Hair Mouse.

Tak's Spruce Moth

Originator: Rick Takahashi
Tier: Rick Takahashi

Hook: #14 Tiemco 2302
Thread: Tan 3/0 Danville's Monocord
Body: Callibaetis color Nature's Spirit peacock herl
Underwing: Light olive Whiting Brahma Hen Hackle
Wing: Deer hair
Antennae: Pearl Krystal Flash

TYING TAK'S SPRUCE MOTH

1. Attach the tying thread to the shank two eye widths back from the hook eye. Wrap the thread to the hook bend (opposite the barb) then back to the original tie-in point.

2. Take three dyed peacock herls and trim the tips even. Attach the peacock herls to the hook. Wrap the tying thread over the peacock herls to the hook bend.

3. Attach gold wire with tying thread and wrap thread forward to within two eye widths of the eye of the hook. Then wrap the peacock herl forward in touching wraps.

4. Counterwrap the wire over the peacock body in evenly spaced wraps.

5. Select a body feather from the Whiting Farms Brahma Hen Back. Trim the hen back feather as shown.

6. Attach the hen back feather to the top of the hook.

7. Wrap the tying thread to the hook eye and trim the excess stem.

8. Tie in the Krystal Flash to form the antennae, fold it over to create a loop, and then tie off and trim the excess.

9. Select a small bunch of deer hair about half the diameter of a pencil, stack the hair, and then measure the deer hair to be as long as the feather wing. Trim the butt ends even. Tie in the deer hair with several wraps of thread to flare the hair. Hold the hair so that it doesn't spin.

10. Wrap the thread forward through the deer hair to secure it to the hook.

11. Whip-finish and trim the excess thread.

12. Cut the Krystal Flash in the middle of the strands.

13. The completed Tak's Spruce Moth.

Crackle Back Caterpillar

Originator: Rick Takahashi
Tier: Rick Takahashi

Hook:	#14 Tiemco 2312
Thread:	Yellow 3/0 Danville's Monocord
Body:	Yellow wool yarn
Overbody:	Peacock herl
Rib:	Gold UTC Wire (small)
Hackle:	Yellow Grizzly Whiting Farms saddle hackle

TYING THE CRACKLE BACK CATERPILLAR

1. Attach the tying thread at a point two eye widths behind the hook eye. Wrap the thread to the hook bend and then back to the tie-in point.

2. Take three dyed peacock herls and trim the tips even, then tie in at the one-third position.

3. Attach the wire.

4. Wrap the thread back over the wire and herl to the hook bend, just above the barb.

5. Wrap the thread forward to the one-third position behind the eye.

6. Attach the yarn by its tip. Wrap the thread over the yarn back to the hook bend and then to the one-third position behind the eye.

7. Wrap the yarn forward with touching wraps to the thread and tie off. Trim the excess yarn.

8. Fold the peacock herl forward and tie off.

9. Tie in the saddle hackle in back of the eye of the hook with the dull side facing toward the front of the hook.

10. Reverse palmer the hackle back to the hook bend.

11. Wrap the wire around the hackle stem to secure it to the hook and then wrap the wire forward with evenly spaced wraps.

12. Tie off the wire and whip-finish, then trim the thread.

13. Trim the hackle at the rear of the hook.

14. The completed Crackle Back Caterpillar.

Attractor Patterns

Parachute Madam X

Originator: Unknown
Tier: Spirit River

Hook: #12-16 Tiemco 100
Thread: Red 6/0 Uni-Thread
Body: Red floss
Thorax: Peacock herl
Hackle: Grizzly dry fly saddle
Post: White Spirit River Sparkle Yarn
Wing/Tail: Bleached deer hair
Legs: White round rubber (fine)

Hopper Stimulator (with Eyes)

Originator: Randall Kaufmann
Tier: Tim Mack

Hook: #12 Tiemco 200R
Thread: Fire orange 8/0 Uni-Thread
Body: Wapsi yellow Antron Dubbing
Head: Polar orange Spirit River Brite Blend
Wing: Spirit River bleached elk hair
Underwing: Pearl Hareline Krystal Flash (midge)
Eyes: Black Hareline mono (small)
Legs: Orange Spirit River Rubber Legs (mini)
Hackle: Grizzly and brown Whiting Farms saddle
Rib: Gold Ultra Wire (small) and brown Whiting Farms saddle
Tail: Spirit River bleached elk hair

Penasco Hopper Stimulator

Originator: Tim Mack
Tier: Tim Mack

Hook: #12 Tiemco 200R
Thread: Fire orange 8/0 Uni-Thread
Body: Green Wapsi Antron Dubbing
Head: Polar orange Spirit River Brite Blend
Wing: Spirit River bleached elk hair
Underwing: Pearl Hareline Krystal Flash (midge)
Legs: Orange Spirit River Rubber Legs (mini)
Hackle: Brown and grizzly Whiting Farms saddle
Rib: Gold Ultra Wire (small) and brown Whiting Farms saddle
Tail: Spirit River bleached elk hair

Ugly

Originator: Ken Iwamasa
Tier: Ken Iwamasa

Hook: #12 Tiemco 5210
Thread: Red 6/0 Uni-Thread
Body: Black chenille (medium)
Wing: Calf tail
Tail: Yellow deer hair
Hackle: Brown Whiting Farms
Adhesive: Head cement

Ugly Trude

Originator: Ken Iwamasa
Tier: Ken Iwamasa

Hook: #12 Tiemco 5210
Thread: Red 6/0 Uni-Thread
Body: Black craft foam (2mm)
Wing: Calf tail
Rib: Grizzly dyed yellow Whiting Farms saddle
Tail: Dyed yellow Nature's Spirit coastal deer hair
Hackle: Brown Whiting Farms
Adhesive: Head cement

The Mini Hopper (Brown)

Originator: Ben Smith
Tier: Ben Smith

Hook: #12 Mustad R50 or 94840
Thread: Black 6/0 Uni-Thread
Body: Black Hare-Tron Dubbing
Head: Brown craft foam (2mm)
Wing: Mule deer hair
Legs: Orange and black barred Wapsi Sili Legs
Adhesive: Super Glue

Visible Terrestrial (Tan)

Originator: Masayuki Mori
Tier: Masayuki Mori

Hook: #6 Dai-Riki 070
Thread: Rusty brown 6/0 Uni-Thread
Body: Tan dyed neck hackle
Thorax: Tan dyed CDC
Legs: Tan dyed teal flank

Stink Bug

Originator: Masahiko Ohnishi
Tier: Masahiko Ohnishi

Hook: #10 Gamakatsu R16-2HBV
Thread: Red 6/0 Uni-Thread
Body: Indicator green foam cylinder
Indicator: Orange floating yarn
Eyes: Black permanent marker
Legs: Pumpkin Caterpillar Rubber Legs

MM Kamemushi (Red Stink Bug)

Originator: Masayuki Mori
Tier: Masayuki Mori

Hook: #8-12 Dai-Riki 070
Thread: Dark brown 6/0 Uni-Thread
Underbody: Orange Whiting Farms dry fly hackle
Overbody: Cock pheasant rump patch
Legs: Partridge feather
Note: *Cut bottom hackles.*

MM Kamemushi Ver. 2 (Tan Stink Bug)

Originator: Masayuki Mori
Tier: Masayuki Mori

Hook: #8-12 Dai-Riki 070
Thread: Dark brown 6/0 Uni-Thread
Body: Dun Whiting Farms dry fly hackle
Legs: Partridge feather
Note: *Cut bottom hackles.*

Visible Stimulator (Brown)

Originator: Masayuki Mori
Tier: Masayuki Mori

Hook: #6 Dai-Riki 070
Thread: Dark brown 6/0 Uni-Thread
Body: Brown Whiting Farms dry fly hackle
Hackle: Brown Whiting Farms hen hackle
Tail: Squirrel tail

Hokkaido Orange Stink Bug

Originator: Hideyuki Kawai
Tier: Hideyuki Kawai

Hook: #8 Tiemco 2487
Thread: Red 6/0 Uni-Thread
Body: Orange deer hair
Head: Green deer hair
Legs: Brown Whiting Farms hackle
Note: *Palmer hackle and cut off top and bottom fibers.*

Swisher's Speckled X

Originator: Doug Swisher
Tier: Montana Fly Company

Hook: #10 MFC 7022
Thread: Black 6/0 MFC
Body: Golden tan Antron Dubbing
Wing: Cow elk flank hair
Legs: Speckled yellow Centipede Legs
Hackle Post: White MFC Centipede Leg and white Chickabou feather
Rib: Tying thread
Tail: Cow elk flank hair

Swisher's PMX

Originator: Doug Swisher
Tier: Montana Fly Company

Hook: #10 MFC 7026
Thread: Dark brown 6/0 MFC
Body: Golden stone Gator Hair
Thorax: Peacock herl
Wing: Cow elk flank hair
Indicator: White Widow's Web
Legs: Brown Centipede Legs
Hackle: Grizzly neck
Tail: Cow elk flank hair

Berry's Wing Thing (Clark Fork)

Originator: Patrick Berry
Tier: Montana Fly Company

Hook: #12 MFC 7026
Thread: Red 6/0 MFC
Overbody: Gray foam (2mm)
Body: Raspberry Widow's Web
Egg Sac: Peacock herl
Head: Brown foam (2mm)
Indicator: Yellow foam (2mm)
Legs: White Centipede Legs
Tail: White Centipede Legs

Berry's Wing Thing

Originator: Patrick Berry
Tier: Montana Fly Company

Hook: #12 MFC 7026
Thread: Dark brown 6/0 MFC
Body: Peacock herl
Overbody: Brown foam (2mm)
Head: Brown foam (2mm)
Indicator: Yellow foam (2mm)
Legs: Pearl and black barred Sili Legs
Tail: Pearl and black barred Sili Legs

Swisher's Foam PMX (Tan)

Originator: Doug Swisher
Tier: Montana Fly Company

Hook: #10 MFC 7026
Thread: Dark brown 6/0 MFC
Body: Tan foam (3mm)
Thorax: Peacock herl
Underwing: Pearl MFC Crystal Flash
Wing: Cow elk flank hair
Indicator: White Widow's Web
Legs: Tan/tan LSS 20mm Legs
Hackle: Grizzly neck dyed tan
Note: *Body cut with Tapered Chernobyl cutter.*

Swisher's Madam X

Originator: Doug Swisher
Tier: Montana Fly Company

Hook: #8 MFC 7022
Thread: Yellow 6/0 MFC
Underbody: Cow elk flank hair
Overbody: Tying thread
Head: Cow elk flank hair
Wing: Cow elk flank hair
Legs: White Centipede Legs
Tail: Cow elk flank hair

Perry's Nightmare

Originator: John Perry
Tier: Montana Fly Company

Hook: #8 MFC 7027
Thread: Black 6/0 MFC
Body: Black foam (3mm)
Thorax: Peacock herl
Head: Black foam (3mm)
Overwing: Pearl MFC Crystal Flash
Wing: Purple Supreme Hair
Indicator: Orange foam (2mm)
Legs: Brown Centipede Legs

Terminator

Originator: Richard Pilatzke
Tier: Richard Pilatzke

Hook: #6 Dai-Riki 730
Thread: Black 6/0 Uni-Thread
Underbody: Black marabou under palmered brown saddle
Body: Black over orange craft foam (2mm)
Wing: Black marabou over pearl Krystal Flash
Indicator: Yellow craft foam (2mm)
Legs: Red and black MFC barred rubber legs
Rib: Copper Ultra Wire (x-small)
Tail: Black marabou
Adhesive: Krazy Glue

Madonna's Bloomers

Originator: Richard Pilatzke
Tier: Richard Pilatzke

Hook: #10 Dai-Riki 730
Thread: Hot orange 6/0 Uni-Thread
Underbody: Yellow craft foam (2mm)
Overbody: Orange craft foam (2mm)
Indicator: Yellow craft foam (2mm)
Legs: Orange Rainy's round rubber
Tail: Light tan marabou

McGinty Bee

Originator: Charles McGinty
Tier: Tom Logan

Hook: #10-14 Daiichi 1550
Thread: Black 6/0 Danville's or 8/0 Gudebrod
Body: Bright yellow Antron Steelhead Dubbing
Wing: Paired slips of drake mallard secondary feather tips
Hackle: Red or coachman brown Indian rooster neck
Tail: Red hackle fibers
Rib: Two strands black Danville's flat rayon floss

Deer Hair Bumble Bee

Originator: Tim Jacobs
Tier: Tim Jacobs

Hook: #10 Tiemco 100
Thread: Black 140-denier UTC; white UTC GSP 100
Body: White, black, and yellow deer hair
Head: Black ostrich herl
Wing: Medium dun RRC Speckled River Wing
Legs: Black Spirit River Flex Floss
Adhesive: Zap-A-Gap

Bea's Bumble Bee

Originator: Tim Mack
Tier: Tim Mack

Hook: #8 Mustad R50 or 94840
Thread: Black 6/0 Uni-Thread
Body: Black and yellow Wapsi chenille (medium)
Head: Tying thread
Wing: Black Whiting Farms hen feathers
Hackle: Grizzly dyed yellow Whiting Farms saddle
Tail: Wapsi black goose or turkey biots

Hot Glue Bee

Originator: Katsuhito Saito
Tier: Katsuhito Saito

Hook: #12-16 Tiemco 5210
Thread: Black 6/0 Uni-Thread
Body: Green and black hot glue
Thorax: Yellow and black Fine Dry Fly Dubbing
Post: Pink Tiemco Aero Dry Wing
Hackle: Brown Whiting dry fly hackle

Hot Glue Bee (Yellow)

Originator: Katsuhito Saito
Tier: Katsuhito Saito

Hook: #12-16 Tiemco 5210
Thread: Black 6/0 Uni-Thread
Body: Yellow and black hot glue
Thorax: Yellow and black Fine Dry Fly Dubbing
Post: Pink Tiemco Aero Dry Wing
Hackle: Brown Whiting dry fly hackle

Watana Bee

Originator: Norimasa Watanabe
Tier: Norimasa Watanabe

Hook: #14 Tiemco 2488
Thread: Rusty brown 8/0 Uni-Thread
Body: Pale yellow Super Fine Dubbing
Thorax: Rust Nature's Spirit Emergence Dubbing
Wing: Tan EP Fibers
Eyes: Rainbow black 11/0 glass beads
Rib: Peacock herl
Note: *Twisted body with C&F Extended Body Twister.*

Parachute Foam Bee

Originator: Unknown
Tier: Montana Fly Company

Hook: #10 MFC 7009
Thread: Black 6/0 MFC
Body: Yellow and black MFC Tube Foam (2mm)
Head: Black peacock MFC Phoenix Dubbing
Hackle: Black hackle
Wing: Golden stone Widow's Web
Indicator: White MFC Tube Foam (2mm)

Rydeburg's Humpbee

Originator: Travis Rydeburg
Tier: Montana Fly Company

Hook: #12 MFC 7000
Thread: Black 6/0 MFC
Body: Yellow and black Gator Hair
Wing: White calf tail
Hackle: Brown hackle
Tail/Back: Elk hair

Silverman's Sparkle Bee

Originator: Joel Silverman
Tier: Montana Fly Company

Hook: #12 MFC 7000
Thread: Black 6/0 MFC
Body: Black and yellow Wing N' Flash
Wing: Plain web MFC Etha Wing
Legs: Speckled yellow Centipede Legs
Post: Hot pink Gator Hair
Hackle: Black saddle

Jonny Bee Goode

Originator: Richard Pilatzke
Tier: Richard Pilatzke

Hook: #12 Dai-Riki 305
Thread: Black 6/0 Uni-Thread
Body: Bumble Bee Popper Foam Rainy's
Wing: Pearl metallic craft sheeting
Legs: Black nylon paintbrush bristles
Adhesive: Krazy Glue
Note: *Cut popper in half lengthwise glue to hook shank.*

Haddix's Hovering Wasp

Originator: Jason Haddix
Tier: Jason Haddix

Hook: #10-12 Daiichi X120
Thread: Black 6/0 Danville's
Body: Yellow and black SLF Prism Dubbing
Head: Tying thread coated with adhesive
Wing: Mottled brown Medallion Sheeting
Eyes: Deep Blue mono (50-pound-test)
Legs: Medium brown Whiting Farms dry fly hackle
Back: Clear Wapsi Scudback
Rib: RIO Mono (6X)
Antennae: Black Super Hair
Adhesive: Sally Hansen Hard As Nails
Marker: Black Copic permanent

CNEYE Wasp

Originator: Bubba Smith
Tier: Orvis

Hook: #8-10 Tiemco 100
Thread: Black 6/0 Uni-Thread
Body: Black foam (2mm)
Wing: Pearl Krystal Flash
Indicator: Orange foam (2mm)
Eyes: Doll eyes (4mm)
Legs: Brown/black round rubber (medium)

A&W (Arnie's Wasp)

Originator: Travis Betz
Tier: Travis Betz

Hook: #12 Tiemco 3761
Thread: Black 8/0 MFC; yellow 8/0 Uni-Thread
Body: Goldenrod Darice Foamies Craft Foam (2mm)
Thorax: Black tying thread
Head: Yellow tying thread
Wing: Cereal bag and wing burner
Eyes: Black Loon Outdoors Hard Head Fly Finish
Rib: Black tying thread
Legs: Black Whiting Farms dry fly hackle
Adhesive: Sally Hansen Diamond Strength Instant Nail Hardener

Hang-On Hornet

Originator: Jay Zimmerman
Tier: Jay Zimmerman

Hook: #12 Umpqua C300BL
Thread: Yellow 6/0 Uni-Thread
Body: Tying thread colored with black Sharpie
Thorax: Yellow Hare-Tron Dubbing
Head: Tying thread colored black
Wing: Two white CDC feathers
Hackle: Grizzly Whiting Farms dry fly hackle
Adhesive: Loon UV Knot Sense
Marker: Black Sharpie
Note: *Trim hackle on bottom.*

Hover Fly

Originator: Kenji Kita
Tier: Kenji Kita

Hook: #14-16 Tiemco 2302
Thread: Brown 8/0 Uni-Thread
Body: Yellow Danville's Floss
Thorax: Yellow Danville's Floss
Wing: Tan Darlon
Indicator: Pink Tiemco Aero Dry Wing
Hackle: Coachman brown Whiting Farms hackle
Rib: Brown EP Fiber

Foam Wasp

Originator: Dron Lee
Tier: Dron Lee

Hook: #8 Tiemco 2312
Thread: Black 140-denier UTC
Body: Yellow foam (2mm) Wapsi
Thorax/Neck: Black ostrich herl
Head: Yellow Wapsi foam (2mm)
Wing: Clear Vinyl Raffia
Eyes: Black Loon Hard Head
Legs: Brown barred Wapsi Sili legs
Rib: Tying thread
Antennae: Pheasant tail fibers
Marker: Black permanent

Splayed Yellow Jacket

Originator: Rod Garren
Tier: Rod Garren

Hook: #8-12 Gamakatsu C12U
Thread: Black 70-denier UTC
Body: Yellow foam (2mm)
Thorax: Peacock black Ice Dub
Wing: Black dyed elk hair
Eyes: Black marker
Legs: Yellow and black Crazy Legs
Adhesive: Head cement
Marker: Black Prismacolor

Sting

Originator: Skip Morris
Tier: Skip Morris

Hook: #10-14 Daiichi 1260
Thread: Black 8/0 Uni-Thread
Body: Mustard dry fly dubbing
Head: Black dry fly dubbing
Wing: Brown bucktail, divided
Legs: Chartreuse round rubber
Antennae: Olive MFC Tentacles

Hub's Hornet (Yellow)

Originator: Jerry Hubka
Tier: Jerry Hubka

Hook: #10 Gamakatsu C12U
Thread: Black 140-denier UTC
Underbody: Black Tying thread
Abdomen: Black Tying thread and .5mm yellow Fly Foam Spirit River
Waist: Tying thread
Thorax: Yellow UV Chewee Skin D's Flies and black .5mm Fly Foam Spirit River
Head: Tying thread
Wing: UV Pearl Krystal Flash
Overwing: Black .5mm Fly Foam Spirit River
Legs: Speckled yellow MFC Centipede Legs (medium) and black Sharpie
Antennae: Gold Krystal Flash and black Sharpie
Adhesive: Zap-A-Gap Brush On and CCG Hydro
Marker: Black Sharpie
Note: *Coat abdomen and waist with CCG Hydro.*

Hub's Hornet (Black)

Originator: Jerry Hubka
Tier: Jerry Hubka

Hook: #10 Gamakatsu C12U
Thread: Black 140-denier UTC
Underbody: Tying thread
Abdomen: Tying thread and black UV Chewee Skin
Waist: Tying thread
Thorax: Black UV Chewee Skin and black Spirit River Fly Foam (.5mm)
Head: Tying thread
Wing: UV pearl Krystal Flash
Overwing: Black Spirit River Fly Foam (.5mm)
Legs: Speckled yellow Centipede Legs (medium)
Antennae: Gold Krystal Flash
Adhesive: Zap-A-Gap (Brush On) and CCG Hydro
Marker: Black Sharpie
Note: *Coat abdomen and waist with CCG Hydro.*

Feighny's Wasp

Originator: Mike Feighny
Tier: Mike Feighny

Hook: #14-16 Dai-Riki 270
Thread: Black 8/0 Uni-Thread
Underbody: Yellow Super Fine Dubbing
Wing: Cellophane bag with ridges created by serrated hemostat
Markings: Black Sharpie
Legs: Rusty brown 140-denier thread
Antennae: Rusty brown 140-denier thread
Eyes: CCG Thin
Note: *Coat body, legs, and antennae with CCG Thin.*

Caterpillar Patterns

Mihulka's Cut Bank Caterpillar

Originator: Chris Mihulka
Tier: Rainy's Flies

Hook: #8 Mustad 37160
Thread: Chartreuse 6/0 Uni-Thread
Body: Fluorescent red and chartreuse Ultra Chenille
Back: Fluorescent red Ultra Chenille
Legs: Chartreuse Ultra Chenille
Antennae: Chartreuse Ultra Chenille

Johnston's Cottonwood Caterpillar

Originator: Ray Johnston
Tier: Ray Johnston

Hook: #6 Tiemco 200R
Thread: Black 6/0 Uni-Thread
Body: Black Micro Chenille
Hackle: Tan Whiting Farms dry fly

Mothra's Larva

Originator: LeVern "Vern-O" Burm
Tier: LeVern "Vern-O" Burm

Hook: #4 Daiichi 1730
Thread: Black 6/0 Danville's
Body: Peacock Hareline Ice Dub
Back: Northern lights Loco Foam
Rib: Blue 20-pound-test mono
Antennae: Black goose biots
Note: *Cut foam with a RRC tapered Chernobyl cutter (large).*

Fall Woolly Bear

Originator: Ron Donahue
Tier: Ron Donahue

Hook: #6-8 Tiemco 300
Thread: Black 70-denier UTC
Body: Black and rust Spirit River Sparkle Chenille

Ken's Foam Caterpillar

Originator: Ken Walrath
Tier: Ken Walrath

Hook: #10 Tiemco 200R
Thread: Olive 8/0 Uni-Thread
Body: Green Mainstay Shelf Liner
Legs: Light dun Whiting Farms dry fly hackle
Adhesive: Super Glue

Moja Moja

Originator: Yukihiro Mino
Tier: Yukihiro Mino

Hook: #8-16 Daiichi 1180
Thread: Tan 6/0 Uni-Thread
Body: Peacock herl
Indicator: Pink Tiemco Aero Dry Wing
Hackle: Grizzly Whiting Farms dry fly

Dancing Worm

Originator: Yoshihiro Urushihara
Tier: Yoshihiro Urushihara

Hook: #6-12 Tiemco 2457
Thread: Green and black 8/0 Uni-Thread
Body: Yellow sheet foam (1mm) covered with yellow seal fur dubbing and yellow Ice Dub
Head: Dark brown seal fur dubbing
Rib: Green tying thread
Adhesive: TMC Soft Cement

Mino Kemushi (Brown)

Originator: Yukihiro Mino
Tier: Yukihiro Mino

Hook: #4-6 Daiichi 1270
Thread: Tan 6/0 Uni-Thread
Body: Orange Salmo Web
Rib: Peacock herl and brown Whiting Farms saddle hackle
Antenna/Tail: Tan CDC feathers

CDC Caterpillar

Originator: Ryo Shimazaki
Tier: Ryo Shimazaki

Hook: #13 Tiemco 102Y
Thread: Butter yellow TMC monofilament thread
Underbody: Tan sponge twisted
Overbody: White CDC feather
Head: Brown CDC feather
Adhesive: TMC Multi Glue

Mark's Spider

Originator: Mark McMillian
Tier: Mark Tracy

Hook: #14 Tiemco 2457
Thread: Brown 140-denier UTC
Underbody: Rust/brown Ice Dub
Body: Brown foam (2mm) cut with RRC Caddis wing cutter (small)
Legs: Brown rubber (medium and fine)

Sparky's Secret (Brown)

Originator: Russell Anderson
Tier: Russell Anderson

Hook: #8-12 Tiemco 100
Thread: Reddish brown 6/0 Uni-Thread
Body: Polystyrene ball inside black pantyhose
Thorax: Brown rabbit dubbing under dark brown or black turkey
Legs: Brown/orange flake Hareline Crazy Legs
Tail: Pearl Flashabou
Indicator: Orange foam cylinder ($\frac{1}{16}$")

Russell's Ripper

Originator: Russell Anderson
Tier: Russell Anderson

Hook: #8-12 Tiemco 100
Thread: Gray 6/0 Uni-Thread
Body: Polystyrene ball inside gray pantyhose
Thorax: Brown rabbit dubbing under deer hair
Head: Tying thread
Legs: Black round rubber legs (fine)

Hub's Silver Spider

Originator: Jerry Hubka
Tier: Jerry Hubka

Hook: #8-10 Tiemco 2312
Thread: Black 140-denier UTC
Underbody: Black craft foam (2mm)
Overbody: Northern lights Wapsi Loco Foam (2mm)
Flash: Black Hareline Cactus Chenille (medium)
Indicator: Yellow chartreuse/ green tipped Hareline Crazy Legs
Legs: Chrome silver/black Wapsi Sili Legs
Adhesive: CCG Hydro and Zap-A-Gap (Brush On)
Note: *Foam shapes cut with RRC Tapered Chernobyl cutter (medium).*

KLH Itsy Bitsy Spider

Originator: Kenneth Held
Tier: Kenneth Held

Hook: #10 Dai-Riki 305
Thread: Brown 70-denier UTC
Body: White Wapsi Foam Bug Bodies (#12 Spider)
Legs: Pumpkin barred Wapsi Sili legs
Adhesive: Zap-A-Gap and CCG Hydro
Marker: Taupa, sand, and delta brown Chartpak
Note: *Color body with the lightest color marker then mottle. Coat the body with CCG Hydro.*

PART II

Fishing Terrestrials: Tips from the Masters

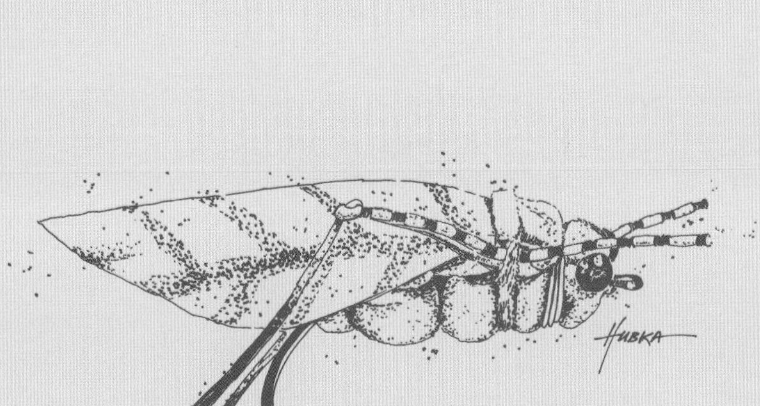

Leaf Hopper

Fishing Terrestrial Fly Patterns

Tak's Olive Ninja Hopper

DENNIS COLLIER

On Colorado's Tarryall River, adjacent hay meadows provide an abundance of terrestrial insects to the delight of large resident trout. DENNIS COLLIER

OVER THE YEARS, much of my fly-fishing guide experience has occurred in the granite amphitheatres of ancient glacial moraines in Colorado's Rocky Mountain National Park. It was here, while coaching anglers on the upper Big Thompson and Fall Rivers during the summer, that I came to fully appreciate the role terrestrial insects play in the diets and survival of the wild resident trout.

At 8,000 feet elevation, and given the substrate characteristics of these freestone watersheds, aquatic insect hatches are sparse. With the receding winter snowpack, ants and beetles make their spring debut and become a frequent menu selection for these fish. During the summer, deep meadow grasses will offer up a banquet of grasshoppers as well. The unfortunate insect that falls in the water next to an undercut bank becomes food in short order.

One of my greatest fly-fishing pleasures is quietly stalking bank-hugging trout in serpentine streams with a good beetle, hopper, or ant pattern. For me, these mountain meadow

At right: Following this Colorado elk herd, an angler takes advantage of the feeding frenzy created by grasshoppers being flushed into the river by the grazing animals. DENNIS COLLIER

Below: This gorgeous Rocky Mountain National Park brook trout found a Charlie Boy Hopper too hard to resist. DENNIS COLLIER

streams provide a magnificent classroom setting for observing angler success and failure, as well as providing for my own fishing enjoyment. With the angling pressure on the more well-known streams, it doesn't take long for the fish to become scared and refuse to eat, or head for cover with the first heavy footstep.

I've found that you can increase your success ratio considerably by quietly slipping down into the stream channel and making fairly long casts upstream to the bank. The high profile of a fisherman walking upright along the bank is guaranteed to start the domino effect of one spooked fish rushing upstream and spooking those ahead of it. Exercising good curve casts around corners where the only thing a fish will see is your fly is another effective technique. As an aside, if you can see waves moving upstream ahead of you, you're wading too fast, so slow down to a snail's pace; otherwise the fish will feel these changes in water pressure along their lateral lines and react accordingly.

Another lesson I learned the hard way is to alternate cast the fly between the obvious deeper runs next to one bank and the shallow areas along the opposite bank. On more occasions than I care to admit, I've spooked some very big fish out from the shallow side in water no more than a few inches deep after I fished out the deeper side and started wading up to the next run.

To many anglers, the only signal to fish a terrestrial pattern is when the hoppers start kicking up ahead of them as they brush the grasses on the way to the river. In my own observations, much of the terrestrial season has been underway long before that happens. Even though I rarely see beetles and ants in any numbers around the water—unless there happens to be a flying ant hatch in progress—nature has programmed the fish to be on the lookout for these high protein morsels and to add them to the daily diet when they come floating by. Consequently, fishing a beetle or ant pattern is a given unless I see specific aquatic insects hatching, and even then odds are the terrestrial will still attract more than its fair share of fish.

In the Rockies, wind is an almost constant factor while fishing. Consequently, I prefer 7-foot 5-inch Umpqua Power Taper leaders tapered to 3X. To this, I'll attach a couple feet of 4X fluorocarbon tippet material. Weight-forward leaders help turn the fly over in even a stiff breeze and facilitate an accurate presentation. When the fish decide they want your terrestrial imitation they generally are not too leader shy and not much stops them from closing the deal. The heavier tippet also discourages breaking off the fly when tugging it off bankside grasses—which you're going to do often if fishing the fly where it should be—tight to the bank. I also tie all my terrestrial patterns on stout, 2X heavy wire hooks, which discourages bend outs from the occasional large brown that was lurking under a deep undercut bank just waiting for dinner to drop in.

On the high-plains lakes and ranch ponds of Colorado and Wyoming, I often use the daily winds as a resource rather than an aggravating hindrance. Flotsam, in the form of hatch remnants, and terrestrials that were blown into the water during the course of the day will stack up in the shallows on the lake's leeward side. Walking the shoreline in the quiet, low-light-level of early dawn, you'll see tails and dorsal fins knifing the surface as the fishcruise around in the bug soup. Some of the best fishing of the day can be had by the angler willing to shed his or her sleeping bag an hour or two earlier than usual, and gently casting a terrestrial pattern on an intercept path with these spotted submarines.

Up close and personal: a wild Rocky Mountain National Park brown trout and the DC's Needle Hopper it mistook for lunch. DENNIS COLLIER

One of my signature fly patterns is the Snoball Beetle, and a number of fellow fly fishermen have reported fishing this creation with great success on many of our most demanding and hard-fished western waters. I have personally fished the Snoball Beetle on Colorado's Fryingpan River during a heavy *Baetis* hatch and caught numerous fish along the banks after my best *Baetis* patterns had been snubbed by the Pan's college-educated trout. This fly has exercised many fish—from the freestone streams of the Canadian Rockies to the San Juan River in New Mexico—and countless other angling venues in between.

My next "go-to" terrestrial fly pattern is the Fall River Flying Ant. The Fall River in Rocky Mountain National Park's Horseshoe Park is filled with wild brown trout that are extremely shy—however they seldom refuse a good parachute ant when presented with stealth. I frequently tie on this same ant pattern when fishing many of our smaller tailwater venues, and even when an aquatic insect hatch is coming off the water, there is just something about an ant floating by that seems irresistible to the opportunistically feeding fish.

If you're a fan of the "hopper-dropper" approach to nymph fishing, I would suggest going large with the hopper indicator. My DC's 1870 Needle Hopper in sizes 4 and 6, is a good choice (but, I'm biased) and the drop bend of the Daiichi 1870 hook is tailor made for attaching the leader for the dropper flies. I usually reserve this approach to larger rivers or float fishing from a drift boat, where visibility for the indicator fly becomes a consideration.

At right: Big and beautiful British Columbia west slope cutthroat that rose to a rubber-legged Stimulator. DENNIS COLLIER

Below: Ants and beetles are favorite fare for stillwater fish, as demonstrated by Tom Druggish on Colorado's Silver Valley Lake. DENNIS COLLIER

Hunting Trout

TIM JACOBS

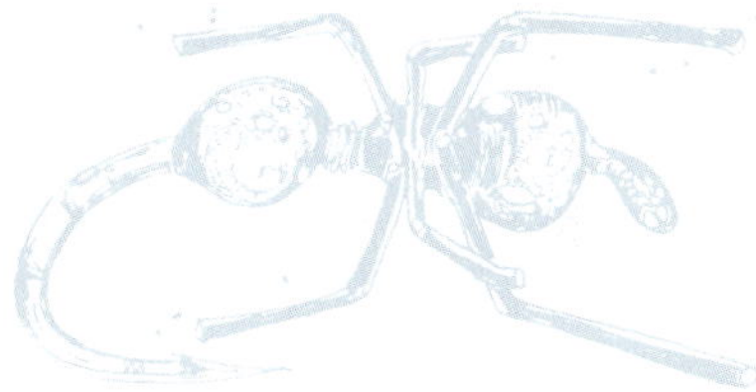

Tak's Bead CCG Ant

MODERN TERRESTRIAL FISHING was effectively born when Vince Marinaro lay down along the banks of the Letort during the 1940s and began to observe the minute insects, including small terrestrials, which were a major food source for those selective trout. Marinaro, along with a cohort of anglers including the likes of Ed Koch, Charlie Fox, and Ernest Schwiebert, began to develop the flies and promote the notion of fishing with something other than the standard dry flies of the day.

Now summer terrestrial fishing is one of the highlights of the trout season. On breezy afternoons when aquatic hatches are sparse, trout will move into the shallows, along the edges of the river, in anticipation of terrestrial insects arriving on the water. Sometimes trout can be very close to the bank, and these fish are easily spooked back into the deeper water at the center of the river. Anglers must wade slowly and cautiously—and spend more time watching than casting.

Early morning on the Yampa River in Colorado. Jerry Hubka lands another fine rainbow caught with an ant pattern drifted close to the grassy river bank. BRIAN YAMAUCHI

If a fish is very shallow, they will normally take an ant or beetle. If you are not seeing any trout along the edges, then use a larger search pattern such as cricket or hopper pattern. Fishing a fairly wooded river such as the Au Sable in Michigan or the Fryingpan in Colorado, use a cricket pattern. If the river has more open banks with grassy open fields next to it, such as the lower Roaring Fork River in Colorado or the Madison River below Quake Lake in Montana, then use a hopper.

In western rivers work upstream, wading near the bank. Make your first cast very close to the edge of the river, and with successive casts work out to the deeper water. If a fish shows to the larger fly, but doesn't eat, then stop, switch to a smaller ant or beetle, and cast to the same spot. Most times the fish will take the smaller pattern without hesitation. Look for current edges, the best of which is where a riffle enters a run. Normally there is a V-shaped section of water right next to the bank just as the run starts. Begin back from that section and work you way into the quiet water along the bank. This is a perfect place for trout, because they have the deeper water of the run to escape into, and the shallow water with less current along the bank to move into to feed. Even if you do not see fish rising or holding in these areas they are normally there and waiting for an opportunity to feed.

I often fish the Au Sable in Michigan during the summer. I will work quietly, moving downstream, casting to the shadows back in the cedar sweepers. Even during the middle of the day, the fish hiding in these shadowed places will respond to a well-cast ant or beetle. While catching mostly smaller brook trout, you will occasionally encounter the larger brown trout that can be a challenge to work out of the wooded cover and out into the river. While the main focus is on edges of the river make the occasional cast to the runs and riffles in the center of the river. Sometimes fish will respond, especially if you are fishing a larger fly.

Don't overlook the unlikely places. Searching along the edges, there will be the deeper cuts along the bank. Sometimes the pocket needs to only be slightly deeper that the surrounding water to hold fish. Look for places in areas that don't get fished by other anglers. One summer in Yellowstone Park I was fishing the Buffalo Ford section of the Yellowstone River. Most of the anglers were out past the gravel flat, nymphing the deeper run. As I was went wading through the gravel flat I discovered that wherever there was a small depression in the gravel there would usually be a one or more Yellowstone Cutthroats. If unaware of my presence, they would readily rise to an ant pattern.

ANTING THE HATCH

In 1982, the late Ken Miyata wrote an article titled "Anting the Hatch." Anting the hatch has been a consistently successful strategy for me over the last three decades. For whatever reasons trout love ants and will normally take them with no hesitation. During hatches of aquatic insects I will always begin by trying to match the hatching insect first; however if I get no interest or short rises, I will quickly try an ant pattern. Trout seem almost always willing to eat an ant even during heavy hatches.

Following hatches, search for eddies along the sides of the river. The Green River in Utah has some huge eddies that collect any insects that have been on the water. Trout will often feed on the smorgasbord of insects floating amid the debris and foam. While trout will rise to an aquatic pattern of the hatch of the day, they seem to especially relish an ant or beetle pattern. I've seen trout move a considerable distance to take an

Jim Browning releases another beautiful rainbow after it succumbed to his hopper pattern. JIM BROWNING

Hitting the Banks. Rick Takahashi fishes the banks as he works his way upstream. JERRY HUBKA

ant when they discover it floating amid the many other insects. Don't overlook small eddies, which often have one or two trout in them.

SHADOWS AND SUN

Finally, be predatory in your fishing. Spend less time casting and more time observing. Pay particular attention to shadowy places along the bank of the river. Trout are nearly impossible to see in these areas, but if you resist casting and observe, they will often reveal themselves with a sipping rise or a tail or caudal fin appearing on the surface. Once you've located a fish, then make a cast. If the fish is unaware of your presence, they will almost always rise to your offering.

Shadows are also good places for an angler to stand to observe the river. It is much harder for trout to be aware of your presence if you are not in the sun. I also find it easer to see the river and trout from a shadowed place.

When looking for fish in a sunlit run, it's not unusual to first see the shadow the fish casts on the bottom of the river rather than the fish itself. Once I have observed and discovered trout, then I can begin to plan my approach so as not to spook the fish.

Feeding Grounds

Rick Takahashi

Tak's Hot Head Beetle

AS SPRING GIVES way to the warmer days of summer and the rivers swollen by runoff start to recede, I begin looking for signs of terrestrials. As I walk to the stream through the fields and hay meadows, I keep a sharp eye out for signs of hopper activity; even the smallest immature hoppers catch my attention. Hoppers are the majorettes in the parade of terrestrial insects that bring promise to a season of fishing opportunities.

Because terrestrials often inhabit areas adjacent to the water's edge, they often find themselves in the water for any number of reasons: wind, miscalculated flight, falling, and being pushed in. With this in mind, fly fishers should concentrate their presentations along the bank, which can provide excellent ambush points for fish, and then work their flies farther away.

Banks. The very edge of a stream or lake is a prime area for holding fish. It is not uncommon to find fish nestled tight to the bank looking for something to eat even if the water appears to be too shallow. If you are approaching a likely spot from

Rick Takahashi prepares to land a trout that was taken on his Simple Cicada pattern in the Big Thompson Canyon, Colorado.
JERRY HUBKA

Drifting a cicada pattern near the bank evokes a splashy rise from an eager trout. Casting a terrestrial pattern so that it slaps down hard on the water's surface can be very effective. The "splat" alerts trout to a meal that has fallen into the water, and the fish will often investigate. JERRY HUBKA

land, stand back from the bank for several feet, crouch down, and gently dap your pattern next to the bank. I often get on my knees to reduce my profile. If fishing tight to the bank from in the river, I'll first try to fish the fly as close to the bank as possible, letting the flies drift into likely holding spots. Fishing close to the bank first ensures that you are getting your flies into a possible feeding lane of the trout. I'll often cast within one or two inches of the bank on the first series of drifts. To reduce my presence in the water, I try to look for and stand in depressions in the streambed.

Undercut banks. Erosion forms depressions in the bank, which provide trout cover from ever-vigilant predators from above. The trout holding in these undercut sections of the river can dart out and snatch any food drifting by. At times larger mature trout hunker down in these undercuts until dusk when they come out to feed.

Overhanging brush or trees. Like undercut banks, brush and trees that have their branches reaching out over the water's edge can also provide a haven the meets the trout need for safety, rest, and food. All sorts of creatures climb around in the bushes and tree branches, and a little breeze or strong gust of wind or a miscalculation on the part of the insect can

Rick Takahashi beams at this large rainbow caught on a blue subsurface beetle pattern. JERRY HUBKA

Surface Strategies

RICK TAKAHASHI

Hub's Peñasco Horse Hopper

Coming in for a landing. Phil Iwane prepares to land a large rainbow trout that has fallen for one of his small floating black ant patterns in the middle section of Eleven Mile Canyon, Colorado. DAVID IWANE

IN FLY FISHING, one of the greatest thrills is seeing a trout take a terrestrial fly off the water's surface. To become an accomplished dry-fly angler, you need to learn to match the insects that the fish are feeding on, slowly get into position, and master the casting skills necessary for a good presentation. Being able to present your fly so that it drifts naturally (dead-drift) is important, but so too is learning to twitch, flutter, and skate your flies, if necessary, to match the movements of the natural you are trying to imitate. These challenges are what make fly fishing fun and rewarding. The topic of dry-fly fishing is so broad, I can't possibly cover everything here; instead, I will focus on covering the major approaches and rigs that I like to use on the water.

PRESENTATION ANGLES

My favorite approach when fishing floating terrestrials is **upstream** or **quartering upstream**. I feel that this angle tends to lessen the chance of the fish hearing or seeing you, and it is easier to eliminate drag caused by casting across many different currents. If I don't spot rising fish, my first casts will be to the bank. I'll allow the fly to drift a short distance, maybe 5 to 10 feet, before using a roll-cast pickup to initiate another cast. My next cast will be a short distance to the side of or slightly ahead of the previous cast.

I work my way across stream until I reach a seam where the shallow water butts up against faster and deeper water. I make a few casts on the side of the seam into the deeper water just in case fish are holding at the seam and will chase the fly in deeper water. If I do not catch any fish, I take one step upstream and repeat the process.

A few pointers: Though a straight cast upstream puts the leader over the fish before the fly, this is rarely a problem for me. I have caught more trout this way than with any other dry-fly fishing method. However, on certain fish a curve cast helps place the fly line off to the side of a fish. Also, when you are casting to rising fish, remember to cast upstream of the rise-form. In moving water, remember that the raise form is traveling at the same speed as the current you are casting to. Remember to compensate for that rise form and cast your fly above where you saw the fish rise—often several feet above a rising fish.

When fishing directly **across stream,** I make my first cast directly in front of where I'm standing and allow the fly to drift drag-free downstream; I'll often extend the drift just in case there is a fish following the fly or perhaps waiting at the end of my drift. I'll keep working my casts just a little farther than the previous drift to ensure I've covered the water thoroughly. Depending on the currents and how the fish are feeding, you can cast a straight line for a short drift, or you can make a reach cast or on-the-water mend to get a longer drag-

Rick Takahashi holds a nice rainbow that fell to one of his hopper patterns. JERRY HUBKA

free drift. At the end of the drift I'll often add a little movement to mimic the struggle to swim back to firm ground. I will often fish the flies quartering downstream using a reach cast to keep the belly of the line upstream to decrease drag.

Across-stream and upstream presentations are common when fishing pocketwater, one of my favorite places to ply a large, buoyant terrestrial such as a Takahopper, Dave's Hopper, or Harder's Ant. I wade carefully into position and fish to both sides of me, often dapping the large dry into the still water behind boulders.

When you need to cast downstream to a feeding fish, the **across and downstream** cast excels. I use this when when

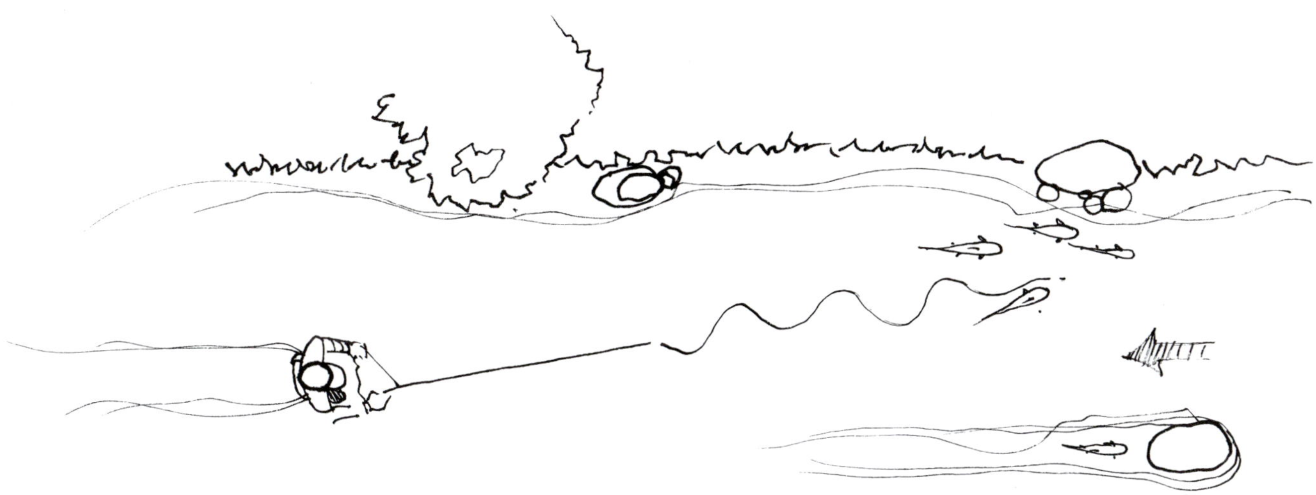

Casting upstream. With an upstream approach, I try to keep my casts in the 15- to 30-foot range with drifts no more than 5 to 10 feet. I do not make more than two or three casts in the same area and only do so if I think fish are holding in that area. Remember, you do not have to see rising fish to fish a dry. Trout are opportunistic and looking up in shallow water. Fish are in shallow water to do only one thing—eat. RICK TAKAHASHI

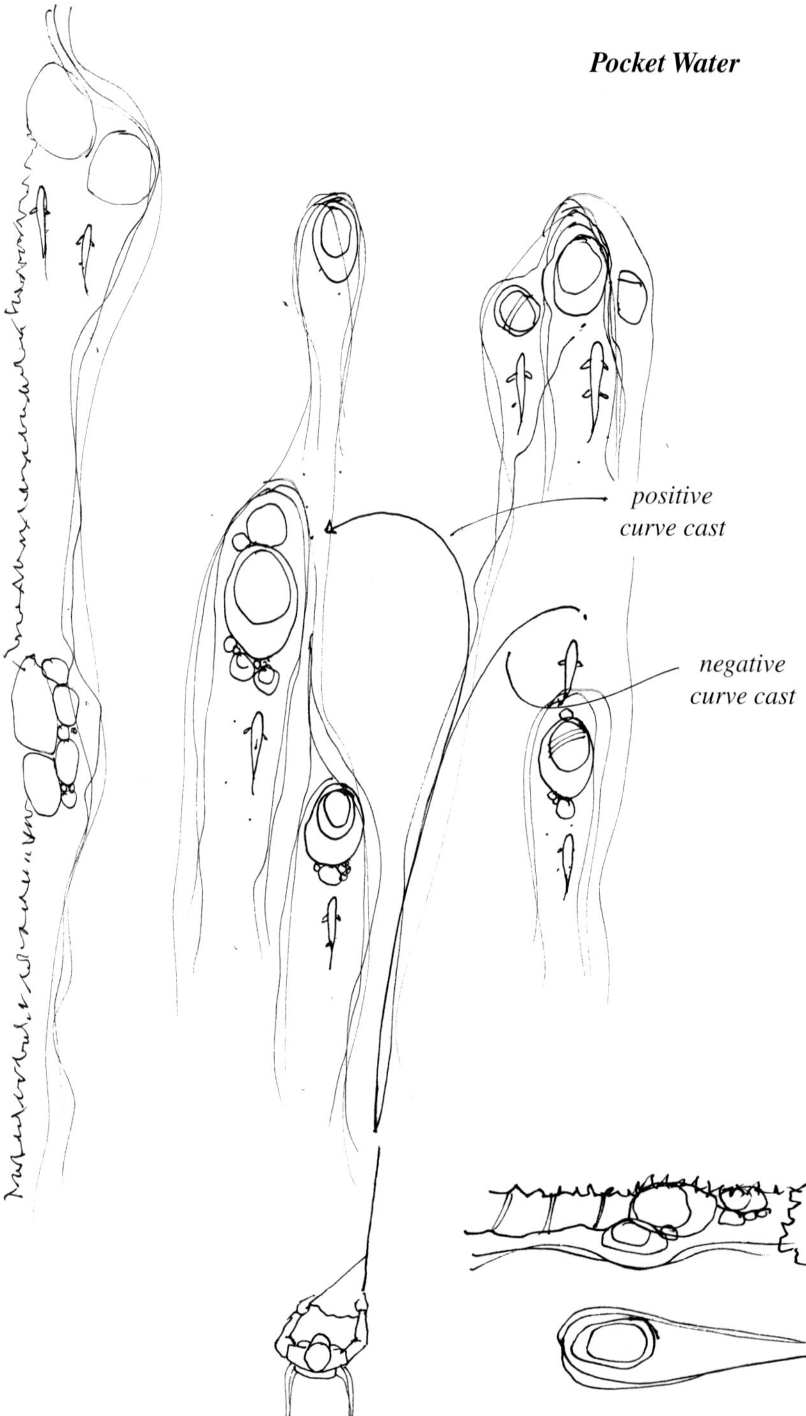

To make a ***positive curve cast****, cant your casting plane at a 45-degree angle to the right of the casting stroke. Slightly overpower the forward cast and stop the rod tip above the horizon. This allows the power of the forward cast to continue and abruptly stop, causing the line to turn over to the left. Lower the rod tip once you have completed the forward cast. The* ***negative curve cast*** *is created by two types of cast. Make your casting stroke on the left side of your body by crossing the rod tip over your left shoulder at a 45 degree plane to the left. Then slightly underpower the forward cast and stop your rod above the horizon to curve the line to the right. Lower the rod tip after the cast.* RICK TAKAHASHI

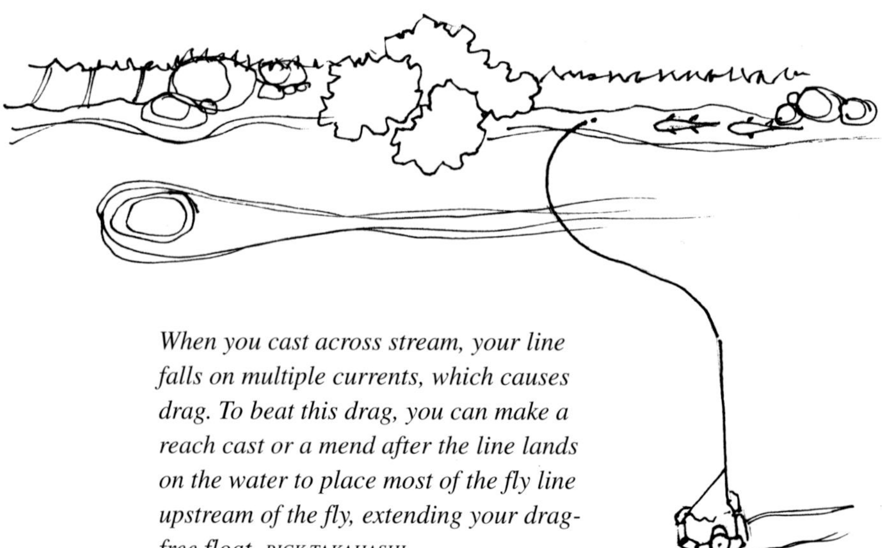

When you cast across stream, your line falls on multiple currents, which causes drag. To beat this drag, you can make a reach cast or a mend after the line lands on the water to place most of the fly line upstream of the fly, extending your drag-free float. RICK TAKAHASHI

presenting small dry flies to feeding fish. I try and make the cast as short as possible to control and see the fly. After the cast, mend your fly line upstream as needed to maintain a drag-free float.

When you are presented with a situation that will require you cast directly **downstream** from your position with a short cast. Make a straight line cast, but at the end of your casting stroke, stop the rod abruptly and drop the rod to create enough slack in the line on the water to allow the fly to drift to the fish unimpeded.

Whenever you approach a fish from upstream, it has a greater chance of detecting your presence. Stealth is always important to success but especially so here. You must be as quiet as you possibly can when moving through the water you plan to fish, as sound carries well in water and any noise you make will surely alert the fish to your presence. Wear neutral

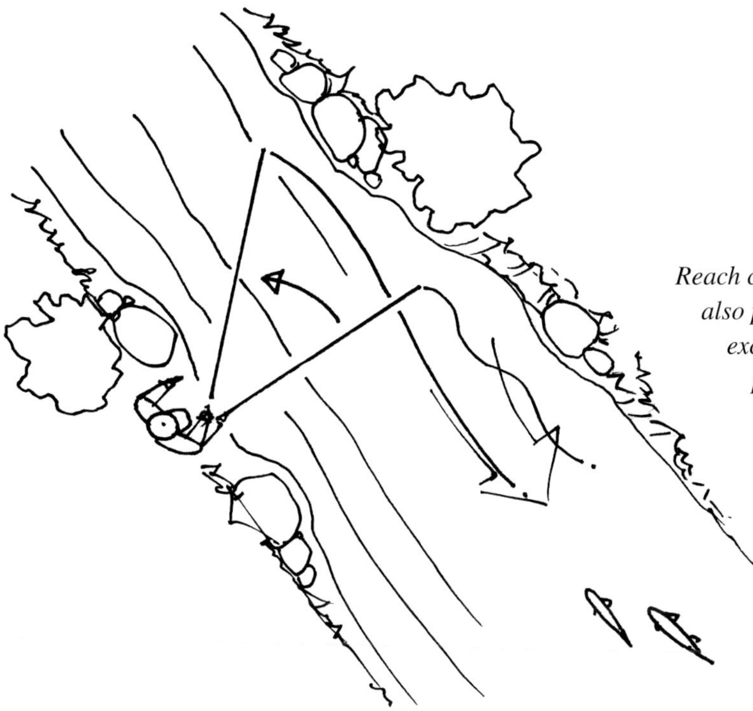

Reach casts help you get a longer drag-free drift and also present the fly first to the fish. They are an excellent option for across or across-and-down presentations. After you stop the rod on the forward cast, reach upstream to place as much fly line upstream of the fly as possible.

RICK TAKAHASHI

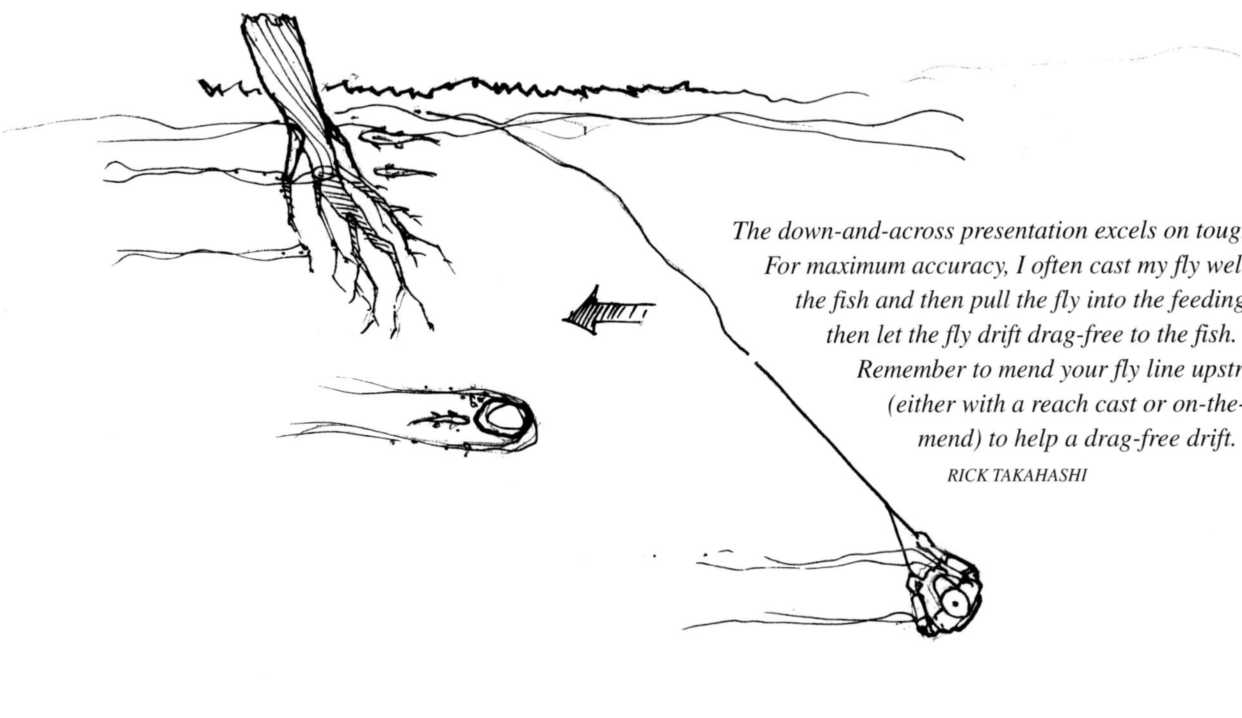

The down-and-across presentation excels on tough fish. For maximum accuracy, I often cast my fly well above the fish and then pull the fly into the feeding lane, then let the fly drift drag-free to the fish. Remember to mend your fly line upstream (either with a reach cast or on-the-water mend) to help a drag-free drift.

RICK TAKAHASHI

Waking Hoppers

Landon Mayer

When taking terrestrials, trout seem to have to have only two speeds—very slow or fast. When trout are quick on the move and feeding on the surface, my favorite presentation is "waking" the fly. I cast at a forty-five degree angle up- or downstream toward the other side of the river from where I am standing. With the rod tip stopping above the water's surface on the forward cast, I slowly elevate the rod tip to twelve o' clock as the fly swings toward the bank I am standing on. This angle causes the fly to wake without sinking.

For less-active trout, I like a still drift after the initial surprise, caused by slapping the imitation on the water and leaving a large moving ring around the fly. Once the fish sees the disturbance followed by a still delivery, it can feel comfortable knowing that the meal will not escape.

colors of clothing that will help you blend into the background, and keep as low a profile as you can when approaching fish.

KEEPING YOUR FLIES FLOATING

Most dry flies require some type of floatant to help them stay on the surface of the water. I recommend using some form of silicon, which repels water and keeps the fly floating for a short period. Most silicon products come in a variety of containers, all requiring rubbing the product onto your fingertips and then applying it to the fly. Once the fly has been has been used for a period of time, it will start to sink.

Dry the fly using amadou (tree fungus), C&F Ruby Cell Foam, or Wonder Cloth. Dip the fly in some form of a desiccant such as Shimizaki Dry Shake or Frog's Fanny. I use Shimizaki Dry Shake for all of my dry flies. The desiccant is applied by opening the top of the container then placing the fly into the container. Close the lid enough to not allow the desiccant to fall out but not tight enough to crimp the tippet. Shake the container to put a light coating of the substance onto the surface of the fly. The excess will come off when you cast the fly. Frog's Fanny has a brush applicator perfect for packing the powder into the crannies of large flies, such as Smith's Cartoon Hopper or Chernobyl-style patterns.

Rick Takahashi and good friend Dave Young capture a 20-inch rainbow on the Henry's Fork. Hoppers and other terrestrials can be excellent "hatch-breakers" and catch fish that are feeding on mayflies or midges. On a number of occasions, we've been able to deliver a hopper to a feeding fish as "dessert." JERRY HUBKA

Dry Dropper Tips

Jake Ruthven

Your rig is one of the most important aspects of your success, falling short only to presentation. Many anglers can't get their two-fly rig to turn over or get the flies to hit the water in a straight line. This may be due to poor casting, but sometimes it's the setup. To prevent this, I like to run standard nylon tippet to my dry fly and fluorocarbon tippet to the dropper. The extra weight of the fluorocarbon pulls the entire rig taut before it lands on the surface. This provides two major advantages. First, less time untangling your once-beautiful rig, and more time fishing. Second, when your rig turns over properly you have an accurate gauge against which to measure your presentations. If you know that your flies are landing in a straight line, you can make minor adjustments to offer up the perfect presentation.

While the extra weight of fluorocarbon helps turn over your rig and sinks your nymph or emerger, the monofilament nylon to the dry fly floats a lot better than fluorocarbon. Nylon tippet material weighs less and is slightly thinner in diameter than fluorocarbon, making it ideal for supporting a dry fly.

For fishing large terrestrials such as grasshoppers, I prefer a 7½-foot 3X nylon leader, which is heavy enough to brave the summer winds, yet light enough to produce a somewhat delicate presentation. When building leaders, I prefer more tippet and less leader. This setup puts wary trout more at ease. Start by clipping 12 inches off of your leader, and tie on 3 feet of 3X nylon tippet using either a triple surgeon's knot or blood knot. Cutting the leader back a foot essentially increases its diameter to the equivalent of 2X tippet, making for a more powerful turnover when transitioned into 3X. This will make casting easier and much more effective. Tie on your dry fly of choice using an improved clinch knot. Attach the dropper to the hook bend of your terrestrial with 2 to 3 feet of 4X or 5X fluorocarbon.

With terrestrials I have found that color is the deciding factor in a day's fishing. Trout, especially large ones, are opportunistic feeders. While size is important in its own way, correct color is what seems to "sell" the imitation time and time again. Try your best to match the color of the terrestrial you plan to imitate, and worry about size later. With your dropper, color and size are often important. When in doubt, go small.

Another tactic to consider is dropping a soft hackle below your terrestrial. Soft hackle patterns perfectly imitate emerging insects, and trout cannot pass them up. During the summer, I like to use Dunnigan's Soft Hackle PMD, as well as many of my own patterns. Soft hackle caddis are also highly effective and worth trying.

Catch and release. A beautiful rainbow is returned to the water to be caught another day.
JIM BROWNING

Fishing ants on the Firehole. RIO's John Harder fishes one of his favorite sections of the Firehole River in Yellowstone National Park. JERRY HUBKA

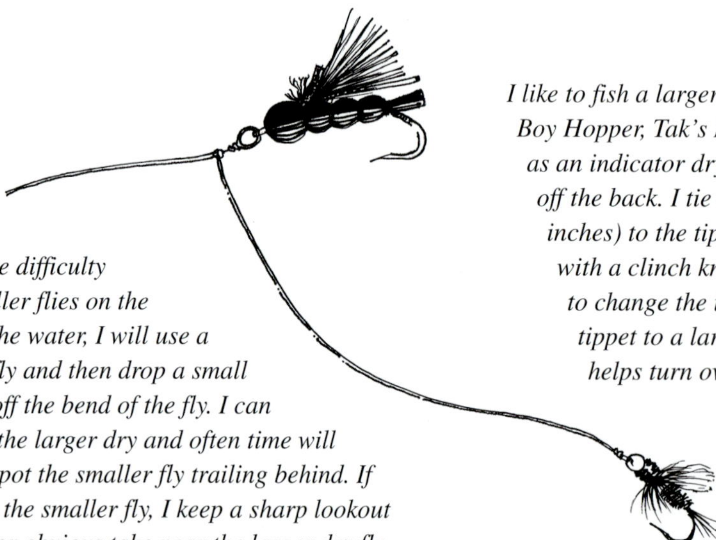

I like to fish a larger hopper pattern like a Dave's Hopper, Charlie Boy Hopper, Tak's Monster Hopper, or Peacock Madam X pattern as an indicator dry with a smaller dry or nymph or midge pattern off the back. I tie my dropper tippet (generally about 18 to 20 inches) to the tippet that is attached to the hopper/indicator with a clinch knot so I can slide the dropper tippet up if I want to change the indicator pattern. Running a larger diameter tippet to a large terrestrial prevents twisting in the air and helps turn over the larger pattern. RICK TAKAHASHI

When I have difficulty seeing smaller flies on the surface of the water, I will use a larger dry fly and then drop a small terrestrial off the bend of the fly. I can easily spot the larger dry and often time will be able to spot the smaller fly trailing behind. If I can't spot the smaller fly, I keep a sharp lookout for a swirl or obvious take near the larger dry fly. RICK TAKAHASHI

Dog Day Droppers

Duane Redford

On the South Platte, near Deckers, Colorado, the dog days of July and August have always been tough. High skies, burning sun, increased angling and recreational pressures, and intermittent hatches can give a guy fits.

Although this time of year we are seeing Pale Morning Duns, the beginning of the Trico invasion, and sporadic Blue Winged Oives coming off at various times of the day, the fishing becomes challenging because of spooky fish and sporadic hatches.

In come the terrestrials. As if on cue, they begin to show up in numbers, and the fish dial in on them. I have found that the best way to leverage the terrestrial invasion is to fish them in combination with the patterns that imitate the other bugs that are hatching. It's a match made in heaven.

Grasshoppers line the banks during the dog days and the fish seem to always be looking up for them. It's amazing to see a fish, often a big fish, come up to the top and yawn in a big hopper during the hottest, most pressured time of the day. And if that fish doesn't come up, it will often eat one of two droppers trailing the hopper. The dry-double-drop rig is my preferred rig on the South Platte from late June though October. I often have a #10-12 Craven's Charlie Boy tied to a 7½-foot, 5X monofilament leader. Then, off of the bend, I tie from 24 to 36 inches of 5X fluorocarbon tippet to a dropper fly. From the dropper I tie off of the eye of the hook another 12 inches of fluorocarbon to my point fly.

I like to run fluorocarbon for my droppers because it sinks faster than monofilament. A small weight directly between the dropper and the point fly finishes the rig off. This weight not only helps break the water's surface tension and aids sinking, but it also helps provide a touch of drag to the rig to clean up most inadequacies one may have with getting a drag-free drift.

The real beauty of this rig is the ability it gives you to fish three different bugs in three different columns. You can fish the terrestrial on top, a PMD emerger in the middle, and a Trico nymph down low, or any other combination. I tie my dropper or middle fly eye-to-eye from the hopper to the bottom or point fly because I want this fly to drift with a flat profile that mimics the emergent or pupae phase of the hatch. The fishes' location and how or what they're eating determines the length of the first dropper.

Most of the time, I will fish a Craven's Charlie Boy Hopper, Amy's Ant, or a Fat Albert on top as my terrestrial imitation, followed by a beadhead Pheasant Tail soft hackle, tied off to a gray or black RS2. With this rig, at the right depth, I'm covering a selection of hatching insects at various depths. A bonus to this rig is that the big floating insect up top acts as a valuable strike indicator. An additional bonus is that I can quickly snip off the droppers to cast a lone terrestrial to fish in tight spots under overhanging banks or vegetation.

Just one more photo before you go. Jim Browning prepares to return a beautifully colored rainbow to the water. JIM BROWNING

The Cycle of Submergence

ERIC ISHIWATA

Tak's Drowned Hopper

SOME DAYS IT simply does not matter. Like when you bushwhack into the high country. Or fish private water. Or it could just be a magical day at your local spot. When the stars align, you can throw almost any fly and it will get clobbered. There is no need to dig deep in the playbook when trout are feeding with reckless abandon.

However, during tougher times such as peak season on pressured waters, you must adjust your tactics. When faced with challenging conditions, conventional wisdom has been to lengthen and lighten leaders, downsize flies, or maybe mix things up with oddball colors such as pink hoppers and purple ants. Admittedly, these tactics often work in tough situations. However, it has always struck me as odd that even the most anemic of boxes are fully equipped with flies to cover aquatic insects throughout the entire water column, yet when it comes to terrestrials, selections are frequently limited to whatever floats best. Those anglers' logic is understandable—midges, mayflies, and caddis hatch so there is a clear need to cover

Dr. Eric Ishiwata, an innovative fly-pattern designer and an avid terrestrial fisherman, holds up a nice trout caught with a two-handed rod, which is well suited for large rivers. JERRY HUBKA

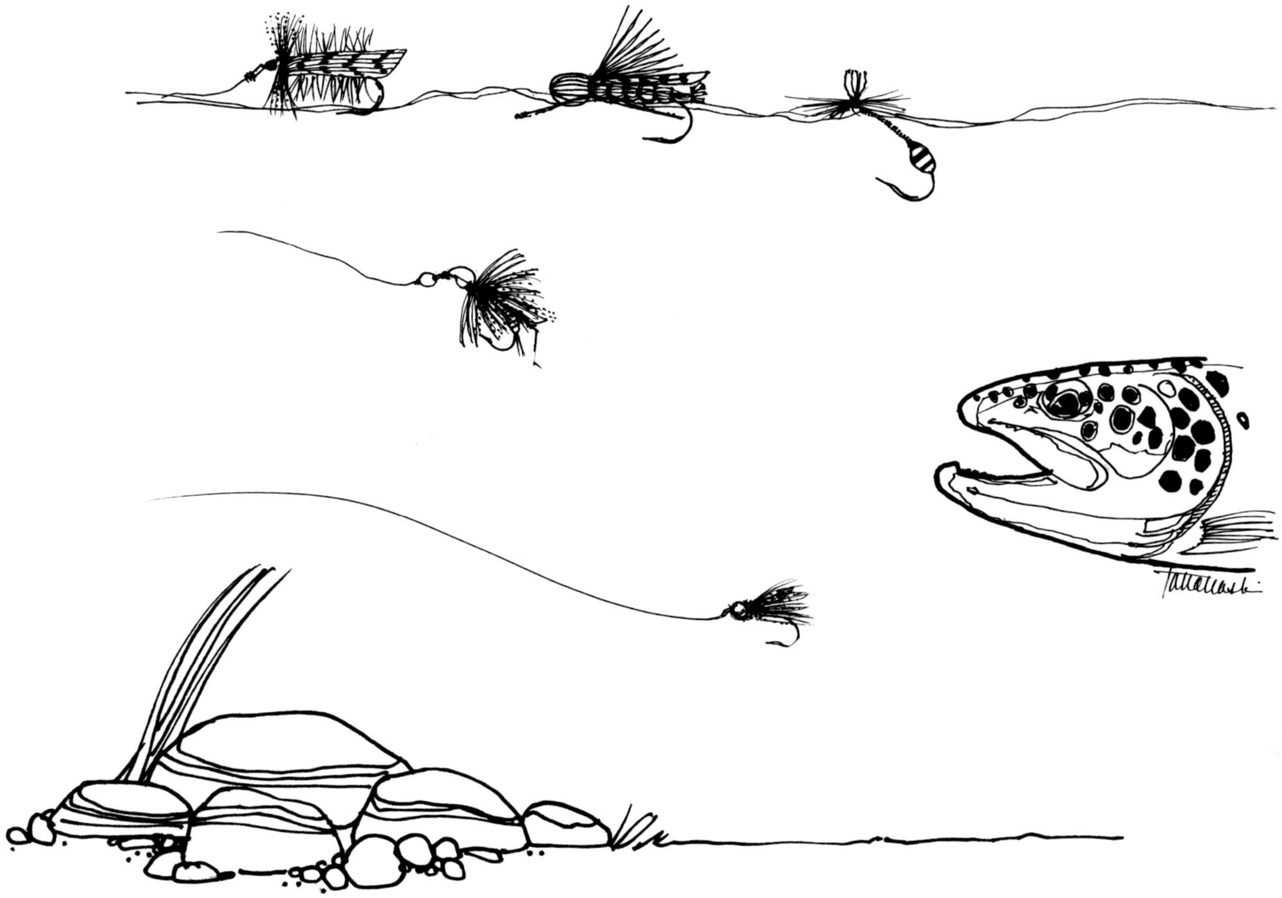

While terrestrials do not emerge like aquatic insects, they do, undeniably, sink. Any time a terrestrial lands in a river, it is almost assuredly a one-way ticket to the depths since they lack the motility required to muster an escape. The cycle of submergence: high floating, flush floating, damp, and deep. RICK TAKAHASHI

each stage of their emergence. But, while it is true that terrestrials do not emerge, they do, undeniably, sink. Any time a terrestrial lands in a river, it is almost assuredly a one-way ticket to the depths since they lack the motility required to muster an escape. In this sense, terrestrials undergo a type of reverse emergence—what I refer to as a cycle of submergence—which begins the moment a terrestrial hits the water and ends with its watery demise: either drowned, eaten, or drowned then eaten. Taking the terrestrial cycle of submergence into account becomes all the more compelling when coupled with the fact that quite often, day in and day out, most large fish feed subsurface.

To cover the different phases of terrestrial submergence, I group my patterns into four principal categories:

- High-Floaters: dry flies designed to ride on top of the surface.
- Flush-Floaters: dry flies designed to imitate terrestrials stuck in the surface film.
- Damp: subsurface patterns that imitate drowned terrestrials drifting in the upper-third of the water column.
- Deep: subsurface patterns that imitate sunk terrestrials dead-drifting along the bottom.

HIGH-FLOATERS

While flush-floaters are without question my go-to dry flies, high-floating patterns are better suited for pocketwater, high flows, and choppy riffles where you need additional floatation due to weaker surface tension (the sticky, film-like phenomenon whereby water molecules along the surface bond more strongly to one another since they have no partners to cling onto in the atmosphere above) and fish that can't afford to scrutinize your patterns—they must make an instantaneous decision whether to pounce or to pass. Although it can be difficult to keep dry flies afloat in this type of water, the upside is these scenarios offer some forgiving fishing situations.

If a terrestrial finds its way to the soft water behind a boulder or the head of a riffle, it is by complete accident—it was either knocked out of its flight path or blown off an overhanging branch. In either case, the entry will be more of a splashy crash landing. Trout know this and, because trout holding in heavy water are forced to be opportunistic feeders, are keenly aware of surface disturbances and ready to pounce the moment something lands on the surface above their lie. Thus, when working through pocketwater, I want a stout leader—maybe $7\frac{1}{2}$ feet of 2X to 4X—that is short enough to manage tight

maximize the time your flies are in the zone. In this regard, tungsten beads, BBs, fluorocarbon, and big bobbers are your keys to success.

I start with a 7½-foot leader tapered to 3X to which I attach 12 to 16 inches of 3X fluorocarbon with a double surgeon's knot. Placing the weight above the surgeon's knot is a much easier way of keeping the weight from sliding down toward the flies. Again, I prefer using fluorocarbon tippet for its faster sink rate, which allows my flies to drop into the midday holding zone quicker. I attach my lead fly, most often a #10 Drunken Hopper, with a non-slip loop knot because it is strong and allows the fly to move. Perhaps most importantly, the open loop knot allows a beadhead to plummet in the most hydrodynamic manner possible: head-first. (This tip was stolen from Frank Smethurst.) Off the bend of the lead fly, I clinch-knot 12 to 15 inches of 4X or 5X fluorocarbon and add a smaller, un- or less-weighted fly (a #12 Soggy Hop or a #14 Drunken or Soggy Beetle), with another non-slip mono loop knot. Once rigged, your only job is to cast and mend well enough to set up a deep, perfect dead-drift since any terrestrial drifting six feet below the surface will have long been rendered immobile.

Another situation that lends itself to fishing terrestrials deep is heavily pressured water. By all means, start off giving dry flies an earnest shot. But, if you get stuck fishing water someone else just covered, or a stretch dozens of people just covered (I'm looking at you, Slough Creek), or you just get caught behind in the count for whatever other reason, think about throwing the fish a curveball with a drowned hopper.

I limit my deep-running drowned terrestrials to hopper and beetle imitations. I have experimented with beadhead ants, and while they've caught some fish, I have never been convinced that they worked any better than a simple Prince or Zebra Midge in a similar size so I've pulled them out of the rotation. It just does not seem as plausible that drowned ants are tumbling along the river bottom with any sort of regularity, let alone in enough numbers to attract feeding fish. My Drunken Hopper, on the other hand, can incite such a laughable rate of takes it sometimes feels like cheating. While the hopper's consistent success has made it my go-to sunken terrestrial and, in the process, one of my favorite ties, there is one distinctive application where it gets routinely outshined by a drowned beetle: high elevations. I am not sure if it is due to elevation or the nightly low temperatures in alpine settings (although they are obviously related), but there is definitely a threshold in the high country where beetles become more prevalent than hoppers, and in my experience drowned beetles will regularly outperform sunken hoppers in upper-altitude lakes.

In terms of design, I follow the same guidelines as my damp patterns, although in this case, I want them to sink rapidly. I like the Nymph-Head Heavy Metal tungsten beads because they look great and sink like stones. A keen tier might twist up some deep terrestrials with brass beads for medium weight, tungsten beads for heavies, and tungsten coupled with lead-free wire wraps for mega-bombs to make sure they had all their bases were covered.

Subsurface Techniques

The Tick

RICK TAKAHASHI

THANKS TO MY co-author and fishing buddy, Jerry Hubka, I have been evolving as a nymph fisherman over the last 25-plus years. I love to see a trout pluck a morsel off the water's surface and nothing gets me stumbling over myself more than to see rising trout; but I've come to understand that most of the trout's feeding activities take place below the surface. Not all terrestrials will be floating on top of the water all the time. At some point terrestrials will be suspended in all parts of the water column.

If I see terrestrial insects on the surface, but do not see the fish rising, I will put enough weight on my tippet so my fly gets down to where the fish are feeding. Add any weight in slight increments until you reach the level at which the trout are feeding. This may require some guesswork on your part, but keep in mind that if you don't get hung up every so often, you are not fishing deep enough. I constantly adjust my weight, check on my rigging, check the flies, and adjust the strike indicator, if I'm using one, as I progress up or down the stream.

Selecting a dropper. Rick Takahashi searches for the right dropper to drift under his Tak's Foam Cicada. JERRY HUBKA

Stream Leaders

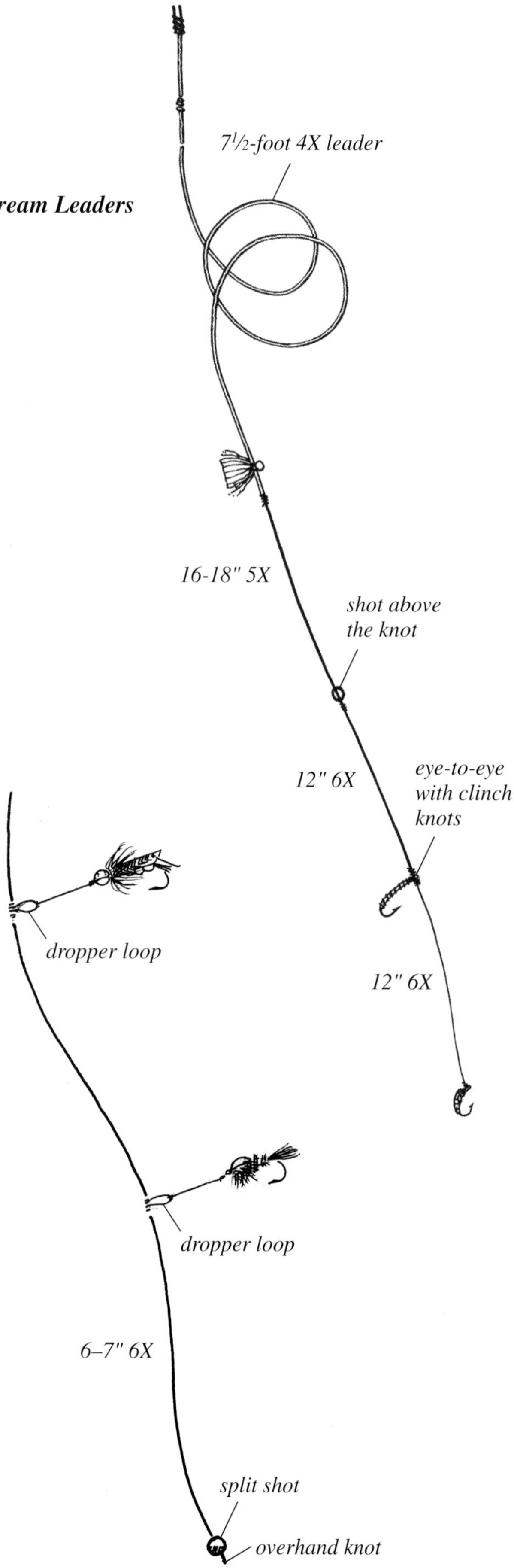

SETTING UP THE SUBSURFACE RIG

My basic set-up for fishing nymphs incorporates a 7½-foot 4X leader attached to approximately 8 inches of fairly stiff butt section such as Mason in .019- to .021-inch diameter with a perfection loop at the tag end. I like to connect the Mason to my fly line with a Super Glue splice (also called a Zap-A-Gap splice). If I use a fly line such as Rio's Gold with a welded loop connection, I will forgo the Mason butt section.

To the 4X leader, I add a 12- to 18-inch section of 5X tippet material using a blood knot. I then add a 10- to 12-inch section of 6X tippet, again with a blood knot. I tie on my first (point) fly to the leader using a clinch knot. If using an additional nymph, I'll attach a 10- to 12-inch piece of tippet to the hook eye and then tie on my bottom (dropper) fly. I will move each knot to the side of the hook eye, forming a T. (This rig is in *Modern Midges: Tying and Fishing the World's Most Effective Patterns.*)

I add weight, if needed, at the junction of the 5X and 6X tippet. If I need to use a strike indicator, I attach it 1 to 1½ times the depth of the water. The distance is calculated from the weight to the indicator. This allows the two-fly rig to be at the lowest level required with the point fly at the lowest level and the dropper pushed a little high by the hydrodynamics of the stream flow. I add additional weight to this setup and position the strike indicator two to three times the depth of the water if fishing faster water. At this time, I prefer fluorocarbon tippet material when fishing nymphs.

The second rig I use is borrowed from my experience steelhead fishing. The prime difference between this rig and the previous one is in the knot used for attaching the flies and the placement of the weight.

For this rig, I use a 9-foot leader tapered to 4X, to which I attach 36 inches of 5X tippet. Approximately 12 inches from the connection of the 4X leader to the 5X tippet, tie in a small dropper loop and then another small dropper loop 12 inches from the previous knot. This will leave a 10- to 12-inch tag end of tippet remaining. Using 6X tippet material I'll tie on a 6- to 7-inch length of tippet. I first make an overhand knot in one end of the tippet, make sure that there is a small section of tippet at the tag end; I'll explain the short end of tippet later.

Thread the knotted end of the tippet through the dropper loop and complete another overhand knot; tighten the over hand knot so that the knotted end with the overhand knot is snug up to the knot. I'll tie on the nymph pattern so that it is no longer than one to two inches away from the dropper loop, which helps prevent the tippet from wrapping around the leader. I will repeat the same process for the dropper fly.

The remaining leader will hold a split-shot on the end of the tippet. I generally will not put a knot on the end of the leader which allows the weight to slip off the tippet should it become lodged on the bottom of the stream. I can also clip the end tippet material if the flies happen to have enough weight to sink them to the desired depth.

Terrestrial magic. Fishing terrestrial patterns in the summer months and into fall pay big rainbow dividends.
DENNIS COLLIER

UPSTREAM STRAIGHT LINE TECHNIQUE

I prefer to use the first rig that I discussed above for this presentation, which unlike a dead-drift keeps tension on the flies. I cast the line directly upstream starting from the bank and work out. I generally look for shallow water that is no deeper than five to six feet, adding sufficient weight to get the fly down but not sink too rapidly. After the cast, I immediately lower the rod tip to the water's surface while I constantly strip in the line with enough speed so the rig doesn't hang up. I try to stay in contact with the flies as they drift downstream, all the while watching the water for signs of movement, flash, or other indication that the fish has intercepted the fly.

I can often feel the take when fishing in this manner, but if I am having trouble staying in contact with my flies, I will put a 2- or 3-inch bend in the tip of my fly line and wait for a take when the bend is straightened out. I will let the flies drift past me and allow to drift downstream before I make my next cast, the dragging fly line will often help me load the rod for the next cast.

UP AND ACROSS

In this presentation, I cast the fly across-stream and then make a series of upstream mends to allow the flies to sink. As the flies drift downstream, I follow them with my rod tip, which is

Trout of Japan. Takashi Nakajima of Japan lands a beautiful, highly sough-after yamame trout. TAKASHI NAKAJIMA

Submerger Patterns

Eric Pettine

I fished the small streams of northern New Mexico sixty years ago with a five-dollar Rexall Drug Store cane fly rod baited with hoppers, beetles, crickets, and moths. We fished bait when the water was high and off color, small Colorado spinners when the water began to clear, and wet flies when the water dropped and cleared. We always fished terrestrials wet. We often fished two hoppers on two hooks with a split-shot between them. It was great training for a future nymph fisher. When I began to tie flies, one of my first patterns was an ant fashioned out of two black lumps of thread on a hook. The fly didn't float, but it caught trout. I still carry both wet and dry terrestrials. Both work very well.

The wet terrestrials, what I call my submerger patterns, are my "secret" weapons when I am guiding and need to find some fish for my clients. Terrestrials are a target of opportunity for trout. The fish don't see them all the time, but they know what they are and like to eat them. While most terrestrials float for a while, all eventually sink. Because of the liquid in their bodies, especially the larger ones, they drift along in the middle of the water column, not on the bottom of the stream. Many of my "submerger" flies are designed to sink into this middle realm. For example, my hopper submerger is tied with deer or elk hair just as the dry version is, but I add a bead in the head of the fly. My submerger ants, crickets, and beetles are tied in a similar fashion.

held up slightly until the line begins to drift below me. I then lower the rod tip and allow the flies to drift below me, and I then lift the rod slightly (Leisenring Lift) before making another cast. Just because the fly pattern is at the end of its drift does not mean the fly and you are done fishing. You will be surprised how many fish follow the fly, and they now realize that their meal is about to get away so they strike to get it before it vanishes from their plate!

A modification of this technique can work wonders when dry-fly fishing. Pull your terrestrial pattern under the surface at the end of the drift and slowly work it back up to the surface; be prepared for a take as soon as the pattern dips under the surface.

INDICATOR FISHING

When I need to suspend my flies at a particular level in the water column, using a strike indicator is the most efficient method. When sight-fishing, I often use a strike indicator to help me judge the proper distance I need to drift the fly into the fish's feeding zone. Because I know the distance of my flies from the strike indicator I can cast above the lie of the fish and adjust for the distance and direction that the flies are traveling. I do not look at the indicator for the take. Rather, I look at what the fish is doing, and if I detect any movement up, down, or sideways, or an opening of the mouth, I set the hook.

If blind indicator fishing, I try to imagine that there is nothing under the surface of the water that impede the strike indicators smooth float down the river. If the strike indicator pauses or its float is disrupted, I lift the rod and hope for a solid hook-up. Of course all sorts of things under the water that can move the indicator, but setting at any movement will increase your catch rate.

Fishing Terrestrials in the High Country

Haley's Hopper

STEVEN B. SCHWEITZER

TERRESTRIALS ARE MOST often associated with subalpine grass-lined meadow streams and ponds. But terrestrials—particularly ants, beetles, hoppers, and crickets—are an important and often overlooked food source in alpine waters (10,000 feet or more above sea level) as well. Reaching these altitudes most often requires hiking, as waters this high rarely have roads near them. And maybe because it requires some modest effort to get to these waters, most fly fishers don't take advantage of the incredible terrestrial fishing they offer, particularly July through September.

Ants are common in and around all waters, regardless of altitude. But if it wasn't for the thermal rising of anabatic winds from lower altitudes, many terrestrials wouldn't have their magic carpet ride to high alpine lakes and streams. As air warms at lower altitudes during a sunny day, it begins to rise, causing a thermal lift strong enough to carry flying insects and small terrestrials upward. When that thermal air, or anabatic wind, meets cooler mountainsides and bodies of water, it slows, dropping the hitchhiking insects on nearby vegetation, rocks, and water. The anabatic process is much more productive in

Banjo and Erin Block fish for native cutthroat on a mountain stream in the Indian Peaks Wilderness, Colorado. JAY ZIMMERMAN

Erin Block searches for high mountain trout in a very steep mountain stream. JAY ZIMMERMAN

early summer as days warm quickly and the juvenile insects are small, almost weightless passengers. As the summer progresses, terrestrials become larger and are less likely to succumb to the anabatic elevator ride.

SEASONAL TACTICS FOR HIGH-ALTITUDE STREAMS

Conditions rapidly change during the short four- to five-month span of an alpine spring-summer-fall cycle. From March through June, high-altitude streams are the highways to drain melting snow and ice from the surrounding terrain and feeder lakes. In good snowpack years, streams can be chock-full of water well into July, but typically runoff subsides by the end of June.

Rarely is an alpine stream accessible in March and April unless by snowshoe. But when "Magical May" comes, die-hard alpine junkies turn their attention to fishing those pre-runoff streams, which are often running crystal clear and ice-cold. And the longer days trigger fish to feed, since they haven't really eaten a good meal in months. Early season midge and BWO hatches can be epic, and on warm days, keep an eye out for early season ants and beetles along the banks and in the budding vegetation. If you see the critters crawling around, fish an ant or small black beetle close to the banks.

Late May into June delivers longer, warmer days, which means runoff and swollen streams. The water can be stained glacial blue to mud-brown, creating challenging fishing conditions. During this period, however, fish gorge on the dislodged streamside bugs, primarily aquatic and terrestrial worms, keeping tight to the banks away from the flushing midstream currents. Fishing a San Juan Worm-style fly under a beetle or hopper in slack-water areas can often be the ticket on a bluebird day. On some occasions, if the water is high but clear, consider fishing a drowned pair of ants close to the bank.

After runoff, typically July onward, terrestrial fishing kicks into high gear. Anabatic winds are a daily event and the bugs that hitched a ride early in the season are now growing at a rapid rate. While you might be fishing a size #16 hopper or #18 beetle in May and June, fish a size or two larger in July and August. A #8-12 hopper, #12-14 beetle, or #16-18 ant will be a bigger, more attractive morsel for opportunistic stream fish later in the summer. Since a fish's growing season is only a few months long, any well-placed terrestrial should entice memory-making rises.

Fall fishing commences in September and October. Fishing becomes more unpredictable by the end of October above 11,000 feet. Snowpack is already forming, and streams are locking up solid for the winter. But September and October often yield the largest fish of the season as they are sensing shorter days and less opportunity for meals. They often charge large hoppers floating by. By this point, fishing hoppers could easily be the only tactic necessary. To increase odds, rig with a #10 hopper trailed by a #18 ant pattern, two high-altitude trout favorites. This combination is my go-to choice after Labor Day.

SEASONAL TACTICS FOR HIGH-ALTITUDE LAKES

High-altitude lake fishing is reserved for a special clan of fly fishers willing to hike in the dark of night to make a lake at 12,000 feet by dawn. These are the same patient brethren who also crave ice-out conditions for the first trout of the year.

Before May, there isn't much alpine fishing to be had as the lakes are still sealed with a lid of ice. But come mid-May, the "magical" time comes. The magic I refer to is those hard-to-predict ice-out days where ice breaks apart and open water is exposed. Depending on the wind, this could easily be near shore, but don't be surprised if it occurs mid-lake as wind and sunny days combine to melt the ice. Fish seek the open water like a magnet orients to the north. They begin cruising the ice shelf looking for food, using the safety of the ice shelf for protection. It seems every fish in the lake is roiling the surface near a sheet of ice. A small #20 ant or Griffith's Gnat can entice some unhesitant rises. To note, hitting ice-out requires

Erin Block hooks a nice cutthroat in an Indian Peaks Wilderness lake in Colorado. JAY ZIMMERMAN

uncanny timing or plenty of recon trips and a smidgeon of luck. Don't forget the snowshoes.

June yields to consistently warmer days and increasingly snow-free trails. By the end of June, expect clear trail travel and consistently good fishing days. Anabatic winds are a daily occurrence and the lakes become littered with blown-in snacks. Early morning fishing—dawn to 10 a.m.—is prime fishing time. The water can be glass smooth and teeming with cruising fish, mostly along the shorelines. By 10 a.m. expect some wind, but that is when the really good fishing starts. Tie on a large hopper and a drowned ant combination. Larger fish lose their shyness and cruise a foot or two below choppy waves, looking for blown-in treats, as if they seem to correlate wind with food.

July, August, and early September are mirror-image months with long days, bigger terrestrials, and cruising fish. Be patient as you approach a lake, looking for cruising fish in the shallow rim of the lake. This shallow area is called the littoral zone. It typically heats up a degree or two sooner than the deeper part of the lake and supports micro plant growth, which harbors insects cruising fish seek. Remember this: cruising fish are hungry fish. During these months, my go-to fly is a #18-20 black ant. There's no better sight than seeing a cruising trout veer three feet out of its way to grab a floating ant or beetle tied to the end of your line.

By late September into October, days are noticeably shorter and snow tends to be a daily event. Longer nights and colder temps make terrestrials lethargic. They become a less important food source for alpine lakes. Windy days, sleet and hail, and freezing rain and snow send trout to the depths. And on cue, terrestrial season has gone to sleep for the season, only to start all over again in another six months.

Fishing High Mountain Lakes

Scott Kemp

IN THE HIGH country, you may not catch the biggest fish, but getting away from the crowds and enjoying the mountains in all sorts of situations packs a reward that will last you a lifetime. The hard part is getting to the water and dealing with the elements that nature will throw back at you. This challenge often neglected by many is savored by a few who capitalize on a vast, pure resource that waits to be explored.

Staying overnight in the backcountry puts you in position for evening fishing, and we all know how good that can be. Unlike decades ago, outdoor shops are now filled with very

Fishing for greenback cutthroat trout at Lake Hustad, Rocky Mountain National Park, Colorado. Ant and beetle patterns are an absolute necessity in this area. The author gathers information on wilderness areas and National Parks for waters that have self-sustaining populations of fish, then target these watersheds for the next adventure. CHRIS KENNEDY

Fly designer Casey Dunnigan holds up a nice sized brown caught on one of his new creations for Montana Fly Company. WILL HUNT

A grayling from Agnes Lake in the Pioneer Mountains, Montana. Later in the year, grayling will often delight in sipping ant patterns off or just under the surface. DOREEN KEMP

lightweight gear that enables you to carry less than 25 pounds for an extended weekend trip. When you research ultra-light camping you will find a multitude of resources and ideas to shave pounds off your pack, which guarantees a more enjoyable experience. As you lighten your load and increase your fitness level, the hike farther upstream doesn't seem nearly as steep, and access to remote lakes once thought unattainable and mostly untouched will become within reach.

Because of the often-opportunistic nature of the fish, equipment can be minimal. A four-piece 5-weight rod with a weight-forward floating line will fit nearly all situations because it has the strength to cast into the wind, yet will provide efficiency in smaller streams. Long leaders with light tippets from 5X to 7X help in the clear waters. A selection of flies that is heavy on beetles, ants, and small hoppers is a must. A fly box should also include mayfly imitations (Parachute Adams, Comparaduns, Pheasant Tails), midges (Brassies, black and green larvae patterns, Griffith's Gnats), caddis (Hare's Ears, Sparkle Caddis, Elk-hair Caddis), subsurface patterns (small Woolly Buggers, Beadhead Prince Nymphs, Zug Bugs), as well as your personal favorite patterns.

The summer and early autumn afternoon winds hold the key to successful dry fly fishing in the high country. In *Fly Fishing the High Country Lakes*, Gary LaFontaine describes the warm anabatic winds that climb from lower elevations and deposit terrestrial insects on lakes that are typically above 7,000 to 9,000 feet in elevation in the mountain west. The beetles, hoppers and especially ants that meet their demise, can literally "rain" onto a lake to provide a critical food source for trout. If they could, the trout would eat all of these terrestrials. In some lakes during the summer it is estimated that more than half of a trout's diet is terrestrial insects that have been blown in from lower altitudes or from the banks by the wind.

Headwater streams and lakes offer us a chance to do more than catch and release fish. They provide us a sense of place and of conservation that we have lost as humans slip deeper into the electronic age. Deep memories of camping, hiking, and friendships have been established throughout my experiences in the backcountry and always leave me invigorated with a clearer focus of what is really important. This enjoyment is magnified because of the lack of distraction that our normal lives bring and forms lasting relationships with family and friends that share a respect and love of the outdoors.

After the Fall

JERRY HUBKA

Hub's San Juan Ant

The San Juan River in New Mexico is reknowed for its epic flying ant falls. PAT DORSEY

MY ENTIRE FLY-FISHING life has been measured by my firm and well-founded belief that fishing midges, nymphs, and streamers below the surface of the water was the best and only way to catch trout.

I learned to fly fish on the Fryingpan River in the late 1960s. My fly fishing mentor, Ralph Coffman, taught me to fish with nymphs and wet flies. Though Ralph designed and patented the famous dry fly, The House and Lot, now tied and sold as the H&L Variant, sadly he never introduced me to the dry fly experience. He showed me the fly more than once, but never offered one to me or told me to fish it. He said I needed to learn to cast and fish under the surface—"that's where you will catch the most trout," he told me. So, that was how I would fish for trout.

When I met Rick Takahashi at an Art Department meeting in the mid-1980s we struck up a friendship around fly fishing. We fished the South Platte River near Deckers, Colorado, above Denver. He fished dry flies and I fished the "best way"—

with nymphs. Over the years I noticed how excited he would become when fish begain to rise. He cast his dry flies and caught fish with ease as I plopped my nymphs and weight nearby in the same water. He gave me some dry flies and taught me to tie them, but they remained in my smallest fly box, alone and ignored in one lint-filled corner of my fly box bag.

My "fall" happened one evening in the mid-1990s when Rick and I were fishing the San Juan River in northern New Mexico. We were becoming accomplished midge fishermen and began to design and test our own patterns on that scenic desert tailwater. We both fished with great success using our larvae, pupae, and emerger designs, but Rick would occasionally fish #26-28 midge adults to rising trout. Meanwhile, I was shaking my head in disbelief that he would waste precious hours casting and catching one or two fish while I was releasing a dozen or more.

This particular early evening I was about to quit fishing, find Rick, walk back to my truck, and drive back to Durango for dinner and a fly tying and designing session that I called, "tyin' flies, tellin' lies, and callin' the wives." Suddenly, Rick popped out of the willows about 50 yards upstream. I watched him unstring his rig, break down his rod, and sit down on a big rock about 10 feet out from the bank. He spotted me, and I yelled that I would be there in two minutes so we could head for town. I also mentioned that there were fish rising to the surface all around me. He said that I should put on a dry adult midge. Yea, I chuckled to myself, and yelled sarcastically that I left *that* box in the truck. He yelled back that there was an ant fall last week before we arrived and that I should put on a large flying ant.

The San Juan ant fall is legendary. Rick and I had been fishing the Juan many times a year for several years and never experienced it, but our friends who have told us fantastic stories of some of the best topwater fishing on the river every year when it happens. We were a week too late, or were we?

I had caught my share of trout that day, and I thought what the heck, I'll find something in one of my boxes that floats and drop a midge off the hook. I had tied, at Rick's insistence, four #10 black-and-white foam Stimulators two evenings before just to shut him up about having some dry flies in one of my San Juan midge boxes. I tied one on and attached one of my #22 black midge emerger patterns to 12 inches of 6X fluorocarbon to the hook bend of the big ugly black fly pattern. I cynically thought, this should be a good waste of my time; we'll be leaving for Durango in five minutes or less.

The reliable black Stimulator and some San Juan Flying foam ant pattern designs by the author. JERRY HUBKA

The winged ant flies for several reasons, including temperature, humidity or damp conditions, flooded or crowded nests, but primarily for reproduction and establishing new colonies. HENRY RAMSAY

I couldn't stop talking about how much fun I had all the way back to the truck, all the way to Durango, and all during dinner. After dinner we tied some flies, told some lies, and called the wives. I had "fallen," and for three hours, until one-o'clock in the morning, I tied dry flies—big ugly terrestrial dry flies!

And Sometimes, Flying Ants

Tak's San Juan Ant

SKIP MORRIS

WASHINGTON STATE IS trout-stream poor and trout-lake rich. If you're a fly fisher who was born here and have lived here most of your life, as I am, you've probably come to see this as a pretty good bargain—there's always a worthwhile lake somewhere nearby, and the wonderful trout rivers of Oregon, Idaho, and Montana aren't so distant, some just half a day's drive. If you know lakes, you know that a good trout lake is all any fly fisher could reasonably want. At a good lake you may find chironomid squirming as wormlike pupae up from the silt and trout gliding among them to take in one after another. Or dragonfly nymphs creeping in waves toward shore as trout hunt them among the weeds or debris of the lake's bed. Or the activity of any of a broad assortment of creatures that gather the trout to feed deep in a variety of ways.

But the action could be on top—right up on the surface of a lake. Insects emerging from or standing on or buzzing across a lake's calm face and trout rising to take them in easy rhythms, or perhaps in explosive attacks. In many ways it's like fishing

Ants come in a wide range of sizes and color schemes, though their hatches can be unpredicatable. The Ant Carol in several sizes and colors for the most common "hatches" will serve you well on the water. JAY NICHOLS

to trout feeding at the surface of a river—that challenging, exciting, visual feast that's always been the heart of fly fishing—and it's part of the reason we Washingtonians see our lakes-for-rivers trade as a good one. There are all sorts of attractions to bring up the trout: mayflies, caddisflies, backswimmers and water boatmen, damselfly adults, even grasshoppers and beetles.

And sometimes, flying ants.

I've encountered flying ants on rivers, too—but rarely. Just this past August I found cutthroat trout rising to a good salting of truly tiny (probably best matched with a #24 hook) black, white-winged ants on the slick water of an Idaho river, and those trout wouldn't settle for any fly less than a fair match for those ants. But that and another river-ant event are my only two in I don't know how many years. During those same years I've found flying ants on lakes a couple of dozen times at least.

Yet, I rarely go seeking flying ants, because they've proven reliably unreliable. I've seen ants on lakes in spring, summer, and fall; in morning, afternoon, and evening; matching size 24 hooks, size 18, up to size 12, and perhaps even size 8. I've seen black, red, and cinnamon-colored flying ants and one batch that were red in the rear and black in front. One might argue that ants are almost as varied in size and color and habit as mayflies. But unlike hatches of Pale Morning Duns and Green Drake mayflies, for example, flying ant "hatches" are unpredictable.

When I talk about flying ants on trout lakes at fly-fishing events and clubs, I start by telling how a few fishing friends and I were crossing a large lake one afternoon and discovered flying ants half a mile from shore, how we caught one dry-fly trout after another for an hour and a half, returned the next day with neat new flies that perfectly matched the naturals we'd brought back, proceeded to the same area we'd fished the day before under exactly the same overcast skies and the same still air, and found nary an ant nor a trout.

Welcome to the flying ant.

There's only one reliable flying ant I've found in all my years of dealing with the fluttering little hard-shell mysteries: our local termite. Large and brown-orange, it comes in late August on into September on hot afternoons—the hotter and calmer the better. If everything comes together and it's a good year for them, the termites can be everywhere—sailing into your car's windshield on your drive to the lake, scattered across the water with their long brown quivering wings gripped by the water's surface, flying all around. Trout come to them, and so do other creatures.

I've seen largemouth bass leave their tangled cover to rise gently like trout fifty feet from shore for termites. I've caught bluegill and pumpkinseed sunfish that were after termites too. Once, in a tidal flow that runs very close to forested bank, I caught sea-run cutthroat gathered for termites. They sipped quietly and took my Ant Carol pattern dead-drift right on top. For the sort of fishing I was doing I might as well have been standing in the Henry's Fork of the Snake. All well and good, but other than our termite, I can't seem to find an ant whose appearance I can even begin to predict.

So rather than seek ants on lakes, or on any water, I just watch for them—when they show, I'm ready. I'm ready with the flies—I pretty much rely only on my Ant Carol now—the tackle, the techniques, and the strategies. The tackle is easy: full-floating lines, nine-foot leaders with three-foot tippets (unless the water's clear and calm, in which case a longer leader might be better). A 4X leader with 5X tippet usually seems about right.

The Ant Carol just keeps catching ant-eating trout for me, so I keep using it when ants appear on the water (you'll find tying step-by-step instructions with photos in *Morris on Tying Flies*). It has a bulging abdomen and thorax. It has a slender waist. It has thin bucktail wings that suggest translucence and venation. Basically, it has everything a flying ant has that matters to trout and it floats well. I tie it in brown, black, and red. I'll tie the brown version with the wings slightly longer than usual and blend a little orange dubbing into the brown when I use it to imitate the termite on size 12 and 10 dry-fly hooks.

When trout start sipping down ants, I catch a sample, and with the sample in hand, I find an Ant Carol of comparable size and coloring, and tie it on. My third move (which I may skip if the urge to fish is too great) is to locate a natural on the water and just watch. Does it struggle, lie quiet, vibrate its wings to make nervous patterns on the water's surface? Whatever is does, I try to make my Ant Carol do the same.

If I think I'm in a good place, I might drop anchors. Or I might first take a long look around for rising fish or ants in the air or on the water so that I can pick my best possible location. If the day is calm or the breeze is light, I might wait to drop anchor to see if I drift to somewhere better than where I started (although, once I find good ant fishing, I'm inclined to stay put). Or I might blow off all these moves and start tossing a quick guess at the right ant-fly out there just because I can't wait—flying ants are a compelling event.

On a lake in the daytime, I expect to see what I call "searching rises," or just "searching" trout, rising to any surface fare, ants included, and moving randomly between their sips at the water's surface. A trout might come up, turn, go off four feet and rise again, double back a foot and then rise, go straight for three feet, and rise twice in close succession. There's no pattern to follow and consequently no way to predict the next rise.

But from sunset on, trout in lakes tend to rise in a predictable pattern—a rise, then, say, three feet away another rise, then in line with the first two rises and three feet further on another rise, and so on, the time between rises nearly consistent. This I've come to call "path-rising." It creates a glorious game of stealth, strategy, and precision—sliding your boat into place, and then setting the fly quietly and accurately where the next rise should occur—well before it occurs so that the fly

Above: Fishing in the clouds. Lakes in the high Rockies provide excellent fishing with terrestrial for those willing to take the road less traveled. JERRY HUBKA
At left: Stillwater treasures. Brian Yamauchi holds up one of the several large rainbows that he caught on Delaney Buttes Lake, Colorado. RICK TAKAHASHI

doesn't drop too close to the cruising fish. Oh, and from a distance that keeps the waving rod and the movements of the boat from safely away from the skittish fish, around 40 or 45 feet. Many things can go wrong. Here are a few: the fly lands a few inches short, the fly comes in too near the trout and spooks it, the boat rocks during the cast and sends warning wavelets across the flat water (you learn to cast without rocking your boat), or the trout just changes direction never seeing your perfectly placed fly. But when everything goes right, and the fly lands gently on target in good time, and then after a long tense moment the water bulges quietly on the smooth surface—that's a thrill. It's bliss.

You'll find both searching rises and path-rising during ant falls on lakes. It just depends on when the ants arrive: before sunset (the former) or sometime during or after sunset (the latter). Either way, it's grand. If the ants come during the day, just try to find them on the water with trout taking them and put your fly out there. The trout will find it; it's what they do.

Of course all these rules are far too neat for trout to respect them—they'll do as they please, which may mean path-rising before sunset or searching after. They may not rise at all, despite the invitation of helpless ants scattered across the lake in abundance. I've seen it. If you're new to fly fishing, get used to it; if you're an old hand, you already know: they're trout, and we'll never truly understand them. Typically, though, they'll follow the rules simply because following the rules fills their bellies.

So, outside of my local termites, flying ant falls are so unpredictable I'd never advise a fly fisher to go looking for them on any lake at any time. But I do advise you to get ant tactics into your head and imitations into your lake fly boxes—at its best, an ant fall can challenge your strategies and skills and reward them handsomely.

Beyond Dusk: To Catch A Natural Born Killer

Hub's Señor Ratón

KEVAN EVANS

FISHING AT NIGHT is an entirely different experience. An incredible stillness, full of unseen life; eyesight beaten into submission by the darkening skies; the heightened sense of awareness to compensate for senses lost; the scenic puzzle of the landscape disappears into the dusk; a scurry on the bank lifts the hair on the back of your neck; primal instincts grab hold over the logical mind; the air cools down to welcome the stars; and, the moon appears as a guardian with authority over the blackened sky.

By this time, all the hordes of fair-weather fly fishermen have broken down their rod and hit the road home. They may feel as if their day was successful or they might be disappointed with the results of their day on the water. Either way, knowledge of all the big fish that they know lurk in the river that they have never caught will haunt them. They ponder each of their outings to this water and wonder, "Why can't I get into those monsters?"

NATURAL BORN KILLERS

I have spent many years dedicated to fishing at night, and while many patterns and tactics work, fishing a mouse is one of the best ways to hunt large nocturnal trout. Trout have eyes that afford them the ability to feed at night. The dark skies provide the absolute best protection from predators of all kinds, allowing them to move freely throughout the water and bully their way up and downstream to their favorite hunting grounds.

Trout that hunt at night are far less "match-the-hatch" fish and are less selective trout. They are opportunistic feeders. They will chow down on any aquatic night hatch, but if a grasshopper comes across their way during the hatch, they will eat it. However, not all night feeders are meat eaters. The meat eaters are, in my opinion, the crème de la crème of trout. These fish are a special breed, cut from different cloth—aggressive as a pike, fast as a bolt of lightning, and downright nasty. They are natural born killers.

Some people say night fishing is only good on a full moon, or the three days before and after. Yet, I believe that the fish that feed at night, feed every night. It makes no sense to believe that these fish only eat seven nights a month. Some of my most spectacular nights fishing have been the darkest nights. So, I beg to differ with these theories that have become accepted as facts. It is a bit easier on the fisherman to fish on those bright nights but that's about it. Success in fishing at night comes down to the fisherman, not the fish. Difficulty fishing on dark nights inspired my development of the glow-in-the-dark mouse patterns. If you can see your fly, you're bound to be more successful while fishing.

At night, the solitude is abundant, and shooting stars rip through the black horizon while the moon reflects off of the surface of the water. The crickets chirp in rhythm trapping their song in the moist, thick air above you while creatures scurry on the river's edge. Night fishing holds many challenges for a fisherman. The action can be unbelievably slow or consistent and rewarding. LANDON MAYER

WHY MICE?

Mice are a staple food of the wilds. They may have the longest predator list of any other creature on earth. Mice are eaten by snakes, cats, coyotes, wolves, hawks, owls, bears, and fish . . . even humans. Mice breed about every six weeks and baby mice are only under mom's care for three weeks. Then, they go out into the night with nothing more than instinct to survive. Mice are not born scared of water; they are actually very good swimmers and divers.

Mice grow to an average of 10 cm and a weight of 30 grams. They will be the color of their surroundings. Because of this small size and long list of predators, mice move around at night. During the day, they will also take advantage of the protection of light, when predators are less likely to be out hunting. No doubt, most of us have seen a mouse or two running around in the daytime.

During the winter mice go into a "torpid" state. They will burrow an extensive tunnel system under snow-covered areas and feed on stockpiled seeds for the most part. Then they can and do come out of these tunnels during the warm days and nights of winter. In other words, you can fish mice year-round.

Steve Hoffman holds a Yampa River brown that fell for a Morrish Mouse. LANDON MAYER

TOPWATER TECHNIQUES

The most common technique is to cast the mouse pattern to the bank and swing it through the current. While this technique is tried and true, there are other ways to fish a mouse. One technique that I like to use to cover water, especially when moving from hole to hole, is to twitch the mouse up against the bank that you're standing on, as if the mouse is struggling to get onto the bank. At the same time, walk slowly downstream.

In shallow riffles, which are full of action, I like to skate the mouse across the skinny water as if the mouse doesn't want to get its feet wet. This is also why I tie my mice with the hook pointed up and legs pointed down. It is a simple and effective technique. After each cast, take one step downstream and repeat.

Bends in the river, typically sharp bends, will create an undercut bank. The night feeders tend to move out of the safety of that bank and into the slack water of the opposite shore. This occurs from inside the current's edge all the way to the bank itself. This is a great area to place your fly into the current and swim it all through the slack water using lots of short twitches with the tip of your rod to create the wakes on the water's surface that a mouse naturally makes while swimming.

Slow moving, glassy water-type sections are the ideal place to employ the "bombing the bank" style of mousing. This is also a good time to swim a lightly weighted drowned mouse right under the surface of the water.

DROWNED MOUSE

As mentioned above, the drowned mouse can be a very effective pattern. The common way to fish it is to dead-drift it, bouncing it off the bottom, imitating a mouse that has drowned. Also, don't forget that mice will dive and swim underwater and can get caught up in the currents and be swept to the bottom. Therefore, the drowned mouse may be used to imitate a mouse swimming underwater. Give it life and trout will respond.

You should fish the drowned mouse just like a streamer from the bottom of the river to just below the surface. Also, you can sink it to the bottom (in a dead-drift) then retrieve it in with strong pulsating strips to the surface with a defined upward retrieve and once it has reached the surface, swim it to shore like you would a topwater mouse. At this time, you should throw a big line mend with your excess line out to the current. The fly line will pull it back away from the bank. Pulsating twitches should be used while it is swinging back and forth from bank to current and current to bank again.

While mousing I always try to make the mouse seem disoriented or somehow disadvantaged from its counterparts. After all, trout are lazy fish and will go for the weakest prey. The laws of nature rule the natural world, so only the strong survive. This type of thinking has served me well while fishing all mouse and streamer patterns.

Mousing is not only effective in summer. I have caught numerous trout during both day and night fishing in the winter,

Mousing Basics

Ken Morrish

Mousing is a unique form of fly fishing. Practically speaking, it is the only time that fly anglers deliberately try to mimic the behavior of a terrestrial mammal, one that struggles for its life in a dangerous aquatic environment. Fish often react in unpredictable ways to these furry morsels, making mousing, in my opinion, the most entertaining form of freshwater fly fishing.

Trying to control its fear, a mouse attempts to cross a river or stream. Invariably, it attempts to swim at an up- and across-stream angle but is swept downstream instead. The rate of flow affects the angle of the swim. The angle increases with the speed of the current.

Morrish Mouse

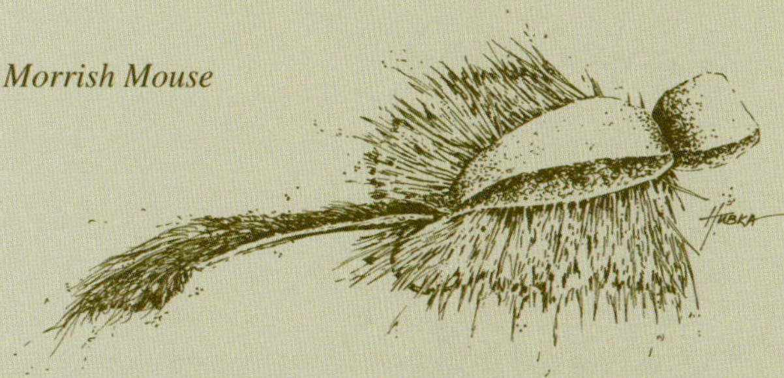

A wise angler will take advantage of this tendency. Place the fly a few inches from the opposite bank. While keeping the rod tip high, lead the fly toward the near bank. Applying the right amount of pressure on the line will allow the fly to sweep down with the current, mimicking a live mouse's swim pattern. Enhance the effect by putting a pulsing action on the fly. Be careful not to overdo this action because mice are weak swimmers. They are incapable of fast acceleration or popping-type movements in the water. Thinking about how a mouse might look as it struggles in the water helps to mimic this movement through the water.

As in most forms of topwater fishing, when the boil comes, react only when certain that the fly has been taken under. Violent boils and wild explosions where the fish never commits to the fly are common. In many cases, the fly will "swim" out of the chaos and then be attacked later. When the fly is under, lift it slowly and firmly. Last but not least, avoid patterns with big bass-style stingers (unless fishing for bass), always fish barbless, and don't hesitate to use a heavy tippet.

though trout seem to prefer smaller (#10) mouse patterns at this time. Towns and cities that have rivers running through them also have bridges over those rivers. Mice use our bridges as well. They can and do fall from the bridges. Trout also like bridges. This makes a pretty good cocktail for successful fishing.

The notoriously intense winters of my home in Summit County, Colorado, provide icy bridges, and no matter how sure footed a mouse is, some will make a bad step and slip into the trout's hunting grounds. So, fish that frequent bridges and downstream of bridges are more accustomed to seeing and eating these mammal morsels. In the winter, in areas where tailwaters are the only open waters, I find that trout tend to stack up in drop-offs and the back ends of deep pools. During these frigid times, shallow riffles seem barren of fish at night.

INDEX